Les Enseignements Secrets Intemporels

Discovery Publisher

®2015, Discovery Publisher

All rights reserved. No part of this book may be reproduced in any form or by any electronic or mechanical means including information storage and retrieval systems, without permission in writing from the publisher.

DISCOVERY PUBLISHER

616 Corporate Way, Suite 2-4933
Valley Cottage, New York, 10989
www.discoverypublisher.com
books@discoverypublisher.com
facebook.com/DiscoveryPublisher
twitter.com/DiscoveryPB

New York • Tokyo • Paris • Hong Kong

PART I

Chapter 1 : Birth and parentage

The Gandhis belong to the Bania caste and seem to have been originally grocers. But for three generations, from my grandfather, they have been Prime Ministers in several Kathiawad States. Uttamchand Gandhi, aliasOta Gandhi, my grandfather, must have been a man of principle. State intrigues compelled him to leave Porbandar, where he was Diwan, and to seek refuge in Junagadh. There he saluted the Nawab with the left hand. Someone, noticing the apparent discourtesy, asked for an explanation, which was thus given: 'The right hand is already pledged to Porbandar.'

Ota Gandhi married a second time, having lost his first wife. He had four sons by his first wife and two by his second wife. I do not think that in my childhood I ever felt or knew that these sons of Ota Gandhi were not all of the same mother. The fifth of these six brothers was Karamchand Gandhi, alias Kaba Gandhi, and the sixth was Tulsidas Gandhi. Both these brothers were Prime Ministers in Porbandar, one after the other. Kaba Gandhi was my father. He was a member of the Rajasthanik Court. It is now extinct, but in those days it was a very influential body for settling disputes between the chiefs and their fellow clansmen. He was for some time Prime Minister in Rajkot and then in Vankaner. He was a pensioner of the Rajkot State when he died.

Kaba Gandhi married four times in succession, having lost his wife each time by death. He had two daughters by his first and second marriages. His last wife, Putlibai, bore him a daughter and three sons, I being the youngest.

My father was a lover of his clan, truthful, brave and generous, but short-tempered. To a certain extent he might have been even given to carnal pleasures. For he married for the fourth time when he was over forty. But he was incorruptible and had earned a name for strict impartiality in his family as well as outside. His loyalty to the state was well known. An Assistant Political Agent spoke insultingly of the Rajkot Thakore Saheb, his chief, and he stood up to the insult. The Agent was angry and asked Kaba Gandhi to apologize. This he refused to do and was therefore kept under detention for a few hours. But when the Agent saw that Kaba Gandhi was adamant, he ordered him to be released.

My father never had any ambition to accumulate riches and left us very little property.

He had no education, save that of experience. At best, he might be said to have read up to the fifth Gujarati standard. Of history and geography he was innocent. But his rich experience of practical affairs stood him in good stead in the solution of the most intricate questions and in managing hundreds of men. Of religious training he had very little, but he had that kind of religious culture which frequent visits to temples and listening to religious discourses make available to many Hindus. In his last days he began reading the Gita at the instance of a learned Brahman friend of the family, and he used to repeat aloud some verses every day at the time of worship.

The outstanding impression my mother has left on my memory is that of saintliness. She was deeply religious. She would not think of taking her meals without her daily prayers. Going to Haveli-the Vaishnava temple-was one of her daily duties. As far as my memory can go back, I do not remember her having ever missed the Chaturmas[*]. She would take the hardest vows and keep them without flinching. Illness was no excuse for relaxing them. I can recall her once falling ill when she was observing the Chandrayana[†] vow, but the illness was not allowed to interrupt the observance. To keep two or three consecutive fasts was nothing to her. Living on one meal a day during Chaturmas was a habit with her. Not content with that she fasted every alternate day during one Chaturmas. During another Chaturmas she vowed not to have food without seeing the sun. We children on those days would stand, staring at the sky, waiting to announce the appearance of the sun to our mother. Everyone knows that at the height of the rainy season the sun often does not condescend to show his face. And I remember days when, at his sudden appearance, we would rush and announce it to her, she would run out to se with her own eyes, but by that time the fugitive sun would be gone, thus depriving her of her meal. "That does not matter;" she would say cheerfully, "God did not want me to eat today." And then she would return to her round of duties.

My mother had strong commonsense. She was well informed about all matters of state, and ladies of the court thought highly of her intelligence. Often I would accompany her, exercising the privilege of childhood, and I still remember many lively discussions she had with the widowed mother of the Thakore Saheb.

Of these parents I was born at Porbandar, otherwise known as Sudamapuri, on the 2nd October, 1869. I passed my childhood in Porbandar. I recollect having been put to school. It was with some difficulty that I got through the multiplication tables. The fact that I recollect nothing more of those days than having learnt, in company with other boys, to call our teacher all kinds of names, would strongly suggest that my intellect must have been sluggish, and my memory raw.

Chapter 2: Childhood

I must have been about seven when my father left Porbandar for Rajkot to become a member of the Rajasthanik Court. There I was put into a primary school, and I can well recollect those days, including the names and other particulars of the teachers who taught me. As at Porbandar, so here, there is hardly anything to note about my studies. I could have been only a mediocre student. From this school I went to the suburban

[*] Literally a period of four months. A vow of fasting and semi-fasting during the four months of the rains. The period is a sort of long Lent.

[†] A sort of fast in which the daily quantity of food is increased or diminished according as the moon waxes or wanes.

school and thence to the high school, having already reached my twelfth year. I do not remember having ever told a lie, during this short period, either to my teachers or to my schoolmates. I used to be very shy and avoided all company. My books and my lessons were my sole companions. To be at school at the stroke of the hour and to run back home as soon as the school closed — that was my daily habit. I literally ran back, because I could not bear to talk to anybody. I was even afraid lest anyone should poke fun at me.

There is an incident which occurred at the examination during my first year at the high school and which is worth recording. Mr. Giles, the Educational Inspector, had come on a visit of inspection. He had set us five words to write as a spelling exercise. One of the words was 'kettle'. I had mis-spelt it. The teacher tried to prompt me with the point of his boot, but I would not be prompted. It was beyond me to see that he wanted me to copy the spelling from my neighbour's slate, for I had thought that the teacher was there to supervise us against copying. The result was that all the boys, except myself, were found to have spelt every word correctly. Only I had been stupid. The teacher tried later to bring this stupidity home to me. but without effect. I never could learn the art of 'copying'.

Yet the incident did not in the least diminish my respect for my teacher. I was by nature blind to the faults of elders. Later I came to know of many other failings of this teacher, but my regard for him remained the same. For I had learnt to carry out the orders of elders, not to scan their actions.

Two other incidents belonging to the same period have always clung to my memory. As a rule I had a distaste for any reading beyond my school books. The daily lessons had to be done, because I disliked being taken to task by my teacher as much as I disliked deceiving him. Therefore I would do the lessons, but often without my mind in them. Thus when even the lessons could not be done properly, there was of course no question of any extra reading. But somehow my eyes fell on a book purchased by my father. It was Shravana Pitribhakti Nataka (a play about Sharavana's devotion to his parents). I read it with intense interest. There came to our place about the same time itinerant showmen. One of the pictures I was shown was of Shravana carrying, by means of slings fitted for his shoulders, his blind parents on a pilgrimage. The book and the picture left an indelible impression on my mind. 'Here is an example for you to copy,' I said to myself. The agonized lament of the parents over Shravana's death is still fresh in my memory. The melting tune moved me deeply, and I played it on a concertina which my father had purchased for me.

There was a similar incident connected with another play. Just about this time, I had secured my father's permission to see a play performed by a certain dramatic company. This play-Harishchandra-captured my heart. I could never be tired of seeing it. But how often should I be permitted to go? It haunted me and I must have acted Harishchandra to myself times without number. 'Why should not all be truthful like Harishchandra?' was the question I asked myself day and night. To follow truth and to go through all the ordeals Harishchandra went through was the one ideal it inspired in me. I literally believed in the story of Harishchandra. The thought of it all often made me weep. My commonsense tells me today that Harishchandra could not have been a historical character. Still both Harishchandra and Shravana are living realities for me, and I am sure I should be moved as before if I were to read those plays again today.

Chapter 3: Child marriage

Much as I wish that I had not to write this chapter, I know that I shall have to swallow many such bitter draughts in the course of this narrative. And I cannot do otherwise, if I claim to be a worshipper of Truth. It is my painful duty to have to record here my marriage at the age of thirteen. As I see the youngsters of the same age about me who are under my care, and think of my own marriage, I am inclined to pity myself and to congratulate them on having escaped my lot. I can see no moral argument in support of such a preposterously early marriage.

Let the reader make no mistake. I was married, not betrothed. For in Kathiawad there are two distinct rites — betrothal and marriage. Betrothal is a preliminary promise on the part of the parents of the boy and the girl to join them in marriage, and it is not inviolable. The death of the boy entails no widowhood on the girl. It is an agreement purely between the parents, and the children have no concern with it. Often they are not even informed of it. It appears that I was betrothed thrice, though without my knowledge. I was told that two girls chosen for me had died in turn, and therefore I infer that I was betrothed three times. I have a faint recollection, however, that the third betrothal took place in my seventh year. But I do not recollect having been informed about it. In the present chapter I am talking about my marriage, of which I have the clearest recollection.

It will be remembered that we were three brothers. The first was already married. The elders decided to marry my second brother, who was two or three years my senior, a cousin, possibly a year older, and me, all at the same time. In doing so there was no thought of our welfare, much less our wishes. It was purely a question of their own convenience and economy.

Marriage among Hindus is no simple matter. The parents of the bride and the bridegroom often bring themselves to ruin over it. They waste their substance, they waste their time. Months are taken up over the preparations — in making clothes and ornaments and in preparing budgets for dinners. Each tries to outdo the other in the number and variety of courses to be prepared. Women, whether they have a voice or no, sing themselves hoarse, even get ill, and disturb the peace of their neighbours. These in their turn quietly put up with all the turmoil and bustle, all the dirt and filth, representing the remains of the feasts, because they know that a time will come when they also will be behaving in the same manner.

It would be better, thought my elders, to have all this bother over at one and the same time. Less expense and greater éclat. For money could be freely spent if it had only to be spent once instead of thrice. My father and my uncle were both old, and we were the last children they had to marry. It is likely that they wanted to have the last best time of their lives. In view of all these considerations, a triple wedding was decided upon, and as I have said before, months were taken up in preparation for it.

It was only through these preparations that we got warning of the coming event. I do not think it meant to me anything more than the prospect of good clothes to wear, drum beating, marriage processions, rich dinners and a strange girl to play with. The carnal desire came later. I propose to draw a curtain over my shame, except for a few details worth recording. To these I shall come later. But even they have little to do with the central idea I have kept before me in writing this story.

So my brother and I were both taken to Porbandar from Rajkot. There are some amusing details of the preliminaries to the final drama — e.g., smearing our bodies all over with turmeric paste — but I must omit them.

My father was a Diwan, but nevertheless a servant, and all the more so because he was in favour with the Thakore Saheb. The latter would not let him go until the last moment. And when he did so, he ordered for my father special stage coaches, reducing the journey by two days. But the fates had willed otherwise. Porbandar is 120 miles from Rajkot — a cart journey of five days. My father did the distance in three, but the coach toppled over in the third stage, and he sustained severe injuries. He arrived bandaged all over. Both his and our interest in the coming event was half destroyed, but the ceremony had to be gone through. For how could the marriage dates be changed? However, I forgot my grief over my father's injuries in the childish amusement of the wedding.

I was devoted to my parents. But no less was I devoted to the passions that flesh is heir to. I had yet to learn that all happiness and pleasure should be sacrificed in devoted service to my parents. And yet, as though by way of punishment for my desire for pleasures, an incident happened, which has ever since rankled in my mind and which I will relate later. Nishkulanand sings:

> 'Renunciation of objects, without the renunciation of desires, is short-lived, however hard you may try'.

Whenever I sing this song or hear it sung, this bitter untoward incident, rushes to my memory and fills me with shame.

My father put on a brave face in spite of his injuries, and took full part in the wedding. As I think of it, I can even today call before my mind's eye the places where he sat as he went through the different details of the ceremony. Little did I dream then that one day I should severely criticize my father for having married me as a child. Everything on that day seemed to me right and proper and pleasing. There was also my own eagerness to get married. And as everything that my father did then struck me as beyond reproach, the recollection of those things is fresh in my memory. I can picture to myself, even today, how we sat on our wedding dais, how we performed the Saptapadi*, how we, the newly wedded husband and wife, put the sweet Kansar† into each other's mouth, and how we began to live together. And oh! that first night. Two innocent children all unwittingly hurled themselves into the ocean of life. My brother's wife had thoroughly coached me about my behaviour on the first night. I do not know who had coached my wife. I have never asked her about it, nor am I inclined to do so now. The reader may be sure that we were too nervous to face each other. We were certainly too shy. How was I to talk to her, and what was I to say? The coaching could not carry me far. But no coaching is really necessary in such matters. The impressions of the former birth are potent enough to make all coaching superfluous. We gradually began to know each other, and to speak freely together. We were the same age. but I took no time in assuming the authority of a husband.

Chapter 4: Playing the husband

About the time of my marriage, little pamphlets costing a pice, or a pie (I now forget how much), used to be issued, in which conjugal love, thrift, child marriages, and other such subjects were discussed. Whenever I came across any of these, I used to go through them cover to cover, and it was a habit with me to forget what I did not like, and to carry out in practice whatever I liked. Lifelong faithfulness to the wife, inculcated in these booklets as the duty of the husband, remained permanently imprinted on my heart. Furthermore, the passion for truth was innate in me, and to be false to her was therefore out of the question. And then there was very little chance of my being faithless at that tender age.

But the lesson of faithfulness had also an untoward effect. 'If I should be pledged to be faithful to my wife, she also should be pledged to be faithful to me', I said to myself. The thought made me a jealous husband. Her duty was easily converted into my right to exact faithfulness from her, and if it had to be exacted, I should be watchfully tenacious of the right. I had absolutely no reason to suspect my wife's fidelity, but jealousy does

* 'Saptapadi' are seven steps the Hindu bride and groom walk together, making at the same time promises of mutual fidelity and devotion, after which the marriage becomes irrevocable.

† 'Kansar' is a preparation of wheat which the pair partake of together after the completion of the ceremony.

not wait for reasons. I must needs be forever on the look-out regarding her movements, and therefore she could not go anywhere without my permission. This sowed the seeds of a bitter quarrel between us. The restraint was virtually a sort of imprisonment. And Kasturbai was not the girl to brook any such thing. She made it a point to go out whenever and wherever she liked. More restraint on my part resulted in more liberty being taken by her, and in my getting more and more cross. Refusal to speak to one another thus became the order of the day with us, married children. I think it was quite innocent of Kasturbai to have taken those liberties with my restrictions. How could a guileless girl brook any restraint on going to the temple or on going on visits to friends? If I had the right to impose restrictions on her, had not she also similar right? All this is clear to me today. But at that time I had to make good my authority as a husband!

Let not the reader think, however, that ours was a life of unrelieved bitterness. For my severities were all based on love. I wanted to make my wife an ideal wife. My ambition was to make her live a pure life, learn what I learnt, and identify her life and thought with mine.

I do not know whether Kasturbai had any such ambition. She was illiterate. By nature she was simple, independent, persevering and, with me at least, reticent. She was not impatient of her ignorance and I do not recollect my studies having ever spurred her to go in for a similar adventure. I fancy, therefore, that my ambition was all one-sided. My passion was entirely centered on one woman, and I wanted it to be reciprocated. But even if there were no reciprocity, it could not be all unrelieved misery because there was active love on one side at least.

I must say I was passionately fond of her. Even at school I used to think of her, and the thought of nightfall and our subsequent meeting was ever haunting me. Separation was unbearable. I used to keep her awake till late in the night with my idle talk. If with this devouring passion there had not been in me a burning attachment to duty, I should either have fallen a prey to disease and premature death, or have sunk into a burdensome existence. But the appointed tasks had to be gone through every morning, and lying to anyone was out of the question. It was this last thing that saved me from many a pitfall.

I have already said that Kasturbai was illiterate. I was very anxious to teach her, but lustful love left me no time. For one thing the teaching had to be done against her will, and that too at night. I dared not meet her in the presence of the elders, much less talk to her. Kathiawad had then, and to a certain extent has even today, its own peculiar, useless and barbarous Purdah. Circumstances were thus unfavourable. I must therefore confess that most of my efforts to instruct Kasturbai in our youth were unsuccessful. And when I awoke from the sleep of lust, I had already launched forth into public life, which did not leave me much spare time. I failed likewise to instruct her through private tutors. As a result Kasturbai can now with difficulty write simple letters and understand simple Gujarati. I am sure that, had my love for her been absolutely untainted with lust, she would be a learned lady today; for I could than have conquered her dislike for studies. I know that nothing is impossible for pure love.

I have mentioned one circumstance that more or less saved me from the disasters of lustful love. There is another worth noting. Numerous examples have convinced me that God ultimately saves him whose motive is pure. Along with the cruel custom of child marriages, Hindu society has another custom which to a certain extent diminishes the evils of the former. Parents do not allow young couples to stay long together. The child-wife spends more than half her time at her father's place. Such was the case with us. That is to say, during the first five years of our married life (from the age of 13 to 18), we could not have lived together longer than an aggregate period of three years. We would hardly have spent six months together, when there would be a call to my wife from her parents. Such calls were very unwelcome in those days, but they saved us both. At the age of eighteen I went to England, and this meant a long and healthy spell of separation. Even after my return from England we hardly stayed together longer than six months. For I had to run up and down between Rajkot and Bombay. Then came the call from South Africa, and that found me already fairly free from the carnal appetite.

Chapter 5: At the high school

I have already said that I was learning at the high school when I was married. We three brothers were learning at the same school. The eldest brother was in a much higher class, and the brother who was married at the same time as I was only one class ahead of me. Marriage resulted in both of us wasting a year. Indeed the result was even worse for my brother, for he gave up studies altogether. Heaven knows how many youths are in the same plight as he. Only in our present Hindu society do studies and marriage go thus hand in hand.

My studies were continued. I was not regarded as a dunce at the high school. I always enjoyed the affection of my teachers. Certificates of progress and character used to be sent to the parents every year. I never had a bad certificate. In fact I even won prizes after I passed out of the second standard. In the fifth and sixth I obtained scholarships of rupees four and ten respectively, an achievement for which I have to thank good luck more than my merit. For the scholarships were not open to all, but reserved for the best boys amongst those coming from the Sorath Division of Kathiawad. And in those days there could not have been many boys from Sorath in a class of forty to fifty.

My own recollection is that I had not any high regard for my ability. I used to be astonished whenever I won prizes and scholarships. But I very jealously guarded my character. The least little blemish drew tears from my eyes. When I merited, or seemed to the teacher to merit, a rebuke, it was unbearable for me. I remember having once received corporal punishment. I did not so much mind the punishment as the fact that it was considered my desert. I wept piteously. That was when I was in the first or second standard. There was another such incident during the time when I was in the seventh standard. Dorabji Edulji Gimi was the headmaster then. He was popular among boys, as he was a disciplinarian, a man of method and a good teacher. He had made gymnastics and cricket compulsory for boys of the upper standards. I disliked both. I never took part in any exercise, cricket or football, before they were made compulsory. My shyness was one of the reasons for this aloofness, which I now see was wrong. I then had the false notion that gymnastics had nothing to do with education. Today I know that physical training should have as much place in the curriculum as mental training.

I may mention, however, that I was none the worse for abstaining from exercise. That was because I had read in books about the benefits of long walks in the open air, and having liked the advice, I had formed a habit of taking walks, which has still remained with me. These walks gave me a fairly hardy constitution.

The reason for my dislike for gymnastics was my keen desire to serve as nurse to my father. As soon as the school closed, I would hurry home and begin serving him. Compulsory exercise came directly in the way of this service. I requested Mr. Gimi to exempt me from gymnastics so that I might be free to serve my father. But he would not listen to me. Now it happened that one Saturday, when we had school in the morning, I had to go from home to the school for gymnastics at four o'clock in the afternoon. I had no watch, and the clouds deceived me. Before I reached the school the boys had all left. The next day Mr. Gimi, examining the roll, found me marked absent. Being asked the reason for absence, I told him what had happened. He refused to believe me and ordered me to pay a fine of one or two annas (I cannot now recall how much).

I was convicted of lying! That deeply pained me. How was I to prove my innocence? There was no way. I cried in deep anguish. I saw that a man of truth must also be a man of care. This was the first and last instance of my carelessness in school. I have a faint recollection that I finally succeeded in getting the fine remitted. The exemption from exercise was of course obtained, as my father wrote himself to the headmaster saying that he wanted me at home after school.

But though I was none the worse for having neglected exercise, I am still paying the penalty of another neglect. I do not know whence I got the notion that good handwriting was not a necessary part of education, but I retained it until I went to England. When later, especially in South Africa, I saw the beautiful handwriting of lawyers and young men born and educated in South Africa, I was ashamed of myself and repented of my neglect. I saw that bad handwriting should be regarded as a sign of an imperfect education. I tried later to improve mine, but it was too late. I could never repair the neglect of my youth. Let every young man and woman be warned by my example, and understand that good handwriting is a necessary part of education. I am now of opinion that children should first be taught the art of drawing before learning how to write. Let the child learn his letters by observation as he does different objects, such as flowers, birds, etc., and let him learn handwriting only after he has learnt to draw objects. He will then write a beautifully formed hand.

Two more reminiscences of my school days are worth recording. I had lost one year because of my marriage, and the teacher wanted me to make good the loss by skipping a class — a privilege usually allowed to industrious boys. I therefore had only six months in the third standard and was prompted to the forth after the examinations which are followed by the summer vacation. English became the medium of instruction in most subjects from the fourth standard. I found myself completely at sea. Geometry was a new subject in which I was not particularly strong, and the English medium made it still more difficult for me. The teacher taught the subject very well, but I could not follow him. Often I would lose heart and think of going back to the third standard, feeling that the packing of two years' studies into a single year was too ambitious. But this would discredit not only me, but also the teacher; because, counting on my industry, he had recommended my promotion. So the fear of the double discredit kept me at my post. When however, with much effort I reached the thirteenth proposition of Euclid, the utter simplicity of the subject was suddenly revealed to me. A subject which only required a pure and simple use of one's reasoning powers could not be difficult. Ever since that time geometry has been both easy and interesting for me.

Samskrit, however, proved a harder task. In geometry there was nothing to memorize, whereas in Samskrit, I thought, everything had to be learnt by heart. This subject also was commenced from the fourth standard. As soon as I entered the sixth I became disheartened. The teacher was a hard taskmaster, anxious, as I thought, to force the boys. There was a sort of rivalry going on between the Samskrit and the Persian teachers. The Persian teacher was lenient. The boys used to talk among themselves that Persian was very easy and the Persian teacher very good and considerate to the students. The 'easiness' tempted me and one day I sat in the Persian class. The Samskrit teacher was grieved. He called me to his side and said: 'How can you forget that you are the son of a Vaishnava father? Won't you learn the language of your own religion? If you have any difficulty, why not come to me? I want to teach you students Samskrit to the best of my ability. As you proceed further, you will find in it things of absorbing interest. You should not lose heart. Come and sit again in the Samskrit class.'

This kindness put me to shame. I could not disregard my teacher's affection. Today I cannot but think with gratitude of Krishnashankar Pandya. For if I had not acquired the little Samskrit that I learnt then, I should have found it difficult to take any interest in our sacred books. In fact I deeply regret that I was not able to acquire a more thorough knowledge of the language, because I have since realized that every Hindu boy and girl should possess sound Samskrit learning. It is now my opinion that in all Indian curricula of higher education there should be a place for Hindi, Samskrit, Persian, Arabic and English, besides of course the vernacular. This big list need not frighten anyone. If our education were more systematic, and the boys free from the burden of having to learn their subjects through a foreign medium, I am sure learning all these languages would not be an irksome task, but a perfect pleasure. A scientific knowledge of one language makes a knowledge of other languages comparatively easy.

In reality, Hindi, Gujarati and Samskrit may be regarded as one language, and Persian and Arabic also as one. Though Persian belongs to the Aryan, and Arabic to the Semitic family of languages, there is a close relationship between Persian and Arabic, because both claim their full growth through the rise of Islam. Urdu I have not regarded as a distinct language, because it has adopted the Hindi grammar and its vocabulary is mainly Persian and Arabic, and he who would learn good Urdu must learn Persian and Arabic, as one who would learn good Gujarati, Hindi, Bengali, or Marathi must learn Samskrit.

Chapter 6: A tragedy

Amongst my few friends at the high school I had, at different times, two who might be called intimate. One of these friendships did not last long, though I never forsook my friend. He forsook me, because I made friends with the other. This latter friendship I regard as a tragedy in my life. It lasted long. I formed it in spirit of a reformer.

This companion was originally my elder brother's friend. They were classmates. I knew his weakness, but I regarded him as a faithful friend. My mother, my eldest brother, and my wife warned me that I was in bad company. I was too proud to heed my wife's warning. But I dared not go against the opinion of my mother and my eldest brother. Nevertheless I pleaded with them saying, 'I know he has the weaknesses you attribute to him, but you do not know his virtues. He cannot lead me astray, as my association with him is meant to reform him. For I am sure that if he reforms his ways, he will be a splendid man. I beg you not to be anxious on my account.'

I do not think this satisfied them, but they accepted my explanation and let me go my way.

I have seen since that I had calculated wrongly. A reformer cannot afford to have close intimacy with him whom he seeks to reform. True friendship is an identity of souls rarely to be found in this world. Only between like natures can friendship be altogether worthy and enduring. Friends react on one another. Hence in friendship there is very little scope for reform. I am of opinion that all exclusive intimacies are to be avoided; for man takes in vice far more readily than virtue. And he who would be friends with

God must remain alone, or make the whole world his friend. I may be wrong, but my effort to cultivate an intimate friendship proved a failure.

A wave of 'reform' was sweeping over Rajkot at the time when I first came across this friend. He informed me that many of our teachers were secretly taking meat and wine. He also named many well-known people of Rajkot as belonging to the same company. There were also, I was told, some high-school boys among them.

I was surprised and pained. I asked my friend the reason and he explained it thus: 'We are a weak people because we do not eat meat. The English are able to rule over us, because they are meat-eaters. You know how hardy I am, and how great a runner too. It is because I am a meat-eater. Meat-eaters do not have boils or tumours, and even if they sometimes happen to have any, these heal quickly. Our teachers and other distinguished people who eat meat are no fools. They know its virtues. You should do likewise. There is nothing like trying. Try, and see what strength it gives.'

All these pleas on behalf of meat-eating were not advanced at a single sitting. They represent the substance of a long and elaborate argument which my friend was trying to impress upon me from time to time. My elder brother had already fallen. He therefore supported my friend's argument. I certainly looked feeble-bodied by the side of my brother and this friend. They were both hardier, physically stronger, and more daring. This friend's exploits cast a spell over me. He could run long distances and extraordinarily fast. He was an adept in high and long jumping. He could put up with any amount of corporal punishment. He would often display his exploits to me and, as one is always dazzled when he sees in others the qualities that he lacks himself, I was dazzled by this friend's exploits. This was followed by a strong desire to be like him. I could hardly jump or run. Why should not I also be as strong as he?

Moreover, I was a coward. I used to be haunted by the fear of thieves, ghosts, and serpents. I did not dare to stir out of doors at night. Darkness was a terror to me. It was almost impossible for me to sleep in the dark, as I would imagine ghosts coming from one direction, thieves from another and serpents from a third. I could not therefore bear to sleep without a light in the room. How could I disclose my fears to my wife, no child, but already at the threshold of youth, sleeping by my side? I knew that she had more courage than I, and I felt ashamed of myself. She knew no fear of serpents and ghosts. She could go out anywhere in the dark. My friend knew all these weaknesses of mine. He would tell me that he could hold in his hand live serpents, could defy thieves and did not believe in ghosts. And all this was, of course, the result of eating meat.

A doggerel of the Gujarati poet Narmad was in vogue amongst us schoolboys, as follows:

Behold the mighty Englishman He rules the Indian small, Because being a meat-eater He is five cubits tall.

All this had its due effect on me. I was beaten. It began to grow on me that meat-eating was good, that it would make me strong and daring, and that, if the whole county took to meat-eating, the English could be overcome.

A day was thereupon fixed for beginning the experiment. It had to be conducted in secret. The Gandhis were Vaishnavas. My parents were particularly staunch Vaishnavas. They would regularly visit the Haveli. The family had even its own temples. Jainism was strong in Gujarat, and its influence was felt everywhere and on all occasions. The opposition to and abhorrence of meat-eating that existed in Gujarat among the Jains and Vaishnavas were to be seen nowhere else in India or outside in such strength. These were the traditions in which I was born and bred. And I was extremely devoted to my parents. I knew that the moment they came to know of my having eaten meat, they would be shocked to death. Moreover, my love of truth made me extra cautious. I cannot say that I did not know then that I should have to deceive my parents if I began eating meat. But my mind was bent on the 'reform'. It was not a question of pleasing the palate. I did not know that it had a particularly good relish. I wished to be strong and daring and wanted my countrymen also to be such, so that we might defeat the English and make India free. The word Swaraj I had not yet heard. But I knew what freedom meant. The frenzy of the 'reform' blinded me. And having ensured secrecy, I persuaded myself that mere hiding the deed from parents was no departure from truth.

Chapter 7: A tragedy (continued)

So the day came. It is difficult fully to describe my condition. There were, on the one hand, the zeal for 'reform', and the novelty of making a momentous departure in life. There was, on the other, the shame of hiding like a thief to do this very thing. I cannot say which of the two swayed me more. We went in search of a lonely spot by the river, and there I saw, for the first time in my life — meat. There was baker's bread also. I relished neither. The goat's meat was as tough as leather. I simply could not eat it. I was sick and had to leave off eating.

I had a very bad night afterwards. A horrible night-mare haunted me. Every time I dropped off to sleep it would seem as though a live goat were bleating inside me, and I would jump up full of remorse. But then I would remind myself that meat-eating was a duty and so become more cheerful.

My friend was not a man to give in easily. He now began to cook various delicacies with meat, and dress them neatly. And for dining, no longer was the secluded spot on the river chosen, but a State house, with its dining hall, and tables and chairs, about which my friend had made arrangements in collusion with the chief cook there.

This bait had its effect. I got over my dislike for bread, forswore my compassion for the goats, and became a relisher of meat-dishes, if not of meat itself. This went on for about a year. But not more than half a dozen meat-feasts were enjoyed in all; because the State house was not available every day, and there was the obvious difficulty about frequently preparing expensive savoury meat-dishes. I had no money to pay for this 'reform'. My friend had therefore always to find the wherewithal. I had no knowledge where he found it. But find it he did, because he was bent on turning me into a meat-eater.

But even his means must have been limited, and hence these feasts had necessarily to be few and far between.

Whenever I had occasion to indulge in these surreptitious feasts, dinner at home was out of the question. My mother would naturally ask me to come and take my food and want to know the reason why I did not wish to eat. I would say to her, 'I have no appetite today; there is something wrong with my digestion.' It was not without compunction that I devised these pretexts. I knew I was lying, and lying to my mother. I also knew that, if my mother and father came to know of my having become a meat-eater, they would be deeply shocked. This knowledge was gnawing at my heart.

Therefore I said to myself: 'Though it is essential to eat meat, and also essential to take up food 'reform' in the country, yet deceiving and lying to one's father and mother is worse than not eating meat. In their lifetime, therefore, meat-eating must be out of the question. When they are no more and I have found my freedom, I will eat meat openly, but until that moment arrives I will abstain from it.'

This decision I communicated to my friend, and I have never since gone back to meat. My parents never knew that two of their sons had become meat-eaters.

I abjured meat out of the purity of my desire not to lie to my parents, but I did not abjure the company of my friend. My zeal for reforming him had proved disastrous for me, and all the time I was completely unconscious of the fact.

The same company would have led me into faithlessness to my wife. But I was saved by the skin of my teeth. My friend once took me to a brothel. He sent me in with the necessary instructions. It was all prearranged. The bill had already been paid. I went into the jaws of sin, but God in His infinite mercy protected me against myself. I was almost struck blind and dumb in this den of vice. I sat near the woman on her bed, but I was tongue-tied. She naturally lost patience with me, and showed me the door, with abuses and insults. I then felt as though my manhood had been injured, and wished to sink into the ground for shame. But I have ever since given thanks to God for having saved me. I can recall four more similar incidents in my life, and in most of them my good fortune, rather than any effort on my part, saved me. From a strictly ethical point of view, all these occasions must be regarded as moral lapses; for the carnal desire was there, and it was as good as the act. But from the ordinary point of view, a man who is saved from physically committing sin is regarded as saved. And I was saved only in that sense. There are some actions from which an escape is a godsend both for the man who escapes and for those about him. Man, as soon as he gets back his consciousness of right, is thankful to the Divine mercy for the escape. As we know that a man often succumbs to temptation, however much he say resist it, we also know that Providence often intercedes and saves him in spite of himself. How all this happens — how far a man is free and how far a creature of circumstances — how far free-will comes into play and where fate enters on the scene — all this is a mystery and will remain a mystery.

But to go on with the story. Even this was far from opening my eyes to the viciousness of my friend's company. I therefore had many more bitter draughts in store for me, until my eyes were actually opened by an ocular demonstration of some of his lapses quite unexpected by me. But of them later, as we are proceeding chronologically.

One thing, however, I must mention now, as it pertains to the same period. One of the reasons of my differences with my wife was undoubtedly the company of this friend. I was both a devoted and a jealous husband, and this friend fanned the flame of my suspicions about my wife. I never could doubt his veracity. And I have never forgiven myself the violence of which I have been guilty in often having pained my wife by acting on his information. Perhaps only a Hindu wife would tolerate these hardships, and that is why I have regarded woman as an incarnation of tolerance. A servant wrongly suspected may throw up his job, a son in the same case may leave his father's roof, and a friend may put an end to the friendship. A wife, if she suspects her husband, will keep quiet, but if her husband suspects her, she is ruined. Where is she to go? A Hindu wife may not seek divorce in a law-court. Law has no remedy for her. And I can never forget or forgive myself for a having driven my wife to that desperation.

The canker of suspicion was rooted out only when I understood Ahimsa* in all its bearings. I saw then the glory of Brahmacharya† and realized that the wife is not the husband's bondslave, but his companion and his helpmate, and an equal partner in all his joys and sorrows — as free as the husband to choose her own path. Whenever I think of those dark days of doubts and suspicions, I am filled with loathing of my folly and my lustful cruelty, and I deplore my blind devotion to a friend.

Chapter 8: Stealing and atonement

I have still to relate some of my failings during this meat-eating period and also previous to it, which date from before my marriage or soon after.

A relative and I became fond of smoking. Not that we saw any good in smoking, or were enamoured of the smell of a cigarette. We simply imagined a sort of pleasure in

---

* 'Ahimsa' means literally not-hurting, non-violence.

† 'Brahmacharya' means literally conduct that leads one to God. Its technical meaning is self-restraint, particularly mastery over the sexual organ.

emitting clouds of smoke from our mouths. My uncle had the habit, and when we saw him smoking, we thought we should copy his example. But we had no money. So we began to pilfer stumps of cigarettes thrown away by my uncle.

The stumps, however, were not always available, and could not emit much smoke either. So we began to steal coppers from the servant's pocket money in order to purchase Indian cigarettes. But the question was where to keep them. We could not of course smoke in the presence of elders. We managed somehow for a few weeks on these stolen coppers. In the meantime we heard that the stalks of a certain plant were porous and could be smoked like cigarettes. We got them and began this kind of smoking.

But we were far from being satisfied with such things as these. Our want of independence began to smart. It was unbearable that we should be unable to do anything without the elders' permission. At last, in sheer disgust, we decided to commit suicide!

But how were we to do it? From where were we to get the poison? We heard that Dhatura seeds were an effective poison. Off we went to the jungle in search of these seeds, and got them. Evening was thought to be the auspicious hour. We went to Kedarji Mandir, put ghee in the temple-lamp, had the darshan and then looked for a lonely corner. But our courage failed us. Supposing we were not instantly killed? And what was the good of killing ourselves? Why not rather put up with the lack of independence? But we swallowed two or three seeds nevertheless. We dared not take more. Both of us fought shy of death, and decided to go toRamji Mandir to compose ourselves, and to dismiss the thought of suicide.

I realized that it was not as easy to commit suicide as to contemplate it. And since then, whenever I have heard of someone threatening to commit suicide, it has had little or on effect on me.

The thought of suicide ultimately resulted in both of us bidding good-bye to the habit of smoking stumps of cigarettes and of stealing the servant's coppers for the purpose of smoking.

Ever since I have been grown up, I have never desired to smoke and have always regarded the habit of smoking as barbarous, dirty and harmful. I have never understood why there is such a rage for smoking throughout the world. I cannot bear to travel in a compartment full of people smoking. I become choked.

But much more serious than this theft was the one I was guilty of a little later. I pilfered the coppers when I was twelve or thirteen, possibly less. The other theft was committed when I was fifteen. In this case I stole a bit of gold out of my meat-eating brother's armlet. This brother had run into a debt of about twenty-five rupees. He had on his arm an armlet of solid gold. It was not difficult to clip a bit out of it.

Well, it was done, and the debt cleared. But this became more than I could bear. I resolved never to steal again. I also made up my mind to confess it to my father. But I did not dare to speak. Not that I was afraid of my father beating me. No I do not recall his ever having beaten any of us. I was afraid of the pain that I should cause him. But I felt that the risk should be taken; that there could not be a cleansing without a confession.

I decided at last to write out the confession, to submit it to my father, and ask his forgiveness. I wrote it on a slip of paper and handed it to him myself. In this note not only did I confess my guilt, but I asked adequate punishment for it, and closed with a request to him not to punish himself for my offence. I also pledged myself never to steal in future.

I was trembling as I handed the confession to my father. He was then suffering from a fistula and was confined to bed. His bed was a plain wooden plank. I handed him the note and sat opposite the plank.

He read it through, and pearl-drops trickled down his cheeks, wetting the paper. For a moment he closed his eyes in thought and then tore up the note. He had sat up to read it. He again lay down. I also cried. I could see my father's agony. If I were a painter I could draw a picture of the whole scene today. It is still so vivid in my mind.

Those pearl-drops of love cleansed my heart, and washed my sin away. Only he who has experienced such love can know what it is. As the hymn says:

Only he Who is smitten with the arrows of love, Knows its power.

This was, for me, an object-lesson in Ahimsa. Then I could read in it nothing more than a father's love, but today I know that it was pure Ahimsa. When such Ahimsa becomes all-embracing, it transforms everything it touches. There is no limit to its power.

This sort of sublime forgiveness was not natural to my father. I had thought that he would be angry, say hard things, and strike his forehead. But he was so wonderfully peaceful, and I believe this was due to my clean confession. A clean confession, combined with a promise never to commit the sin again, when offered before one who has the right to receive it, is the purest type of repentance. I know that my confession made my father feel absolutely safe about me, and increased his affection for me beyond measure.

Chapter 9: My father's death and my double shame

The time of which I am now speaking is my sixteenth year. My father, as we have seen, was bed-ridden, suffering from a fistula. My mother, an old servant of the house, and I were his principal attendants. I had the duties of a nurse, which mainly consisted in dressing the wound, giving my father his medicine, and compounding drugs whenever they had to be made up at home. Every night I massaged his legs and retired only when he asked me to do so or after he had fallen asleep. I loved to do this service. I do not remember ever having neglected it. All the time at my disposal, after the performance of the daily duties, was divided between school and attending on my father. I would only go out for an evening walk either when he permitted me or when he was feeling well.

This was also the time when my wife was expecting a baby — a circumstance which, as I can see today, meant a double shame for me. For one thing I did not restrain myself, as I should have done, whilst I was yet a student. And secondly, this carnal lust got the better of what I regarded as my duty to study, and of what was even a greater duty, my devotion to my parents, Shravana having been my ideal since childhood. Every night whilst my hands were busy massaging my father's legs, my mind was hovering about the bed-room — and that too at a time when religion, medical science and commonsense alike forbade sexual intercourse. I was always glad to be relieved from my duty, and went straight to the bed-room after doing obeisance to my father.

At the same time my father was getting worse every day. Ayurvedic physicians had tried all their ointments, Hakims their plasters, and local quacks their nostrums. An English surgeon had also used his skill. As the last and only resort he had recommended a surgical operation. But the family physician came in the way. He disapproved of an operation being performed at such an advanced age. The physician was competent and well known, and his advice prevailed. The operation was abandoned, and various medicines purchased for the purpose were of no account. I have an impression that, if the physician had allowed the operation, the wound would have been easily healed. The operation also was to have been performed by a surgeon who was then well known in Bombay. But God had willed otherwise. When death is imminent, who can think of the right remedy? My father returned from Bombay with all the paraphernalia of the operation, which were now useless. He despaired of living any longer. He was getting weaker and weaker, until at last he had to be asked to perform the necessary functions in bed. But up to the last he refused to do anything of the kind, always insisting on going through the strain of leaving his bed. The Vaishnavite rules about external cleanliness are so inexorable.

Such cleanliness is quite essential no doubt, but Western medical science has taught us that all the functions, including a bath, can be done in bed with the strictest regard to cleanliness, and without the slightest discomfort to the patient, the bed always remaining spotlessly clean. I should regard such cleanliness as quite consistent with Vaishnavism. But my father's insistence on leaving the bed only struck me with wonder then, and I had nothing but admiration for it.

The dreadful night came. My uncle was then in Rajkot. I have a faint recollection that he came to Rajkot having had news that my father was getting worse. The brothers were deeply attached to each other. My uncle would sit near my father's bed the whole day, and would insist on sleeping by his bedside after sending us all to sleep. No one had dreamt that this was to be the fateful night. The danger of course was there.

It was ten-thirty or eleven p.m. I was giving the massage. My uncle offered to relieve me. I was glad and went straight to the bed-room. My wife, poor thing, was fast asleep. But how could she sleep when I was there? I woke her up. In five or six minutes, however, the servant knocked at the door. I started with alarm. 'Get up,' he said, 'Father is very ill.' I knew of course that he was very ill, and so I guessed what 'very ill' meant at that moment. I sprang out of bed.

'What is the matter? Do tell me!'

'Father is no more.'

So all was over! I had but to wring my hands. I felt deeply ashamed and miserable. I ran to my father's room. I saw that, if animal passion had not blinded me, I should have been spared the torture of separation from my father during his last moments. I should have been massaging him, and he would have died in my arms. But now it was my uncle who had this privilege. He was so deeply devoted to his elder brother that he had earned the honour of doing him the last services! My father had forebodings of the coming event. He had made a sign for pen and paper, and written: 'Prepare for the last rites.' He had then snapped the amulet off his arm and also his gold necklace of tulasi-beads and flung them aside. A moment after this he was no more.

The shame, to which I have referred in a foregoing chapter, was this shame of my carnal desire even at the critical hour of my father's death, which demanded wakeful service. It was a blot I have never been able to efface or forget, and I have always thought that, although my devotion to my parents knew no bounds and I would have given up anything for it, yet it was weighed and found unpardonably wanting because my mind was at the same moment in the grip of lust. I have therefore always regarded myself as a lustful, though a faithful, husband. It took me long to get free from the shackles of lust, and I had to pass through many ordeals before I could overcome it.

Before I close this chapter of my double shame, I may mention that the poor mite that was born to my wife scarcely breathed for more than three or four days. Nothing else could be expected. Let all those who are married be warned by my example.

Chapter 10: Glimpses of religion

From my sixth or seventh year up to my sixteenth I was at school, being taught all sorts of things except religion. I may say that I failed to get from the teachers what they could have given me without any effort on their part. And yet I kept on picking up things here and there from my surroundings. The term 'religion' I am using in its broadest sense, meaning thereby self-realization or knowledge of self.

Being born in the Vaishnava faith, I had often to go to the Haveli. But it never appealed to me. I did not like its glitter and pomp. Also I heard rumours of immorality being practised there, and lost all interest in it. Hence I could gain nothing from the Haveli.

But what I failed to get there I obtained from my nurse, an old servant of the family, whose affection for me I still recall. I have said before that there was in me a fear of ghosts and spirits. Rambha, for that was her name, suggested, as a remedy for this fear, the repetition of Ramanama. I had more faith in her than in her remedy, and so at a tender age I began repeating Ramanama to cure my fear of ghosts and spirits. This was of course short-lived, but the good seed sown in childhood was not sown in vain. I think it is due to the seed sown by that good woman Rambha that today Ramanama is an infallible remedy for me.

Just about this time, a cousin of mine who was a devotee of the Ramayana arranged for my second brother and me to learn Ram Raksha. We got it by heart, and made it a rule to recite it every morning after the bath. The practice was kept up as long as we were in Porbandar. As soon as we reached Rajkot, it was forgotten. For I had not much belief in it. I recited it partly because of my pride in being able to recite Ram Raksha with correct pronunciation.

What, however, left a deep impression on me was the reading of the Ramayana before my father. During part of his illness my father was in Porbandar. There every evening he used to listen to the Ramayana. The reader was a great devotee of Rama — Ladha Maharaj of Bileshvar. It was said of him that he cured himself of his leprosy not by any medicine, but by applying to the affected parts bilva leaves which had been cast away after being offered to the image of Mahadeva in Bileshvar temple, and by the regular repetition of Ramanama. His faith it, it was said, had made him whole. This may or may not be true. We at any rate believed the story. And it is a fact that when Ladha Maharaj began his reading of the Ramayana his body was entirely free from leprosy. He had a melodious voice. He would sing the Dohas (couplets) and Chopais (quatrains), and explain them, losing himself in the discourse and carrying his listeners along with him. I must have been thirteen at that time, but I quite remember being enraptured by his reading. That laid the foundation of my deep devotion to the Ramayana. Today I regard the Ramayana of Tulasidas as the greatest book in all devotional literature.

A few months after this we came to Rajkot. There was no Ramayana reading there. The Bhagavat, however, used to be read on every Ekadashi* day. Sometimes I attended the reading, but the reciter was uninspiring. Today I see that the Bhagavat is a book which can evoke religious fervour. I have read it in Gujarati with intense interest. But when I heard portions of the original read by Pandit Madan Mohan Malaviya during my twenty-one day's fast, I wished I had heard it in my childhood from such a devotee as he is, so that I could have formed a liking for it at an early age. Impressions formed at that age strike roots deep down into one's nature, and it is my perpetual regret that I was not fortunate enough to hear more good books of this kind read during that period.

In Rajkot, however, I got an early grounding in toleration for all branches of Hinduism and sister religions. For my father and mother would visit the Haveli as also Shiva's and Rama's temples, and would take or send us youngsters there. Jain monks also would

---

* Eleventh day of the bright and the dark half of a lunar month.

pay frequent visits to my father, and would even go out of their way to accept food from us — non-Jains. They would have talks with my father on subjects religious and mundane.

He had, besides, Musalman and Parsi friends, who would talk to him about their own faiths, and he would listen to them always with respect, and often with interest. Being his nurse, I often had a chance to be present at these talks.

These many things combined to inculcate in me a toleration for all faiths.

Only Christianity was at that time an exception. I developed a sort of dislike for it. And for a reason. In those days Christian missionaries used to stand in a corner near the high school and hold forth, pouring abuse on Hindus and their gods. I could not endure this. I must have stood there to hear them once only, but that was enough to dissuade me from repeating the experiment. About the same time, I heard of a well known Hindu having been converted to Christianity. It was the talk of the town that, when he was baptized, he had to eat beef and drink liquor, that he also had to change his clothes, and that thenceforth he began to go about in European costume including a hat. These things got on my nerves. Surely, thought I, a religion that compelled one to eat beef, drink liquor, and change one's own clothes did not deserve the name. I also heard that the new convert had already begun abusing the religion of his ancestors, their customs and their country. All these things created in me a dislike for Christianity.

But the fact that I had learnt to be tolerant to other religions did not mean that I had any living faith in God. I happened, about this time, to come across Manusmriti* which was amongst my father's collection. The story of the creation and similar things in it did not impress me very much, but on the contrary made me incline somewhat towards atheism.

There was a cousin of mine, still alive, for whose intellect I had great regard. To him I turned with my doubts. But he could not resolve them. He sent me away with this answer: 'When you grow up, you will be able to solve these doubts yourself. These questions ought not to be raised at your age.' I was silenced, but was not comforted. Chapters about diet and the like in Manusmriti seemed to me to run contrary to daily practice. To my doubts as to this also, I got the same answer. 'With intellect more developed and with more reading I shall understand it better', I said to myself.

Manusmriti at any rate did not then teach me ahimsa. I have told the story of my meat-eating. Manusmriti seemed to support it. I also felt that it was quite moral to kill serpents, bugs and the like. I remember to have killed at that age bugs and such other insects, regarding it as a duty.

But one thing took deep root in me — the conviction that morality is the basis of things, and that truth is the substance of all morality. Truth became my sole objective. It began to grow in magnitude every day, and my definition of it also has been ever widening.

A Gujarati didactic stanza likewise gripped my mind and heart. Its precept — return good for evil — became my guiding principle. It became such a passion with me that I

---

* Laws of Manu, a Hindu law-giver. They have the sanction of religion.

began numerous experiments in it. Here are those (for me) wonderful lines:
For a bowl of water give a goodly meal:
For a kindly greeting bow thou down with zeal: For a simple penny pay thou back with gold:
If thy life be rescued, life do not withhold.
Thus the words and actions of the wise regard;
Every little service tenfold they reward. But the truly noble know all men as one,
And return with gladness good for evil done.

Chapter 11: Preparation for England

I passed the matriculation examination in 1887. It then used to be held at two centres, Ahmedabad and Bombay. The general poverty of the country naturally led Kathiawad students to prefer the nearer and the cheaper centre. The poverty of my family likewise dictated to me the same choice. This was my first journey from Rajkot to Ahmedabad and that too without a companion.

My elders wanted me to pursue my studies at college after the matriculation. There was a college in Bhavnagar as well as in Bombay, and as the former was cheaper, I decided to go there and join the Samaldas College. I went, but found myself entirely at sea. Everything was difficult. I could not follow, let alone taking interest in, the professors' lectures. It was no fault of theirs. The professors in that College were regarded as first rate. But I was so raw. At the end of the first term, I returned home.

We had, in Mavji Dave, who was a shrewd and learned Brahman an old friend and adviser of the family. He had kept up his connection with the family even after my father's death. He happened to visit us during my vacation. In conversation with my mother and elder brother, he inquired about my studies. Learning that I was at Samaldas College, he said: 'The times are changed. And none of you can expect to succeed to your father's gadi without having had a proper education. Now as this boy is still pursuing his studies, you should all look to him to keep the gadi. It will take him four or five years to get his B.A. degree, which will at best qualify him for a sixty rupees' post, not for a Diwanship. If like my son he went in for law, it would take him longer still, by which time there would be a host of lawyers aspiring for a Diwan's post. I would far rather that you sent him to England. My son Kevalram says it is very easy to become a barrister. In three years' time he will return. Also expenses will not exceed four to five thousand rupees. Think of that barrister who has just come back from England. How stylishly he lives! He could get the Diwanship for the asking. I would strongly advise you to send Mohandas to England this very year. Kevalram has numerous friends in England. He will give notes of introduction to them, and Mohandas will have an easy time of it there.'

Joshiji — that is how we used to call old Mavji Dave — turned to me with complete assurance, and asked: 'Would you not rather go to England than study here?' Nothing could have been more welcome to me. I was fighting shy of my difficult studies. So I jumped at the proposal and said that the sooner I was sent the better. It was no easy business to pass examinations quickly. Could I not be sent to qualify for the medical profession?

My brother interrupted me: 'Father never liked it. He had you in mind when he said that we Vaishnavas should have nothing to do with dissection of dead bodies. Father intended you for the bar.'

Joshiji chimed in: 'I am not opposed to the medical profession as was Gandhiji. Our Shastras are not against it. But a medical degree will not make a Diwan of you, and I want you to be Diwan, or if possible something better. Only in that way could you take under your protecting care your large family. The times are fast changing and getting harder every day. It is the wisest thing therefore to become a barrister.' Turning to my mother he said: 'Now, I must leave. Pray ponder over what I have said. When I come here next I shall expect to hear of preparations for England. Be sure to let me know if I can assist in any way.'

Joshiji went away, and I began building castles in the air.

My elder brother was greatly exercised in his mind. How was he to find the wherewithal to send me? And was it proper to trust a young man like me to go abroad alone?

My mother was sorely perplexed. She did not like the idea of parting with me. This is how she tried to put me off: 'Uncle,' she said, 'is now the eldest member of the family. He should first be consulted. If he consents we will consider the matter.'

My brother had another idea. He said to me: 'We have a certain claim on the Porbandar State. Mr. Lely is the Administrator. He thinks highly of our family and uncle is in his good books. It is just possible that he might recommend you for some State help for your education in England.'

I liked all this and got ready to start off for Porbandar. There was no railway in those days. It was a five days' bullock-cart journey. I have already said that I was a coward. But at that moment my cowardice vanished before the desire to go to England, which completely possessed me. I hired a bullock-cart as far as Dhoraji, and from Dhoraji I took a camel in order to get to Porbandar a day quicker. This was my first camel-ride.

I arrived at last, did obeisance to my uncle, and told him everything. He thought it over and said: 'I am not sure whether it is possible for one to stay in England without prejudice to one's own religion. From all I have heard, I have my doubts. When I meet these big barristers, I see no difference between their life and that of Europeans. They know no scruples regarding food. Cigars are never out of their mouths. They dress as shamelessly as Englishmen. All that would not be in keeping with our family tradition. I am shortly going on a pilgrimage and have not many years to live. At the threshold of death, how dare I give you permission to go to England, to cross the seas? But I will not stand in your way. It is your mother's permission which really matters. If she permits you, then godspeed! Tell her I will not interfere. You will go with my blessings.'

'I could expect nothing more from you,' said I. 'I shall now try to win mother over. But would you not recommend me to Mr. Lely?'

'How can I do that?' said he. 'But he is a good man. You ask for an appointment telling him how you are connected. He will certainly give you one and may even help you.'

I cannot say why my uncle did not give me a note of recommendation. I have a faint idea that he hesitated to co-operate directly in my going to England, which was in his opinion an irreligious act.

I wrote to Mr. Lely, who asked me to see him at his residence. He saw me as he was ascending the staircase; and saying curtly, 'Pass your B.A. fist and then see me. No help can be given to you now,' he hurried upstairs. I had made elaborate preparations to meet him. I had carefully learnt up a few sentences and had bowed low and saluted him with both hands. But all to no purpose!

I thought of my wife's ornaments. I thought of my elder brother, in whom I had the utmost faith. He was generous to a fault, and he loved me as his own son.

I returned to Rajkot from Porbandar and reported all that had happened. I consulted Joshiji, who of course advised even incurring a debt if necessary. I suggested the disposal of my wife's ornaments, which could fetch about two or three thousand rupees. My brother promised to find the money somehow.

My mother, however, was still unwilling. She had begun making minute inquiries. Someone had told her that young men got lost in England. Someone else had said that they took to meat; and yet another that they could not live there without liquor. 'How about all this?' she asked me. I said: 'Will you not trust me? I shall not lie to you. I swear that I shall not touch any of those things. If there were any such danger, would Joshiji let me go?'

'I can trust you,' she said. 'But how can I trust you in a distant land? I am dazed and know not what to do. I will ask Becharji Swami.'

Becharji Swami was originally a Modh Bania, but had now become a Jain monk. He too was a family adviser like Joshiji. He came to my help, and said: 'I shall get the boy solemnly to take the three vows, and then he can be allowed to go.' He administered the oath and I vowed not to touch wine, woman and meat. This done, my mother gave her permission.

The high school had a send-off in my honour. It was an uncommon thing for a young man of Rajkot to go to England. I had written out a few words of thanks. But I could scarcely stammer them out. I remember how my head reeled and how my whole frame shook as I stood up to read them.

With the blessings of my elders, I started for Bombay. This was my first journey from Rajkot to Bombay. My brother accompanied me. But there is many a slip, 'twixt the cup and the lip. There were difficulties to be faced in Bombay.

Chapter 12: Outcaste

With my mother's permission and blessings, I set off exultantly for Bombay, leaving my wife with a baby of a few months. But on arrival there friends told my brother that the Indian Ocean was rough in June and July, and as this was my first voyage, I should not be allowed to sail until November. Someone also reported that a steamer had just been sunk in a gale. This made my brother uneasy, and he refused to take the risk of allowing me to sail immediately. Leaving me with a friend in Bombay, he returned to Rajkot to resume his duty. He put the money for my travelling expenses in the keeping of a brother-in-law, and left word with some friends to give me whatever help I might need.

Time hung heavily on my hands in Bombay. I dreamt continually of going to England.

Meanwhile my caste-people were agitated over my going abroad. No Modh Bania had been to England up to now, and if I dared to do so, I ought to be brought to book! A general meeting of the caste was called and I was summoned to appear before it. I went. Now I suddenly managed to muster up courage I do not know. Nothing daunted, and without the slightest hesitation, I came before the meeting. The Sheth — theheadman of the community — who was distantly related to me and had been on very good terms with my father, thus accosted me:

'In the opinion of the caste, your proposal to go to England is not proper. Our religion forbids voyages abroad. We have also heard that it is not possible to live there without compromising out religion. One is obliged to eat and drink with Europeans!'

To which I replied: 'I do not think it is at all against our religion to go to England. I intend going there for further studies. And I have solemnly promised to my mother to abstain from three things you fear most. I am sure the vow will keep me safe.'

'But we tell you,' rejoined the Sheth, 'that it is not possible to keep our religion there. You know my relations with your father and you ought to listen to my advice.'

'I know those relations.' said I. 'And you are as an elder to me. But I am helpless in this matter. I cannot alter my resolve to go to England. My father's friend and adviser, who is a learned Brahman, sees no objection to my gong to England, and my mother and brother have also given me their permission.'

'But will you disregard the orders of the caste?'

'I am really helpless. I think the caste should not interfere in the matter.'

This incensed the Sheth. He swore at me. I sat unmoved. So the Sheth pronounced his order: 'This boy shall be treated as an outcaste from today. Whoever helps him or goes to see him off at the dock shall be punishable with a fine of one rupee four annas.'

The order had no effect on me, and I took my leave of the Sheth. But I wondered how my brother would take it. Fortunately he remained firm and wrote to assure me that I had his permission to go, the Sheth's order notwithstanding.

The incident, however, made me more anxious than ever to sail. What would happen if they succeeded in bringing pressure to bear on my brother? Supposing something unforeseen happened? As I was thus worrying over my predicament, I heard that a Junagadh vakil was going to England, for being called to the bar, by a boat sailing on the 4th of September. I met the friends to whose care my brother had commended me. They also agreed that I should not let go the opportunity of going in such company. There was no time to be lost. I wired to my brother for permission, which he granted. I asked my brother-in-law to give me the money. But he referred to the order of the Sheth and said that he could not afford to lose caste. I then sought a friend of the family and requested him to accommodate me to the extent of my passage and sundries, and to recover the loan from my brother. The friend was not only good enough to accede to my request, but he cheered me up as well. I was so thankful. With part of the money I at once purchased the passage. Then I had to equip myself for the voyage. There was another friend who had experience in the matter. He got clothes and other things ready. Some of the clothes I liked and some I did not like at all. The necktie, which I delighted in wearing later, I then abhorred. The short jacket I looked upon as immodest. But this dislike was nothing before the desire to go to England, which was uppermost in me. Of provisions also I had enough and to spare for the voyage. A berth was reserved for me by my friends in the same cabin as that of Sjt. Tryambakrai Mazmudar, the Junagadh vakil. They also commended me to him. He was an experienced man of mature age and knew the world. I was yet a stripling of eighteen without any experience of the world. Sjt. Mazmudar told my friends not to worry about me.

I sailed at last from Bombay on the 4th of September.

Chapter 13: In London at last

I did not feel at all sea-sick. But as the days passed, I became fidgety. I felt shy even in speaking to the steward. I was quite unaccustomed to talking English, and except for Sjt. Mazmudar all the other passengers in the second saloon were English. I could not speak to them. For I could rarely follow their remarks when they came up to speak to me, and even when I understood I could not reply. I had to frame every sentence in my mind, before I could bring it out. I was innocent of the use of knives and forks and had not the boldness to inquire what dishes on the menu were free of meat, I therefore never took meals at table but always had them in my cabin, and they consisted principally of sweets and fruits which I had brought with me. Sjt. Mazmudar had no difficulty, and he mixed with everybody. He would move about freely on deck, while I hid myself in the cabin the whole day, only venturing up on deck when there were but few people. Sjt. Mazmudar kept pleading with me to associate with the passengers and to talk with them freely. He told me that lawyers should have a long tongue, and related to me his legal experiences. He advised me to take every possible opportunity of talking English, and not to mind making mistakes which were obviously unavoidable with a foreign tongue. But nothing could make me conquer my shyness.

An English passenger, taking kindly to me, drew me into conversation. He was older than I. He asked me what I ate, what I was, where I was going, why I was shy, and so on. He also advised me to come to table. He laughed at my insistence on abjuring meat, and said in a friendly way when we were in the Red Sea: 'It is all very well so far but you will have to revise your decision in the Bay of Biscay. And it is so cold in England that one cannot possibly live there without meat.'

'But I have heard that people can live there without eating meat,' I said.

'Rest assured it is a fib,' said he. 'No one, to my knowledge, lives there without being a meat-eater. Don't you see that I am not asking you to take liquor, though I do so? But I do think you should eat meat, for you cannot live without it.'

'I thank you for your kind advice, but I have solemnly promised to my mother not to touch meat, and therefore I cannot think of taking it. If it be found impossible to get on without it, I will far rather go back to India than eat meat in order to remain there.'

We entered the Bay of Biscay, but I did not begin to feel the need either of meat or liquor. I had been advised to collect certificates of my having abstained from meat, and I asked the English friend to give me one. He gladly gave it and I treasured it for some time. But when I saw later that one could get such a certificate in spite of being a meat-eater, it lost all its charm for me. If my word was not to be trusted, where was the use of possessing a certificate in the matter?

However, we reached Southampton, as far as I remember, on a Saturday. On the boat I had worn a black suit, the white flannel one, which my friends had got me, having been kept especially for wearing when I landed. I had thought that white clothes would suit me better when I stepped ashore, and therefore I did so in white flannels. Those were the last days of September, and I found I was the only person wearing such clothes. I left in charge of an agent of Grindlay and Co. all my kit, including the keys, seeing that many others had done the same and I must follow suit.

I had four notes of introduction: to Dr. P. J. Mehta, to Sjt. Dalpatram Shukla, to Prince Ranjitsinhji and to Dadabhai Naoroji. Someone on board had advised us to put up at the Victoria Hotel in London. Sjt Mazmudar and I accordingly went there. The shame of being the only person in white clothes was already too much for me. And when at the Hotel I was told that I should not get my thing from Grindlay's the next day, it being a Sunday, I was exasperated.

Dr. Mehta, to whom I had wired from Southampton, called at about eight o'clock the same evening. He gave me a hearty greeting. He smiled at my being in flannels. As we were talking, I casually picked up his top-hat, and trying to see how smooth it was, passed my hand over it the wrong way and disturbed the fur. Dr. Mehta looked somewhat angrily at what I was doing and stopped me. But the mischief had been done. The incident was a warning for the future. This was my first lesson in European etiquette, into the details of which Dr. Mehta humorously initiated me. 'Do not touch other people's things,' he said. 'Do not ask questions as we usually do in India on first acquaintance; do not talk loudly; never address people as "sir" whilst speaking to them as we do in India; only servants and subordinates address their masters that way.' And so on and so forth. He also told me that it was very expensive to live in a hotel and recommended that I should live with a private family. We deferred consideration of the matter until Monday.

Sjt. Mazmudar and I found the hotel to be a trying affair. It was also very expensive. There was, however, a Sindhi fellow-passenger from Malta who had become friends with Sjt. Mazmudar, and as he was not a stranger to London, he offered to find rooms for us. We agreed, and on Monday, as soon as we got our baggage, we paid up our bills and went to the rooms rented for us by the Sindhi friend. I remember my hotel bill came to £3, an amount which shocked me. And I had practically starved in spite of this heavy bill! For I could relish nothing. When I did not like one thing, I asked for another, but had to pay for both just the same. The fact is that all this while I had depended on the provisions which I had brought with me from Bombay.

I was very uneasy even in the new rooms. I would continually think of my home and country. My mother's love always haunted me. At night the tears would stream down my cheeks, and home memories of all sorts made sleep out of the question. It was impossible to share my misery with anyone. And even if I could have done so, where was the use? I knew of nothing that would soothe me. Everything was strange — the people, their ways, and even their dwellings. I was a complete novice in the matter of English etiquette and continually had to be on my guard. There was the additional inconvenience of the vegetarian vow. Even the dishes that I could eat were tasteless and insipid. I thus found myself between Scylla and Charybdis. England I could not bear, but to return to India was not to be thought of. Now that I had come, I must finish the three years, said the inner voice.

Chapter 14: My choice

Dr. Mehta went on Monday to the Victoria Hotel expecting to find me there. He discovered that we had left, got our new address, and met me at our rooms. Through sheer folly I had managed to get ringworm on the boat. For washing and bathing we used to have sea-water, in which soap is not soluble. I, however, used soap, taking its use to be a sign of civilization, with the result that instead of cleaning the skin it made it greasy. This gave me ringworm. I showed it to Dr. Mehta, who told me to apply acetic acid. I remember how the burning acid made me cry. Dr. Mehta inspected my room and its appointments and shook his head in disapproval. 'This place won't do,' he said. 'We come to England not so much for the purpose of studies as for gaining experience of English life and customs. And for this you need to live with a family. But before you do so, I think you had better serve a period of apprenticeship with . I will take you there.'

I gratefully accepted the suggestion and removed to the friend's rooms. He was all kindness and attention. He treated me as his own brother, initiated me into English ways and manners, and accustomed me to talking the language. My food, however, became a serious question. I could not relish boiled vegetables cooked without salt or condiments. The landlady was at a loss to know what to prepare for me. We had oatmeal porridge for breakfast, which was fairly filling, but I always starved at lunch and dinner. The friend continually reasoned with me to eat meat, but I always pleaded my vow and then remained silent. Both for luncheon and dinner we had spinach and bread and jam too. I was a good eater and had a capacious stomach; but I was ashamed to ask for more than two or three slices of bread, as it did not seem correct to do so. Added to this, there was no milk either for lunch or dinner. The friend once got disgusted with this state of things, and said: 'Had you been my own brother, I would have sent you packing. What is the value of a vow made before an illiterate mother, and in ignorance of conditions here? It is no vow at all. It would not be regarded as a vow in law. It is pure superstition to stick to such a promise. And I tell you this persistence will not help you to gain anything here. You confess to having eaten and relished meat. You took it where it was absolutely unnecessary, and will not where it is quite essential. What a pity!'

But I was adamant.

Day in and day out the friend would argue, but I had an eternal negative to face him with. The more he argued, the more uncompromising I became. Daily I would pray for God's protection and get it. Not that I had any idea of God. It was faith that was at work — faith of which the seed had been sown by the good nurse Rambha.

One day the friend began to read to me Bentham's Theory of Utility. I was at my wits' end. The language was too difficult for me to understand. He began to expound it. I said: 'Pray excuse me. These abstruse things are beyond me. I admit it is necessary to eat meat. But I cannot break my vow. I cannot argue about it. I am sure I cannot meet you in argument. But please give me up as foolish or obstinate. I appreciate your love for me and I know you to be my well-wisher. I also know that you are telling me again and again about this because you feel for me. But I am helpless. A vow is a vow. It cannot be broken.'

The friend looked at me in surprise. He closed the book and said: 'All right. I will not argue any more.' I was glad. He never discussed the subject again. But he did not cease to worry about me. He smoked and drank, but he never asked me to do so. In fact he asked me to remain away from both. His one anxiety was lest I should become very weak without meat, and thus be unable to feel at home in England.

That is how I served my apprenticeship for a month. The friend's house was in Richmond, and it was not possible to go to London more than once or twice a week. Dr. Mehta and Sjt. Dalpatram Shukla therefore decided that I should be put with some family. Sjt. Shukla hit upon an Anglo-Indian's house in West Kensington and placed me there. The landlady was a widow. I told her about my vow. The old lady promised to look after me properly, and I took up my residence in the house. Here too I practically had to starve. I had sent for sweets and other eatables from home, but nothing had yet come. Everything was insipid. Every day the old lady asked me whether I liked the food, but what could she do? I was still as shy as ever and dared not ask for more than was put before me. She had two daughters. They insisted on serving me with an extra slice or two of bread. But little did they know that nothing less than a loaf would have filled me.

But I had found my feet now. I had not yet started upon my regular studies. I had just begun reading newspapers, thanks to Sjt. Shukla. In India I had never read a newspaper. But here I succeeded in cultivating a liking for them by regular reading. I always glanced over The Daily News, The Daily Telegraph, and The Pall Mall Gazette. This took me hardly an hour. I therefore began to wander about. I launched out in search of a vegetarian restaurant. The landlady had told me that there were such places in the city. I would trot ten or twelve miles each day, go into a cheap restaurant and eat my fill of bread, but would never be satisfied. During these wanderings I once hit on a vegetarian restaurant in Farringdon Street.

The sight of it filled me with the same joy that a child feels on getting a thing after its own heart. Before I entered I noticed books for sale exhibited under a glass window near the door. I saw among them Salt's Plea for Vegetarianism. This I purchased for a shilling and went straight to the dining room. This was my first hearty meal since my arrival in England. God had come to my aid.

I read Salt's book from cover to cover and was very much impressed by it. From the date of reading this book, I may claim to have become a vegetarian by choice. I blessed the day on which I had taken the vow before my mother. I had all along abstained from meat in the interests of truth and of the vow I had taken, but had wished at the same time that every Indian should be a meat-eater, and had looked forward to being one myself freely and openly some day, and to enlisting others in the cause. The choice was now made in favour of vegetarianism, the spread of which henceforward became my mission.

Chapter 15: Playing the English gentleman

My faith in vegetarianism grew on me from day to day. Salt's book whetted my appetite for dietetic studies. I went in for all books available on vegetarianism and read them. One of these, Howard Williams' The Ethics of Diet, was a 'biographical history of the literature of humane dietetics from the earliest period to the present day'. It tried to make out, that all philosophers and prophets from Pythagoras and Jesus down to those of the present age were vegetarians. Dr. Anna Kingsford's The Perfect Way in Diet was also an attractive book. Dr. Allinson's writings on health and hygiene were likewise very helpful. He advocated a curative system based on regulation of the dietary of patients. Himself a vegetarian, he prescribed for his patients also a strictly vegetarian diet. The result of reading all this literature was that dietetic experiments came to take an important place in my life. Health was the principal consideration of these experiments to begin with. But later on religion became the supreme motive.

Meanwhile my friend had not ceased to worry about me. His love for me led him to think that, if I persisted in my objections to meat-eating, I should not only develop a weak constitution, but should remain a duffer, because I should never feel at home in English society. When he came to know that I had begun to interest myself in books on vegetarianism, he was afraid lest these studies should muddle my head; that I should fritter my life away in experiments, forgetting my own work, and become a crank. He therefore made one last effort to reform me. He one day invited me to go to the theatre. Before the play we were to dine together at the Holborn Restaurant, to me a palatial place and the first big restaurant I had been to since leaving the Victoria Hotel. The stay at that hotel had scarcely been a helpful experience for I had not lived there with my wits about me. The friend had planned to take me to this restaurant evidently imagining that modesty would forbid any questions. And it was a very big company of diners in the midst of which my friend and I sat sharing a table between us. The first course was soup. I wondered what it might be made of, but dared not ask the friend about it. I therefore summoned the waiter. My friend saw the movement and sternly asked across the table what was the matter. With considerable hesitation I told him that I wanted to inquire if the soup was a vegetable soup. 'You are too clumsy for decent society,' he passionately exclaimed 'If you cannot behave yourself, you had better go. Feed in some other restaurant and await me outside.' This delighted me. Out I went. There was a vegetarian restaurant close by, but it was closed. So I went without food that night. I accompanied my friend to the theatre, but he never said a word about the scene I had created. On my part of course there was nothing to say.

That was the last friendly tussle we had. It did not affect our relations in the least. I could see and appreciate the love by which all my friend's efforts were actuated, and my respect for him was all the greater on account of our differences in thought and action.

But I decided that I should put him at ease, that I should assure him that I would be clumsy no more, but try to become polished and make up for my vegetarianism by cultivating other accomplishments which fitted one for polite society. And for this purpose I undertook the all too impossible task of becoming an English gentleman.

The clothes after the Bombay cut that I was wearing were, I thought, unsuitable for English society, and I got new ones at the Army and Navy stores. I also went in for a chimney-pot hat costing nineteen shillings — an excessive price in those days. Not content with this, I wasted ten pounds on an evening suit made in Bond Street, the centre of fashionable life in London; and got my good and noble-hearted brother to send me a double watch-chain of gold. It was not correct to wear a ready-made tie and I learnt the art of tying one for myself. While in India, the mirror had been a luxury permitted on the days when the family barber gave me a shave. Here I wasted ten minutes every day before a huge mirror, watching myself arranging my tie and parting my hair in the correct fashion. My hair was by no means soft, and every day it meant a regular struggle with the brush to keep it in position. Each time the hat was put on and off, the hand would automatically move towards the head to adjust the hair, not to mention the other civilized habit of the hand every now and then operating for the same purpose when sitting in polished society.

As if all this were not enough to make me look the thing, I directed my attention to other details that were supposed to go towards the making of an English gentleman. I was told it was necessary for me to take lessons in dancing, French and elocution. French was not only the language of neighbouring France, but it was the lingua franca of the Continent over which I had a desire to travel. I decided to take dancing lessons at a class and paid down £3 as fees for a term. I must have taken about six lessons in three weeks. But it was beyond me To achieve anything like rhythmic motion. I could not follow the piano and hence found it impossible to keep time. What then was I to do? The recluse in the fable kept a cat to keep off the rats, and then a cow to feed the cat with milk, and a man to keep the cow and so on. My ambitions also grew like the family of the recluse. I thought I should learn to play the violin in order to cultivate an ear for Western music. So I invested £3 in a violin and something more in fees. I sought a third teacher to give me lessons in elocution and paid him a preliminary fee of a guinea. He recommended Bell's Standard Elocutionist as the text-book, which I purchased. And I began with a speech of Pitt's.

But Mr. Bell rang the bell of alarm in my ear and I awoke.

I had not to spend a lifetime in England, I said to myself. What then was the use of learning elocution? And how could dancing make a gentleman of me? The violin I could learn even in India. I was a student and ought to go on with my studies. I should qualify myself to join the Inns of Court. If my character made a gentleman of me, so much the better. Otherwise I should forego the ambition.

These and similar thoughts possessed me, and I expressed them in a letter which I addressed to the elocution teacher, requesting him to excuse me from further lessons. I had taken only two or three. I wrote a similar letter to the dancing teacher, and went personally to the violin teacher with a request to dispose of the violin for any price it might fetch. She was rather friendly to me, so I told her how I had discovered that I was pursuing a false ideal. She encouraged me in the determination to make a complete change.

This infatuation must have lasted about three months. The punctiliousness in dress persisted for years. But henceforward I became a student.

Chapter 16: Changes

Let no one imagine that my experiments in dancing and the like marked a stage of indulgence in my life. The reader will have noticed that even then I had my wits about me. That period of infatuation was not unrelieved by a certain amount of self-introspection on my part. I kept account of every farthing I spent, and my expenses were carefully calculated. Every little item such as omnibus fares or postage or a couple of coppers spent on newspapers, would be entered, and the balance struck every evening before going to bed. That habit has stayed with me ever since, and I know that as a result, though I have had to handle public funds amounting to lakhs, I have succeeded in exercising strict economy in their disbursement, and instead of outstanding debts have had invariably a surplus balance in respect of all the movements I have led. Let every youth take a leaf out of my book and make it a point to account for everything that comes into and goes out of his pocket, and like me he is sure to be a gainer in the end.

As I kept strict watch over my way of living, I could see that it was necessary to economize. I therefore decided to reduce my expenses by half. My accounts showed numerous items spent on fares. Again my living with a family meant the payment of a regular weekly bill. It also included the courtesy of occasionally taking members of the family out to dinner, and likewise attending parties with them. All this involved heavy items for conveyances, especially as, if the friend was a lady, custom required that the man should pay all the expenses. Also dining out meant extra cost, as no deduction could be made from the regular weekly bill for meals not taken. It seemed to me that all these items could be saved, as likewise the drain on my purse caused through a false sense of propriety.

So I decided to take rooms on my own account, instead of living any longer in a family, and also to remove from place to place according to the work I had to do, thus gaining experience at the same time. The rooms were so selected as to enable me to reach the place of business on foot in half an hour, and so save fares. Before this I had always taken some kind of conveyance whenever I went anywhere, and had to find extra time for walks. The new arrangement combined walks and economy, as it meant a saving of fares and gave me walks of eight or ten miles a day. It was mainly this habit of long walks that kept me practically free from illness throughout my stay in England and gave me a fairly strong body.

Thus I rented a suite of rooms; one for a sitting room and another for a bedroom. This was the second stage. The third was yet to come.

These changes saved me half the expense. But how was I to utilize the time? I knew that Bar examinations did not require much study, and I therefore did not feel pressed for time. My weak English was a perpetual worry to me. Mr. (afterwards Sir Frederic) Lely's words, 'Graduate first and then come to me', still rang in my ears. I should, I thought, not only be called to the Bar, but have some literary degree as well. I inquired about the Oxford and Cambridge University courses, consulted a few friends, and found that, if I elected to go to either of these places, that would mean greater expense and a much longer stay in England than I was prepared for. A friend suggested that, if I really wanted to have the satisfaction of taking a difficult examination, I should pass the London Matriculation. It meant a good deal of labour and much addition to my stock of general knowledge, without any extra expense worth the name. I welcomed the suggestion. But the syllabus frightened me. Latin and a modern language were compulsory! How was I to manage Latin? But the friend entered a strong plea for it: 'Latin is very valuable to lawyers. Knowledge of Latin is very useful in understanding law books. And one paper in Roman Law is entirely in Latin. Besides a knowledge of Latin means greater command over the English language.' It went home and I decided to learn Latin, no matter how difficult it might be. French I had already begun, so I thought that should be the modern language. I joined a private Matriculation class. Examinations were held every six months and I had only five months at my disposal. It was an almost impossible task for me. But the aspirant after being an English gentleman chose to convert himself into a serious student. I framed my own time-table to the minute; but neither my intelligence nor memory promised to enable me to tackle Latin and French besides other subjects within the given period. The result was that I was ploughed in Latin. I was sorry but did not lose heart. I had acquired a taste for Latin, also I thought my French would be all the better for another trial and I would select a new subject in the science group. Chemistry which was my subject in science had no attraction for want of experiments, whereas it ought to have been a deeply interesting study. It was one of the compulsory subjects in India and so I had selected it for the London Matriculation. This time, however, I chose Heat and Light instead of Chemistry. It was said to be easy and I found it to be so.

With my preparation for another trial, I made an effort to simplify my life still further. I felt that my way of living did not yet befit the modest means of my family. The thought of my struggling brother, who nobly responded to my regular calls for monetary help, deeply pained me. I saw that most of those who were spending from eight to fifteen pounds monthly had the advantage of scholarships. I had before me examples of much simpler living. I came across a fair number of poor students living more humbly than I. One of them was staying in the slums in a room at two shillings a week and living on two pence worth of cocoa and bread per meal from Lockhart's cheap Cocoa Rooms. It was far from me to think of emulating him, but I felt I could surely have one room instead of two and cook some of my meals at home. That would be a saving of four to five pounds each month. I also came across books on simple living. I gave up the suite of rooms and rented one instead, invested in a stove, and began cooking my breakfast at home.

The process scarcely took me more than twenty minutes for there was only oatmeal porridge to cook and water to boil for cocoa. I had lunch out and for dinner bread and cocoa at home. Thus I managed to live on a shilling and three pence a day. This was also a period of intensive study. Plain living saved me plenty of time and I passed my examination.

Let not the reader think that this living made my life by any means a dreary affair. On the contrary the change harmonized my inward and outward life. It was also more in keeping with the means of my family. My life was certainly more truthful and my soul knew no bounds of joy.

Chapter 17: Experiments in dietetics

As I searched myself deeper, the necessity for changes both internal and external began to grow on me. As soon as, or even before, I made alterations in my expenses and my way of living, I began to make changes in my diet. I saw that the writers on vegetarianism had examined the question very minutely, attacking it in its religious, scientific, practical and medical aspects. Ethically they had arrived at the conclusion that man's supremacy over the lower animals meant not that the former should prey upon the latter, but that the higher should protect the lower, and that there should be mutual aid between the two as between man and man. They had also brought out the truth that man eats not for enjoyment but to live. And some of them accordingly suggested and effected in their lives abstention not only from flesh-meat but from eggs and milk. Scientifically some had concluded that man's physical structure showed that he was not meant to be a cooking but a frugivorous animal, that he could take only his mother's milk and, as soon as he had teeth, should begin to take solid foods. Medically they had suggested the rejection of all spices and condiments. According to the practical and economic argument they had demonstrated that a vegetarian diet was the least expensive. All these considerations had their effect on me, and I came across vegetarians of all these types in vegetarian restaurants. There was a Vegetarian Society in England with a weekly journal of its own. I subscribed to the weekly, joined the society and very shortly found myself on the Executive Committee. Here I came in contact with those who were regarded as pillars of vegetarianism, and began my own experiments in dietetics.

I stopped taking the sweets and condiments I had got from home. The mind having taken a different turn, the fondness for condiments wore away, and I now relished the boiled spinach which in Richmond tasted insipid, cooked without condiments. Many such experiments taught me that the real seat of taste was not the tongue but the mind.

The economic consideration was of course constantly before me. There was in those days a body of opinion which regarded tea and coffee as harmful and favoured cocoa. And as I was convinced that one should eat only articles that sustained the body, I gave up tea and coffee as a rule, and substituted cocoa.

There were two divisions in the restaurants I used to visit. One division, which was patronized by fairly well-to-do people, provided any number of courses from which one chose and paid for a la carte, each dinner thus costing from one to two shillings. The other division provided six-penny dinners of three courses with a slice of bread. In my days of strict frugality I usually dined in the second division.

There were many minor experiments going on along with the main one; as for example, giving up starchy foods at one time, living on bread and fruit alone at another, and once living on cheese, milk and eggs. This last experiments is worth noting. It lasted not even a fortnight. The reformer who advocated starchless food had spoken highly of eggs and held that eggs were not meat. It was apparent that there was no injury done to living creatures in taking eggs. I was taken in by this plea and took eggs in spite of my vow. But the lapse was momentary. I had no business to put a new interpretation on the vow. The interpretation of my mother who administered the vow was there for me. I knew that her definition of meat included eggs. And as soon as I saw the true import of the vow I gave up eggs and the experiment alike.

There is a nice point underlying the argument, and worth noting. I came across three definitions of meat in England. According to the first, meat denoted only the flesh of birds and beasts. Vegetarians who accepted that definition abjured the flesh of birds and beasts, but ate fish, not to mention eggs. According to the second definition, meat meant flesh of all living creatures. So fish was here out of the question, but eggs were allowed. The third definition included under meat the flesh of living beings, as well as all their products, thus covering eggs and milk alike. If I accepted the first definition, I could take not only eggs, but fish also. But I was convinced that my mother's definition was the definition binding on me. If, therefore, I would observe the vow I had taken, I must abjure eggs. I therefore did so. This was a hardship inasmuch as inquiry showed that even in vegetarian restaurants many courses used to contain eggs. This meant that unless I knew what was what, I had to go through the awkward process of ascertaining whether a particular course contained eggs or no, for many puddings and cakes were not free from them. But though the revelation of my duty caused this difficulty, it simplified my food. The simplification in its turn brought me annoyance in that I had to give up several dishes I had come to relish. These difficulties were only passing, for the strict observance of the vow produced an inward relish distinctly more healthy, delicate and permanent.

The real ordeal, however, was still to come, and that was in respect of the other vow. But who dare harm whom God protects?

A few observations about the interpretation of vows or pledges may not be out of place here. Interpretation of pledges has been a fruitful source of strife all the world over. No matter how explicit the pledge, people will turn and twist the text to suit their own purposes. They are to be met with among all classes of society, from the rich down to the poor, from the prince down to the peasant. Selfishness turns them blind, and by a use of the ambiguous middle they deceive themselves and seek to deceive the world and God. One golden rule is to accept the interpretation honestly put on the pledge by the party administering it. Another is to accept the interpretation of the weaker party, where there are two interpretations possible. Rejection of these two rules gives rise to strife and iniquity, which are rooted in untruthfulness. He who seeks truth alone easily follows the golden rule. He need not seek learned advice for interpretation. My mother's interpretation of meat was, according to the golden rule, the only true one for me, and not the one my wider experience or my pride of better knowledge might have taught me.

My experiments in England were conducted from the point of view of economy and hygiene. The religious aspect of the question was not considered until I went to South Africa where I undertook strenuous experiments which will be narrated later. The seed, however, for all of them was sown in England.

A convert's enthusiasm for his new religion is greater than that of a person who is born in it. Vegetarianism was then a new cult in England, and likewise for me, because, as we have seen, I had gone there a convinced meat-eater, and was intellectually converted to vegetarianism later. Full of the neophyte's zeal for vegetarianism, I decided to start a vegetarian club in my locality, Bayswater. I invited Sir Edwin Arnold, who lived there, to be Vice-President. Dr. Oldfield who was Editor of the The Vegetarian became President. I myself became the Secretary. The club went well for a while, but came to an end in the course of a few months. For I left the locality, according to my custom of moving from place to place periodically. But this brief and modest experience gave me some little training in organizing and conducting institutions.

Chapter 18: Shyness my shield

I was elected to the Executive Committee of the Vegetarian Society, and made it a point to attend every one of its meetings, but I always felt tongue-tied. Dr. Oldfield once said to me, 'You talk to me quite all right, but why is it that you never open your lips at a committee meeting? You are a drone.' I appreciated the banter. The bees are ever busy, the drone is a thorough idler. And it was not a little curious that whilst others expressed their opinions at these meetings, I sat quite silent. Not that I never felt tempted to speak. But I was at a loss to know how to express myself. All the rest of the members appeared to me to be better informed than I. Then it often happened that just when I had mustered up courage to speak, a fresh subject would be started. This went on for a long time.

Meantime a serious question came up for discussion. I thought it wrong to be absent, and felt it cowardice to register a silent vote. The discussion arose somewhat in this wise. The President of the Society was Mr. Hills, proprietor of the Thames Iron Works. He was a puritan. It may be said that the existence of the Society depended practically on his financial assistance. Many members of the Committee were more or less his protégés. Dr. Allinson of vegetarian fame was also a member of the Committee. He was an advocate of the then new birth control movement, and preached its methods among the working classes. Mr. Hills regarded these methods as cutting at the root of morals. He thought that the Vegetarian Society had for its object not only dietetic but also moral reform, and that a man of Dr. Allinson's anti-puritanic views should not be allowed to remain in the Society. A motion was therefore brought for his removal. The question deeply interested me. I considered Dr. Allinson's views regarding artificial methods of birth control as dangerous, and I believed that Mr. Hills was entitled, as a puritan, to oppose him. I had a high regard for Mr. Hills and his generosity. But I thought it was quite improper to exclude a man from a vegetarian society simply because he refused to regard puritan morals as one of the objects of the society. Mr. Hills' view regarding the exclusion of anti-puritans from the Society was personal to himself, and it had nothing to do with the declared object of the Society, which was simply the promotion of vegetarianism and not of any system of morality. I therefore held that any vegetarian could be a member of the Society irrespective of his views on other morals.

There were in the Committee others also who shared my view, but I felt myself personally called upon to express my own. How to do it was the question. I had not the courage to speak and I therefore decided to set down my thoughts in writing. I went to the meeting with the document in my pocket. So far as I recollect, I did not find myself equal even to reading it, and the President had it read by someone else. Dr. Allinson lost the day. Thus in the very first battle of the kind I found myself siding with the losing party. But I had comfort in the thought that the cause was right. I have a faint recollection that, after this incident, I resigned from the Committee. This shyness I retained throughout my stay in England. Even when I paid a social call the presence of half a dozen or more people would strike me dumb.

I once went to Ventnor with Sjt. Mazmudar. We stayed there with a vegetarian family. Mr. Howard, the author of The Ethics of Diet, was also staying at the same watering-place. We met him, and he invited us to speak at a meeting for the promotion of vegetarianism. I had ascertained that it was not considered incorrect to read one's speech. I knew that many did so to express themselves coherently and briefly. To speak ex tempore would have been out of the question for me. I had therefore written down my speech. I stood up to read it, but could not. My vision became blurred and I trembled, though the speech hardly covered a sheet of foolscap. Sjt. Mazmudar had to read it for me. His own speech was of course excellent and was received with applause. I was ashamed of myself and sad at heart for my incapacity.

My last effort to make a public speech in England was on the eve of my departure for home. But this time too I only succeeded in making myself ridiculous. I invited my vegetarian friends to dinner in the Holborn Restaurant referred to in these chapters. 'A vegetarian dinner could be had,' I said to myself, 'in vegetarian restaurants as a matter of course. But why should it not be possible in a non-vegetarian restaurant too?' And I arranged with the manager of the Holborn Restaurant to provide a strictly vegetarian meal. The vegetarians hailed the new experiment with delight. All dinners are meant for enjoyment, but the West has developed the thing into an art. They are celebrated with great éclat, music and speeches. And the little dinner party that I gave was also not unaccompanied by some such display. Speeches, therefore, there had to be. When my turn for speaking came, I stood up to make a speech. I had with great care thought out one which would consist of a very few sentences. But I could not proceed beyond the first sentence. I had read of Addison that he began his maiden speech in the House of Commons, repeating 'I conceive' three times, and when he could proceed no further, a wag stood up and said, 'The gentleman conceived thrice but brought forth nothing.' I had thought of making a humorous speech taking this anecdote as the text. I therefore began with it and stuck there. My memory entirely failed me and in attempting a humorous speech I made myself ridiculous. 'I thank you, gentlemen, for having kindly responded to my invitation,' I said abruptly, and sat down.

It was only in South Africa that I got over this shyness, though I never completely overcame it. It was impossible for me to speak impromptu. I hesitated whenever I had to face strange audiences and avoided making a speech whenever I could. Even today I do not think I could or would even be inclined to keep a meeting of friends engaged in idle talk.

I must say that, beyond occasionally exposing me to laughter, my constitutional shyness has been no disadvantage whatever. In fact I can see that, on the contrary, it has been all to my advantage. My hesitancy in speech, which was once an annoyance, is now a pleasure. Its greatest benefit has been that it has taught me the economy of words. I have naturally formed the habit of restraining my thoughts. And I can now give myself the certificate that a thoughtless word hardly ever escapes my tongue or pen. I do not recollect ever having had to regret anything in my speech or writing. I have thus been spared many a mishap and waste of time. Experience has taught me that silence is part of the spiritual discipline of a votary of truth. Proneness to exaggerate, to suppress or modify the truth, wittingly or unwittingly, is a natural weakness of man, and silence is necessary in order to surmount it. A man of few words will rarely be thoughtless in his speech; he will measure every word. We find so many people impatient to talk. There is no chairman of a meeting who is not pestered with notes for permission to speak. And whenever the permission is given the speaker generally exceeds the time-limit, asks for more time, and keeps on talking without permission. All this talking can hardly be said to be of any benefit to the world. It is so much waste of time. My shyness has been in reality my shield and buckler. It has allowed me to grow. It has helped me in my discernment of truth.

Chapter 19: The canker of untruth

There were comparatively few Indian students in England forty years ago. It was a practice with them to affect the bachelor even though they might be married. School or college students in England are all bachelors, studies being regarded as incompatible with married life. We had that tradition in the good old days, a student then being invariably known as a brahmachari1. But in these days we have child-marriages, a thing practically unknown in England. Indian youths in England, therefore, felt ashamed to confess that they were married. There was also another reason for dissembling, namely that in the event of the fact being known it would be impossible for the young men to go about or flirt with the young girls of the family in which they lived. The flirting was more or less innocent. Parents even encouraged it; and that sort of association between young men and young women may even be a necessity there, in view of the fact that every young man has to choose his mate. If, however, Indian youths on arrival in England indulge in these relations, quite natural to English youths, the result is likely to be disastrous, as has often been found. I saw that our youths had succumbed to the temptation and chosen a life of untruth for the sake of companionships which, however innocent in the case of English youths, were for them undesirable. I too caught the contagion. I did not hesitate to pass myself off as a bachelor though I was married and the father of a son. But I was none the happier for being a dissembler. Only my reserve and my reticence saved me from going into deeper waters. If I did not talk, no girl would think it worth her while to enter into conversation with me or to go out with me.

My cowardice was on a par with my reserve. It was customary in families like the one in which I was staying at Ventnor for the daughter of the landlady to take out guests for a walk. My landlady's daughter took me one day to the lovely hills round Ventnor. I was no slow walker, but my companion walked even faster, dragging me after her and chattering away all the while. I responded to her chatter sometimes with a whispered 'yes' or 'no', or at the most 'yes, how beautiful!' She was flying like a bird whilst I was wondering when I should get back home. We thus reached the top of a hill. How to get down again was the question. In spite of her high-heeled boots this sprightly young lady of twenty-five darted down the hill like an arrow. I was shamefacedly struggling to get down. She stood at the foot smiling and cheering me and offering to come and drag me. How could I be so chicken hearted? With the greatest difficulty, and crawling at intervals, I somehow managed to scramble to the bottom. She loudly laughed 'bravo' and shamed me all the more, as well she might.

But I could not escape scatheless everywhere. For God wanted to rid me of the canker of untruth. I once went to Brighton, another watering-place like Ventnor. This was before the Ventnor visit. I met there at a hotel an old widow of moderate means. This was my first year in England. The courses on the menu were all described in French, which I did not understand. I sat at the same table as the old lady. She saw that I was a stranger and puzzled, and immediately came to my aid. 'You seem to be a stranger,' she said, 'and look perplexed. Why have you not ordered anything?' I was spelling through the menu and preparing to ascertain the ingredients of the courses from the waiter, when the good lady thus intervened. I thanked her, and explaining my difficulty told her that I was at a loss to know which of the courses were vegetarian as I did not understand French.

'Let me help you,' she said. 'I shall explain the card to you and show you what you may eat.' I gratefully availed myself of her help. This was the beginning of an acquaintance that ripened into friendship and was kept up all through my stay in England and long after. She gave me her London address and invited me to dine at her house every Sunday. On special occasions also she would invite me, help me to conquer my bashfulness and introduce me to young ladies and draw me into conversation with them. Particularly marked out for these conversations was a young lady who stayed with her, and often we would be left entirely alone together.

I found all this very trying at first. I could not start a conversation nor could I indulge in any jokes. But she put me in the way. I began to learn; and in course of time looked forward to every Sunday and came to like the conversations with the young friend. The old lady went on spreading her net wider every day. She felt interested in our meetings. Possibly she had her own plans about us.

I was in a quandary. 'How I wished I had told the good lady that I was married!' I said to myself. 'She would then have not thought of an engagement between us. It is, however, never too late to mend. If I declare the truth, I might yet be saved more misery.' With these thoughts in my mind, I wrote a letter to her somewhat to this effect:

'Ever since we met at Brighton you have been kind to me. You have taken care of me even as a mother of her son. You also think that I should get married and with that view you have been introducing me to young ladies. Rather than allow matters to go further, I must confess to you that I have been unworthy of your affection. I should have told you when I began my visits to you that I was married. I knew that Indian students in England dissembled the fact of their marriage and I followed suit. I now see that I should not have done so. I must also add that I was married while yet a boy, and am the father of a son. I am pained that I should have kept this knowledge from you so long. But I am glad God has now given me the courage to speak out the truth. Will you forgive me? I assure you I have taken no improper liberties with the young lady you were good enough to introduce to me. I knew my limits. You, not knowing that I was married, naturally desired that we should be engaged. In order that things should not go beyond the present stage, I must tell you the truth.

'If on receipt of this, you feel that I have been unworthy of your hospitality, I assure you I shall not take it amiss. You have laid me under an everlasting debt of gratitude by your kindness and solicitude. If, after this, you do not reject me but continue to regard me as worthy of your hospitality, which I will spare no pains to deserve, I shall naturally be happy and count it a further token of your kindness.'

Let the reader know that I could not have written such a letter in a moment. I must have drafted and redrafted it many times over. But it lifted a burden that was weighing me down. Almost by return post came her reply somewhat as follows:

> 'I have your frank letter. We were both very glad and had a hearty laugh over it. The untruth you say you have been guilty of is pardonable. But it is well that you have acquainted us with the real state of things. My invitation still stands and we shall certainly expect you next Sunday and look forward to hearing all about your child-marriage and to the pleasure of laughing at your expense. Need I assure you that our friendship is not in the least affected by this incident?'

I thus purged myself of the canker of untruth, and I never thenceforward hesitated to talk of my married state wherever necessary.

Chapter 20: Acquaintance with religions

Towards the end of my second year in England I came across two Theosophists, brothers, and both unmarried. They talked to me about the Gita. They were reading Sir Edwin Arnold's translation — The Song Celestial– and they invited me to read the original with them. I felt ashamed, as I had read the divine poem neither in Samskrit nor in Gujarati.

I was constrained to tell them that I had not read the Gita, but that I would gladly read it with them, and that though my knowledge of Samskrit was meagre, still I hoped to be able to understand the original to the extent of telling where the translation failed to bring out the meaning. I began reading the Gita with them. The verses in the second chapter

> "If one Ponders on objects of the sense, there springs Attraction; from attraction grows desire, Desire flames to fierce passion, passion breeds Recklessness; then the memory–all betrayed– Lets noble purpose go, and saps the mind, Till purpose, mind, and man are all undone."

made a deep impression on my mind, and they still ring in my ears. The book struck me as one of priceless worth. The impression has ever since been growing on me with the result that I regard it today as the *book par excellence* for the knowledge of Truth. It has afforded me invaluable help in my moments of gloom. I have read almost all the English translations of it, and I regard Sir Edwin Arnold's as the best. He has been faithful to the text, and yet it does not read like a translation. Though I read the Gita with these friends, I cannot pretend to have studied it then. It was only after some years that it became a book of daily reading.

The brothers also recommended The Light of Asia by Sir Edwin Arnold, whom I knew till then as the author only of The Song Celestial, and I read it with even greater interest than I did the Bhagavadgita. Once I had begun it I could not leave off. They also took me on one occasion to the Blavatsky Lodge and introduced me to Madame Blavatsky and Mrs. Besant. The latter had just then joined the Theosophical Society, and I was following with great interest the controversy about her conversion. The friends advised me to join the Society, but I politely declined saying, 'With my meagre knowledge of my own religion I do not want to belong to any religious body.' I recall having read, at the brothers' instance, Madame Blavatsky's Key to Theosophy. This book stimulated in me the desire to read books on Hinduism, and disabused me of the notion fostered by the missionaries that Hinduism was rife with superstition.

About the same time I met a good Christian from Manchester in a vegetarian boarding house. He talked to me about Christianity. I narrated to him my Rajkot recollections. He was pained to hear them. He said, 'I am a vegetarian. I do not drink. Many Christians are meat-eaters and drink, no doubt; but neither meat-eating nor drinking is enjoined by Scripture. Do please read the Bible.' I accepted his advice, and he got me a copy. I have a faint recollection that he himself used to sell copies of the Bible, and I purchased from him an edition containing maps, concordance, and other aids. I began reading it, but I could not possibly read through the Old Testament. I read the book of Genesis, and the chapters that followed invariably sent me to sleep. But just for the sake of being able to say that I had read it, I plodded through the other books with much difficulty and without the least interest or understanding. I disliked reading the book of Numbers.

But the New Testament produced a different impression, especially the Sermon on the

Mount which went straight to my heart. I compared it with the Gita. The verses, 'But I say unto you, that ye resist not evil: but whosoever shall smite thee on thy right cheek, turn to him the other also. And if any man take away thy coat let him have thy cloke too,' delighted me beyond measure and put me in mind of Shamal Bhatt's 'For a bowl of water, give a goodly meal' etc. My young mind tried to unify the teaching of the Gita, the Light of Asia and the Sermon on the Mount. That renunciation was the highest form of religion appealed to me greatly.

This reading whetted my appetite for studying the lives of other religious teachers. A friend recommended Carlyle's Heroes and Hero-Worship. I read the chapter on the Hero as a prophet and learnt of the Prophet's greatness and bravery and austere living.

Beyond this acquaintance with religion I could not go at the moment, as reading for the examination left me scarcely any time for outside subjects. But I took mental note of the fact that I should read more religious books and acquaint myself with all the principal religions.

And how could I help knowing something of atheism too? Every Indian knew Bradlaugh's name and his so-called atheism. I read some book about it, the name of which I forget. It had no effect on me, for I had already crossed the Sahara of atheism. Mrs. Besant, who was then very much in the limelight, had turned to theism from atheism, and that fact also strengthened my aversion to atheism. I had read her book How I became a Theosophist.

It was about this time that Bradlaugh died. He was buried in the Working Cemetery. I attended the funeral, as I believe every Indian residing in London did. A few clergymen also were present to do him the last honours. On our way back from the funeral we had to wait at the station for our train. A champion atheist from the crowd heckled one of these clergymen. 'Well sir, you believe in the existence of God?'

'I do,' said the good man in a low tone.

'You also agree that the circumference of the Earth is 28,000 miles, don't you?' said the atheist with a smile of self-assurance.

'Indeed.'

'Pray tell me then the size of your God and where he may be?'

'Well, if we but knew, He resides in the hearts of us both.'

'Now, now, don't take me to be a child,' said the champion with a triumphant look at us.

The clergyman assumed a humble silence.

This talk still further increased my prejudice against atheism.

Chapter 21: Nirbal Ke Bala Rama[*]

Though I had acquired a nodding acquaintance with Hinduism and other religions of the world, I should have known that it would not be enough to save me in my trails. Of the thing that sustains him through trials man has no inkling, much less knowledge, at the time. If an unbeliever, he will attribute his safety to chance. If a believer, he will say God saved him. He will conclude, as well he may, that his religious study or spiritual discipline was at the back of the state of grace within him. But in the hour of his deliverance he does not know whether his spiritual discipline or something else saves. Who that has prided himself on his spiritual strength has not seen it humbled to the dust? A knowledge of religion, as distinguished from experience, seems but chaff in such moments of trial.

It was in England that I first discovered the futility of mere religious knowledge. How I was saved on previous occasions is more than I can say, for I was very young then; but now I was twenty and had gained some experience as husband and father.

During the last year, as far as I can remember, of my stay in England, that is in 1890, there was a Vegetarian Conference at Portsmouth to which an Indian friend and I were invited. Portsmouth is a sea-port with a large naval population. It has many houses with women of ill fame, women not actually prostitutes, but at the same time, not very scrupulous about their morals. We were put up in one of these houses. Needles to say, the Reception Committee did not know anything about it. It would have been difficult in a town like Portsmouth to find out which were good lodgings and which were bad for occasional travelers like us.

We returned from the Conference in the evening. After dinner we sat down to play a rubber of bridge, in which our landlady joined, as is customary in England even in respectable households. Every player indulges in innocent jokes as a matter of course, but here my companion and our hostess began to make indecent ones as well. I did not know that my friend was an adept in the art. It captured me and I also joined in. Just when I was about to go beyond the limit, leaving the cards and the game to themselves, God through the good companion uttered the blessed warning: 'Whence this devil in you, my boy? Be off, quick!'

I was ashamed. I took the warning and expressed within myself gratefulness to my friend. Remembering the vow I had taken before my mother, I fled from the scene. To my room I went quaking, trembling, and with beating heart, like a quarry escaped from its pursuer.

I recall this as the first occasion on which a woman, other than my wife, moved me to lust. I passed that night sleeplessly, all kinds of thoughts assailing me. Should I leave this house? Should I run away from the place? Where was I? What would happen to

---

[*] Refrain of Surdas' famous hymn, 'He is the help of the helpless, the strength of the weak.

me if I had not my wits about me? I decided to act thenceforth with great caution; not to leave the house, but somehow leave Portsmouth. The Conference was not to go on for more than two days, and I remember I left Portsmouth the next evening, my companion staying there some time longer.

I did not then know the essence of religion or of God, and how He works in us. Only vaguely I understood that God had saved me on that occasion. On all occasions of trial He has saved me. I know that the phrase 'God saved me' has a deeper meaning for me today, and still I feel that I have not yet grasped its entire meaning. Only richer experience can help me to a fuller understanding. But in all my trials — of a spiritual nature, as a lawyer, in conducting institutions, and in politics — I can say that God saved me. When every hope is gone. 'when helpers fail and comforts flee,' I find that help arrives somehow, from I know not where. Supplication, worship, prayer are no superstition; they are acts more real than the acts of eating, drinking, sitting or walking. It is no exaggeration to say that they alone are real, all else is unreal.

Such worship or prayer is no flight of eloquence; it is no lip-homage. It springs from the heart. If, therefore, we achieve that purity of the heart when it is 'emptied of all but love', if we keep all the chords in proper tune, they 'trembling pass in music out of sight'. Prayer needs no speech. It is in itself independent of any sensuous effort. I have not the slightest doubt that prayer is an unfailing means of cleansing the heart of passions. But it must be combined with the utmost humility.

Chapter 22: Narayan Hemchandra

Just about this time Narayan Hemchandra came to England. I had heard of him as a writer. We met at the house of Miss Manning of the National Indian Association. Miss Manning knew that I could not make myself sociable. When I went to her place I used to sit tongue-tied, never speaking except when spoken to. She introduced me to Narayan Hemchandra. He did not know English. His dress was queer — a clumsy pair of trousers, a wrinkled, dirty, brown coat after the Parsi fashion, no necktie or collar, and a tasseled woolen cap. He grew a long beard.

He was lightly built and short of stature. His round face was scarred with small-pox, and had a nose which was neither pointed nor blunt. With his hand he was constantly turning over his beard.

Such a queer-looking and queerly dressed person was bound to be singled out in fashionable society.

'I have heard a good deal about you,' I said to him. 'I have also read some of your writings. I should be very pleased if you were kind enough to come to my place.'

Narayan Hemchandra had a rather hoarse voice. With a smile on his face he replied:
'Yes, where do you stay?'
'In Store Street.'
'Then we are neighbours. I want to learn English. Will you teach me?'
'I shall be happy to teach you anything I can, and will try my best. If you like, I will go to your place.'
'Oh, no. I shall come to you. I shall also bring with me a Translation Exercise Book.'
So we made an appointment. Soon we were close friends.

Narayan Hemchandra was innocent of grammar. 'Horse' was a verb with him and 'run' a noun. I remember many such funny instances. But he was not to be baffled by his ignorance. My little knowledge of grammar could make no impression on him. Certainly he never regarded his ignorance of grammar as a matter for shame.

With perfect nonchalance he said: 'I have never been to school like you. I have never felt the need of grammar in expressing my thoughts. Well, do you know Bengali? I know it. I have travelled in Bengal. It is I who have given Maharshi Devendranath Tagore's works to the Gujarati-speaking world. And I wish to translate into Gujarati the treasures of many other languages. I always content myself with bringing out the spirit. Others, with their better knowledge, may be able to do more in future. But I am quite satisfied with what I have achieved without the help of grammar. I know Marathi, Hindi, Bengali, and now I have begun to know English. What I want is a copious vocabulary. And do you think my ambition ends here? No fear. I want to go to France and learn French. I am told that language has an extensive literature. I shall go to Germany also, if possible, and there learn German.' And thus he would talk on unceasingly. He had a boundless ambition for learning languages and for foreign travel.

'Then you will go to America also?'
'Certainly. How can I return to India without having seen the New World?'
'But where will you find the money?'
'What do I need money for? I am not a fashionable fellow like you. The minimum amount of food and the minimum amount of clothing suffice for me. And for this what little I get out of my books and from my friends is enough. I always travel third class. While going to America also I shall travel on deck.'

Narayan Hemchandra's simplicity was all his own, and his frankness was on a par with it. Of pride he had not the slightest trace, excepting, of course, a rather undue regard for his own capacity as a writer.

We met daily. There was a considerable amount of similarity between our thoughts and actions. Both of us were vegetarians. We would often have our lunch together. This was the time when I lived on 17s a week and cooked for myself. Sometimes when I would go to his room, and sometimes he would come to mine. I cooked in the English style. Nothing but Indian style would satisfy him. He would not do without dal. I would make soup of carrots etc., and he would pity me for my taste. Once he somehow hunted out mung* cooked it and brought it to my place. I ate it with delight. This led on to a regular system of exchange between us. I would take my delicacies to him and he would bring his to me.

Cardinal Manning's name was then on every lip. The dock labourers' strike had come to an early termination owing to the efforts of John Burns and Cardinal Manning. I told Narayan Hemchandra of Disraeli's tribute to the Cardinal's simplicity. 'Then I must see the sage', said he.

'He is a big man. How do you expect to meet him?'

'Why? I know how. I must get you to write to him in my name. Tell him I am an author and that I want to congratulate him personally on his humanitarian work, and also say that I shall have to take you as interpreter as I do not know English.'

I wrote a letter to that effect. In two or three days came Cardinal Manning's card in reply giving us an appointment. So we both called on the Cardinal. I put on the usual visiting suit. Narayan Hemchandra was the same as ever, in the same coat and the same trousers. I tried to make fun of this, but he laughed me out and said:

'You civilized fellows are all cowards. Great men never look at a person's exterior. They think of his heart.'

We entered the Cardinal's mansion. As soon as we were seated, a thin, tall, old gentleman made his appearance, and shook hands with us. Narayan Hemchandra thus gave his greetings:

'I do not want to take up your time. I had heard a lot about you and I felt I should come and thank you for the good work you have done for the strikers. It has been my custom to visit the sages of the world and that is why I have put you to this trouble.'

This was of course my translation of that he spoke in Gujarati.

'I am glad you have come. I hope your stay in London will agree with you and that you will get in touch with people here. God bless you.'

With these words the Cardinal stood up and said good-bye.

Once Narayan Hemchandra came to my place in a shirt and dhoti. The good landlady opened the door, came running to me in a fright — this was a new landlady who did not know Narayan Hemchandra — and said: 'A sort of a madcap wants to see you.' I went to the door and to my surprise found Narayan Hemchandra. I was shocked. His face, however, showed nothing but his usual smile.

'But did not the children in the street rag you?'

'Well, they ran after me, but I did not mind them and they were quiet.'

Narayan Hemchandra went to Paris after a few months' stay in London. He began studying French and also translating French books. I knew enough French to revise his translation, so he gave it to me to read. It was not a translation, it was the substance.

---

* An Indian pulse.

Finally he carried out his determination to visit America. It was with great difficulty that he succeeded in securing a deck ticket. While in the United States he was prosecuted for 'being indecently dressed', as he once went out in a shirt and dhoti. I have a recollection that he was discharged.

Chapter 23: The Great Exhibition

There was a great Exhibition at Paris in 1890. I had read about its elaborate preparations, and I also had a keen desire to see Paris. So I thought I had better combine two things in one and go there at this juncture. A particular attraction of the Exhibition was the Eiffel Tower, constructed entirely of iron, and nearly 1,000 feet high. There were of course many other things of interest, but the Tower was the chief one, inasmuch as it had been supposed till then that a structure of that height could not safely stand.

I had heard of a vegetarian restaurant in Paris. I engaged a room there and stayed seven days. I managed everything very economically, both the journey to Paris and the sightseeing there. This I did mostly on foot and with the help of a map of Paris, as also a map of and guide to the Exhibition. These were enough to direct one to the main streets and chief places of interest.

I remember nothing of the Exhibition excepting its magnitude and variety. I have fair recollection of the Eiffel Tower as I ascended it twice or thrice. There was a restaurant on the first platform, and just for the satisfaction of being able to say that I had had my lunch at a great height, I threw away seven shillings on it.

The ancient churches of Paris are still in my memory. Their grandeur and their peacefulness are unforgettable. The wonderful construction of Notre Dame and the elaborate decoration of the interior with its beautiful sculptures cannot be forgotten. I felt then that those who expended millions on such divine cathedrals could not but have the love of God in their hearts.

I had read a lot about the fashions and frivolity of Paris. These were in evidence in every street, but the churches stood noticeably apart from these scenes. A man would forget the outside noise and bustle as soon as he entered one of these churches. His manner would change, he would behave with dignity and reverence as he passed someone kneeling before the image of the Virgin. The feeling I had then has since been growing on me, that all this kneeling and prayer could not be mere superstition; the devout souls kneeling before the Virgin could not be worshipping mere marble. They were fired with genuine devotion and they worshipped not stone, but the divinity of which it was symbolic. I have an impression that I felt then that by this worship they were not detracting from, but increasing, the glory of God.

I must say a word about the Eiffel Tower. I do not know what purpose it serves today. But I then heard it greatly disparaged as well as praised. I remember that Tolstoy was the chief among those who disparaged it. He said that the Eiffel Tower was a monument of man's folly, not of his wisdom. Tobacco, he argued, was the worst of all intoxicants, inasmuch as a man addicted to it was tempted to commit crimes which a drunkard never dared to do; liquor made a man mad, but tobacco clouded his intellect and made him build castles in the air. The Eiffel Tower was one of the creations of a man under such influence. There is no art about the Eiffel Tower. In no way can it be said to have contributed to the real beauty of the Exhibition. Men flocked to see it and ascended it as it was a novelty and of unique dimensions. It was the toy of the Exhibition. So long as we are children we are attracted by toys, and the Tower was a good demonstration of the fact that we are all children attracted by trinkets. That may be claimed to be the purpose served by the Eiffel Tower.

Chapter 24: 'Called'—but then?

I have deferred saying anything up to now about the purpose for which I went to England, viz., being called to the bar. It is time to advert to it briefly.

There were two conditions which had to be fulfilled before a student was formally called to the bar: 'keeping terms,' twelve terms equivalent to about three years; and passing examinations. 'Keeping terms' meant eating one's terms, i.e., attending at least six out of about twenty-four dinners in a term. Eating did not mean actually partaking of the dinner, it meant reporting oneself at the fixed hours and remaining present throughout the dinner. Usually, of course, every one ate and drank the good commons and choice wines provided. A dinner cost from two and six to three and six, that is from two to three rupees. This was considered moderate, inasmuch as one had to pay that same amount for wines alone if one dined at a hotel. To us in India it is a matter for surprise, if we are not 'civilized', that the cost of drink should exceed the cost of food. The first revelation gave me a great shock, and I wondered how people had the heart to throw away so much money on drink. Later I came to understand. I often ate nothing at these dinners, for the things that I might eat were only bread, boiled potato and cabbage. In the beginning I did not eat these, as I did not like them; and later, when I began to relish them, I also gained the courage to ask for other dishes.

The dinner provided for the benchers used to be better than that for the students. A Parsi student, who was also a vegetarian, and I applied, in the interests of vegetarianism, for the vegetarian courses which were served to the benchers. The application was granted, and we began to get fruits and other vegetables from the benchers' table.

Two bottles of wine were allowed to each group of four, and as I did not touch them, I was ever in demand to form a quarter, so that three might empty two bottles. And there was a 'grand night' in each term when extra wines, like champagne, in addition to port and sherry were served. I was therefore specially requested to attend and was in great demand on that grand night.

I could not see then, nor have I seen since, how these dinners qualified the students better for the bar. There was once a time when only a few students used to attend these dinners and thus there were opportunities for talks between them and the benchers, and speeches were also made. These occasions helped to give them knowledge of the world with a sort of polish and refinement, and also improved their power of speaking. No such thing was possible in my time, as the benchers had a table all to themselves. The institution had gradually lost all its meaning, but conservative England retained it nevertheless.

The curriculum of study was easy, barristers being humorously known as 'dinner barristers'. Everyone knew that the examinations had practically no value. In my time there were two, one in Roman Law and the other in Common Law. There were regular textbooks prescribed for these examinations which could be taken in compartments, but scarcely any one read them. I have known many to pass the Roman Law examination by scrambling through notes on Roman Law in a couple of weeks, and the Common Law examination by reading notes on the subject in two or three months. Question papers were easy and examiners were generous. The percentage of passes in the Roman Law examination used to be 95 to 99 and of those in the final examination 75 or even more. There was thus little fear of being plucked, and examinations were held not once but four times in the year. They could not be felt as a difficulty.

But I succeeded in turning them into one. I felt that I should read all the text-books. It was a fraud, I thought, not to read these books. I invested much money in them. I decided to read Roman Law in Latin. The Latin which I had acquired in the London Matriculation stood me in good stead. And all this reading was not without its value later on in South Africa, where Roman Dutch is the common law. The reading of Justinian, therefore, helped me a great deal in understanding the South African law.

It took me nine months of fairly hard labour to read through the Common Law of England. For Broom's Common Law, a big but interesting volume, took up a good deal of time. Snell's Equity was full of interest, but a bit hard to understand. White and Tudor's Leading Cases, from which certain cases were prescribed, was full of interest and instruction. I read also with interest Williams' and Edward's Real Property, and Goodeve'sPersonal Property. Williams' book read like a novel. The one book I remember to have read, on my return to India, with the same unflagging interest, was Mayne's Hindu Law. But it is out of place to talk here of Indian law books.

I passed my examinations, was called to the bar on the 10th of June 1891, and enrolled in the High Court on the 11th. On the 12th I sailed for home.

But notwithstanding my study there was no end to my helplessness and fear. I did not feel myself qualified to practise law.

But a separate chapter is needed to describe this helplessness of mine.

Chapter 25: My helplessness

It was easy to be called, but it was difficult to practise at the bar. I had read the laws, but not learnt how to practise law. I had read with interest 'Legal Maxims', but did not know how to apply them in my profession. 'Sic utere tuo ut alienum non laedas' (Use your property in such a way as not to damage that of others) was one of them, but I was at a loss to know how one could employ this maxim for the benefit of one's client. I had read all the leading cases on this maxim, but they gave me no confidence in the application of it in the practice of law.

Besides, I had learnt nothing at all of Indian law. I had not the slightest idea of Hindu and Mahomedan Law. I had not even learnt how to draft a plaint, and felt completely at sea. I had heard of Sir Pherozeshah Mehta as one who roared like a lion in law courts. How, I wondered, could he have learnt the art in England? It was out of the question for me ever to acquire his legal acumen, but I had serious misgivings as to whether I should be able even to earn a living by the profession.

I was torn with these doubts and anxieties whilst I was studying law. I confided my difficulties to some of my friends. One of them suggested that I should seek Dadabhai Naoroji's advice. I have already said that, when I went to England, I possessed a note of introduction to Dadabhai. I availed myself of it very late. I thought I had no right to trouble such a great man for an interview. Whenever an address by him was announced, I would attend it, listen to him from a corner of the hall, and go away after having feasted my eyes and ears. In order to come in close touch with the students he had founded an association. I used to attend its meetings, and rejoiced at Dadabhai's solicitude for the students, and the latter's respect for him. In course of time I mustered up courage to present to him the note of introduction. He said: 'You can come and have my advice whenever you like.' But I never availed myself of his offer. I thought it wrong to trouble him without the most pressing necessity. Therefore I dared not venture to accept my friend's advice to submit my difficulties to Dadabhai at that time. I forget now whether it was the same friend or someone else who recommended me to meet Mr. Frederick Pincutt. He was a Conservative, but his affection for Indian students was pure and unselfish. Many students sought his advice and I also applied to him for an appointment, which he granted. I can never forget that interview. He greeted me as a friend. He laughed away my pessimism. 'Do you think,' he said, 'that everyone must be a Pherozeshah Mehta? Pherozeshahs and Badruddins are rare. Rest assured it takes no unusual skill to be an ordinary lawyer. Common honesty and industry are enough to enable him to make a living. All cases are not complicated. Well, let me know the extent of your general reading.'

When I acquainted him with my little stock of reading, he was, as I could see, rather disappointed. But it was only for a moment. Soon his face beamed with a pleasing smile and he said, 'I understand your trouble. Your general reading is meagre. You have no knowledge of the world, a sine qua non for a vakil. You have not even read the history of India. A vakil should know human nature. He should be able to read a man's character from his face. And every Indian ought to know Indian history. This has no connection with the practice of law, but you ought to have that knowledge. I see that you have not even read Kaye's and Malleson's history of the Mutiny of 1857. Get hold of that at once and also read two more books to understand human nature.' These were Lavator's and Shemmelpennick's books on physiognomy.

I was extremely grateful to this venerable friend. In his presence I found all my fear gone, but as soon as I left him I began to worry again. 'To know a man from his face' was the question that haunted me, as I thought of the two books on my way home. The next day I purchased Lavator's book. Shemmelpennick's was not available at the shop. I read Lavator's book and found it more difficult than Snell's Equity, and scarcely interesting. I studied Shakespeare's physiognomy, but did not acquire the knack of finding out the Shakespeares walking up and down the streets of London.

Lavator's book did not add to my knowledge. Mr. Pincutt's advice did me very little direct service, but his kindliness stood me in good stead. His smiling open face stayed in my memory, and I trusted his advice that Pherozeshah Mehta's acumen, memory and ability were not essential to the making of a successful lawyer; honesty and industry were enough. And as I had a fair share of these last I felt somewhat reassured.

I could not read Kaye's and Malleson's volumes in England, but I did so in South Africa, as I had made a point of reading them at the first opportunity.

Thus with just a little leaven of hope mixed with my despair, I landed at Bombay from S.S. Assam. The sea was rough in the harbour, and I had to reach the quay in a launch.

PART II

Chapter 1 : Raychandbhai

I said in the last chapter that the sea was rough in Bombay harbour, not an unusual thing in the Arabian Sea in June and July. It had been choppy all the way from Aden. Almost every passenger was sick; I alone was in perfect form, staying on deck to see the stormy surge, and enjoying the splash of the waves. At breakfast there would be just one or two people besides myself, eating their oatmeal porridge from plates carefully held in their laps, lest the porridge itself find its place there.

The outer storm was to me a symbol of the inner. But even as the former left me unperturbed, I think I can say the same thing about the latter. There was the trouble with the caste that was to confront me. I have already adverted to my helplessness in starting on my profession. And then, as I was a reformer, I was taxing myself as to how best to begin certain reforms. But there was even more in store for me than I knew.

My elder brother had come to meet me at the dock. He had already made the acquaintance of Dr. Mehta and his elder brother, and as Dr. Mehta insisted on putting me up at his house, we went there. Thus the acquaintance begun in England continued in India and ripened into a permanent friendship between the two families.

I was pining to see my mother. I did not know that she was no more in the flesh to receive me back into her bosom. The sad news was now given me, and I underwent the usual ablution. My brother had kept me ignorant of her death, which took place whilst I was still in England. He wanted to spare me the blow in a foreign land. The news, however, was none the less a severe shock to me. But I must not dwell upon it. My grief was even greater than over my father's death. Most of my cherished hopes were shattered. But I remember that I did not give myself up to any wild expression of grief. I could even check the tears, and took to life just as though nothing had happened.

Dr. Mehta introduced me to several friends, one of them being his brother Shri Revashankar Jagjivan, with whom there grew up a lifelong friendship. But the introduction that I need particularly take note of was the one to the poet Raychand or Rajchandra, the son-in-law of an elder brother of Dr. Mehta, and partner of the firm of jewellers conducted in the name of Revashankar Jagjivan. He was not above twenty-five then, but my first meeting with him convinced me that he was a man of great character and learning. He was also known as Shatavadhani (one having the faculty of remembering or attending to a hundred things simultaneously), and Dr. Mehta recommended me to see some of his memory feats. I exhausted my vocabulary of all the European tongues I knew, and asked the poet to repeat the words. He did so in the precise order in which I had given them. I envied his gift without, however, coming under its spell. The thing that did cast its spell over me I came to know afterwards. This was his wide knowledge of the scriptures, his spotless character, and his burning passion for self-realization. I saw later that this last was the only thing for which he lived. The following lines of Muktanand were always on his lips and engraved on the tablets of his heart:

'I shall think myself blessed only when I see Him in every one of my daily acts;
Verily He is the thread, which supports Muktanand's life.'

Raychandbhai's commercial transactions covered hundreds of thousands. He was a connoisseur of pearls and diamonds. No knotty business problem was too difficult for him. But all these things were not the centre round which his life revolved. That centre was the passion to see God face to face. Amongst the things on his business table there were invariably to be found some religious book and his diary. The moment he finished his business he opened the religious book or the diary. Much of his published writings is a reproduction from this diary. The man who, immediately on finishing his talk about weighty business transaction, began to write about the hidden things of the spirit could evidently not be a businessman at all, but a real seeker after Truth. And I saw him thus absorbed in godly pursuits in the midst of business, not once or twice, but very often. I never saw him lose his state of equipoise. There was no business or other selfish tie that bound him to me, and yet I enjoyed the closest association with him. I was but a brief-less barrister then, and yet whenever I saw him he would engage me in conversation of a seriously religious nature. Though I was then groping and could not be said to have any serious interest in religious discussion, still I found his talk of absorbing interest. I have since met many a religious leader or teacher. I have tried to meet the heads of various faiths, and I must say that no one else has ever made on me the impression that Raychandbhai did. His words went straight home to me. His intellect compelled as great a regard from me as his moral earnestness, and deep down in me was the conviction that he would never willingly lead me astray and would always confide to me his innermost thoughts. In my moments of spiritual crisis, therefore, he was my refuge.

And yet, in spite of this regard for him I could not enthrone him in my heart as my Guru. The throne has remained vacant and my search still continues.

I believe in the Hindu theory of Guru and his importance in spiritual realization. I think there is a great deal of truth in the doctrine that true knowledge is impossible without a Guru. An imperfect teacher may be tolerable in mundane matters, but not in spiritual matters. Only a perfect gnani* deserves to be enthroned as Guru. There must, therefore, be ceaseless striving after perfection. For one gets the Guru that one deserves. Infinite striving after perfection is one's right. It is its own reward. The rest is in the hands of God.

Thus, though I could not place Raychandbhai on the throne of my heart as Guru, we shall see he was, on many occasions, my guide and helper. Three moderns have left a deep impress on my life, and captivated me: Raychandbhai by his living contact; Tolstoy by his book, The Kingdom of God is Within You; and Ruskin by his Unto this Last. But of these more in their proper place.

---

* A knowing one, a seer.

Chapter 2: How I began life

My elder brother had built high hopes on me. The desire for wealth and name and fame was great in him. He had a big heart, generous to a fault. This, combined with his simple nature, had attracted to him many friends, and through them he expected to get me briefs. He had also assumed that I should have a swinging practice and had, in that expectation, allowed the household expenses to become top-heavy. He had also left no stone unturned in preparing the field for my practice.

The storm in my caste over my foreign voyage was still brewing. It had divided the caste into two camps, one of which immediately re-admitted me, while the other was bent on keeping me out. To please the former my brother took me to Nasik before going to Rajkot, gave me a bath in the sacred river and, on reaching Rajkot, gave a caste dinner. I did not like all this. But my brother's love for me was boundless, and my devotion to him was in proportion to it, and so I mechanically acted as he wished, taking his will to be law. The trouble about re-admission to the caste was thus practically over.

I never tried to seek admission to the section that had refused it. Nor did I feel even mental resentment against any of the headmen of that section. Some of these regarded me with dislike, but I scrupulously avoided hurting their feelings. I fully respected the caste regulations about ex-communication. According to these, none of my relations, including my father-in-law and mother-in-law, and even my sister and brother-in-law, could entertain me; and I would not so much as drink water at their houses. They were prepared secretly to evade the prohibition, but it went against the grain with me to do a thing in secret that I would not do in public.

The result of my scrupulous conduct was that I never had occasion to be troubled by the caste; nay, I have experienced nothing but affection and generosity from the general body of the section that still regards me as ex-communicated. They have even helped me in my work, without ever expecting me to do anything for the caste. It is my conviction that all these good things are due to my non-resistance. Had I agitated for being admitted to the caste, had I attempted to divide it into more camps, had I provoked the castemen, they would surely have retaliated, and instead of steering clear of the storm, I should on arrival from England, have found myself in a whirlpool of agitation, and perhaps a party to dissimulation.

My relations with my wife were still not as I desired. Even my stay in England had not cured me of jealousy. I continued my squeamishness and suspiciousness in respect of every little thing, and hence all my cherished desires remained unfulfilled. I had decided that my wife should learn reading and writing and that I should help her in her studies, but my lust came in the way and she had to suffer for my own shortcoming. Once I went the length of sending her away to her father's house, and consented to receive her back only after I had made her thoroughly miserable. I saw later that all this was pure folly on my part.

I had planned reform in the education of children. My brother had children, and my own child which I had left at home when I went to England was now a boy of nearly four. It was my desire to teach these little ones physical exercise and make them hardy, and also to give them the benefit of my personal guidance. In this I had my brother's support and I succeeded in my efforts more or less. I very much liked the company of children, and the habit of playing and joking with them has stayed with me till today. I have ever since thought that I should make a good teacher of children.

The necessity for food 'reform' was obvious. Tea and coffee had already found their place in the house. My brother had thought it fit to keep some sort of English atmosphere ready for me on my return, and to that end, crockery and such other things, which used to be kept in the house only for special occasions, were now in general use. My 'reform' put the finishing touch. I introduced oatmeal porridge, and cocoa was to replace tea and coffee. But in truth it became an addition to tea and coffee. Boots and shoes were already there. I completed the Europeanization by adding the European dress.

Expenses thus went up. New things were added every day. We had succeeded in tying a white elephant at our door. But how was the wherewithal to be found? To start practice in Rajkot would have meant sure ridicule. I had hardly the knowledge of a qualified vakil and yet I expected to be paid ten times his fees! No client would be fool enough to engage me. And even if such a one was to be found, should I add arrogance and fraud to my ignorance, and increase the burden of debt I owed to the world?

Friends advised me to go to Bombay for some time in order to gain experience of the High Court, to study Indian law and to try to get what briefs I could. I took up the suggestion and went.

In Bombay I started a household with a cook as incompetent as myself. He was a Brahman. I did not treat him as a servant but as a member of the household. He would pour water over himself but never wash. His *dhoti* was dirty, as also his sacred thread, and he was completely innocent of the scriptures. But how was I to get a better cook?

'Well, Ravishankar,' (for that was his name), I would ask him, 'you may not know cooking, but surely you must know your sandhya (daily worship), etc.

'Sandhya, sir! the plough is our sandhya and the spade our daily ritual. That is the type of Brahman I am. I must live on your mercy. Otherwise agriculture is of course there for me.'

So I had to be Ravishankar's teacher. Time I had enough. I began to do half the cooking myself and introduced the English experiments in vegetarian cookery. I invested in a stove, and with Ravishankar began to run the kitchen. I had no scruples about inter-dining, Ravishankar too came to have none, and so we went on merrily together. There was only one obstacle. Ravishankar had sworn to remain dirty and to keep the food unclean!

But it was impossible for me to get along in Bombay for more than four or five months, there being no income to square with the ever-increasing expenditure.

This was how I began life. I found the barrister's profession a bad job — much show and little knowledge. I felt a crushing sense of my responsibility.

Chapter 3: The first case

While in Bombay, I began, on the one hand, my study of Indian law and, on the other, my experiments in dietetics in which Virchand Gandhi, a friend, joined me. My brother, for his part, was trying his best to get me briefs.

The study of Indian law was a tedious business. The Civil Procedure Code I could in no way get on with. Not so however, with the Evidence Act. Virchand Gandhi was reading for the solicitor's examination and would tell me all sorts of stories about barristers and vakils. 'Sir Pherozeshah's ability,' he would say, 'lies in his profound knowledge of law. He has the Evidence Act by heart and knows all the cases on the thirty-second section. Badruddin Tyabji's wonderful power of argument inspires the judges with awe.'

The stories of stalwarts such as these would unnerve me.

'It is not unusual', he would add, 'for a barrister to vegetate for five or seven years. That's why I have signed the articles for solicitorship. You should count yourself lucky if you can paddle your own canoe in three years' time.'

Expenses were mounting up every month. To have a barrister's board outside the house, whilst still preparing for the barrister's profession inside, was a thing to which I could not reconcile myself. Hence I could not give undivided attention to my studies. I developed some liking for the Evidence Act and read Mayne's Hindu Law with deep interest, but I had not the courage to conduct a case. I was helpless beyond words, even as the brides come fresh to her father-in-law's house!

About this time, I took up the case of one Mamibai. It was a 'small cause.' 'You will have to pay some commission to the tout,' I was told. I emphatically declined.

'But even that great criminal lawyer Mr. So-and-So, who makes three to four thousand a month, pays commission!'

'I do not need to emulate him,' I rejoined. 'I should be content with Rs. 300 a month. Father did not get more.'

'But those days are gone. Expenses in Bombay have gone up frightfully. You must be business-like.'

I was adamant. I gave no commission, but got Mamibai's case all the same. It was an easy case. I charged Rs. 30 for my fees. The case was not likely to last longer than a day...

This was my début in the Small Causes Court. I appeared for the defendant and had thus to cross-examine the plaintiff's witnesses. I stood up, but my heart sank into my boots. My head was reeling and I felt as though the whole court was doing likewise. I could think of no question to ask. The judge must have laughed, and the vakils no doubt enjoyed the spectacle. But I was past seeing anything. I sat down and told the agent that I could not conduct the case, that he had better engage Patel and have the fee back from me. Mr. Patel was duly engaged for Rs. 51. To him, of course, the case was child's play.

I hastened from the Court, not knowing whether my client won or lost her case, but I was ashamed of myself, and decided not to take up any more cases until I had courage enough to conduct them. Indeed I did not go to Court again until I went to South Africa. There was no virtue in my decision. I had simply made a virtue of necessity. There would be no one so foolish as to entrust his case to me, only to lose it!

But there was another case in store for me at Bombay. It was a memorial to be drafted. A poor Mussalman's land was confiscated in Porbandar. He approached me as the worthy son of a worthy father. His case appeared to be weak, but I consented to draft a memorial for him, the cost of printing to be borne by him. I drafted it and read it out to friends. They approved of it, and that to some extent made me feel confident that I was qualified enough to draft a memorial, as indeed I really was.

My business could flourish if I drafted memorials without any fees. But that would being no grist to the mill. So I thought I might take up a teacher's job. My knowledge of English was good enough, and I should have loved to teach English to Matriculation boys in some school. In this way I could have met part at least of the expenses. I came across an advertisement in the papers:

'Wanted, an English teacher to teach one hour daily. Salary Rs 75.' The advertisement was from a famous high school. I applied for the post and was called for an interview. I went there in high spirits, but when the principal found that I was not a graduate, he regretfully refused me.

'But I have passed the London Matriculation with Latin as my second language.'

'True but we want a graduate.'

There was no help for it. I wrung my hands in despair. My brother also felt much worried. We both came to the conclusion that it was no use spending more time in Bombay. I should settle in Rajkot where my brother, himself a petty pleader, could give me some work in the shape of drafting applications and memorials. And then as there was already a household at Rajkot, the breaking up of the one at Bombay meant a considerable saving. I liked the suggestion. My little establishment was thus closed after a stay of six months in Bombay.

I used to attend High Court daily whilst in Bombay, but I cannot say that I learnt anything there. I had not sufficient knowledge to learn much. Often I could not follow the cases and dozed off. There were others also who kept me company in this, and thus lightened my load of shame. After a time, I even lost the sense of shame, as I learnt to think that it was fashionable to doze in the High Court.

If the present generation has also its briefless barristers like me in Bombay, I would commend them a little practical precept about living. Although I lived in Girgaum I hardly ever took a carriage or a tram-car. I had made it a rule to walk to the High Court. It took me quite forty-five minutes, and of course I invariably returned home on foot. I had inured myself to the heat of the sun. This walk to and from the Court saved a fair amount of money, and when many of my friends in Bombay used to fall ill, I do not remember having once had an illness. Even when I began to earn money, I kept up the practice of walking to and from the office, and I am still reaping the benefits of that practice.

Chapter 4: The first shock

Disappointed, I left Bombay and went to Rajkot where I set up my own office. Here I got along moderately well. Drafting applications and memorials brought me in, on an average, Rs 300 a month. For this work I had to thank influence rather than my own ability, for my brother's partner had a settled practice. All applications etc. which were, really or to his mind, of an important character, he sent to big barristers. To my lot fell the applications to be drafted on behalf of his poor clients.

I must confess that here I had to compromise the principle of giving no commission, which in Bombay I had so scrupulously observed. I was told that conditions in the two cases were different; that whilst in Bombay commissions had to be paid to touts, here they had to be paid to vakils who briefed you; and that here as in Bombay all barristers, without exception, paid a percentage of their fees as commission. The argument of my brother was, for me, unanswerable. 'You see,' said he, 'that I am in partnership with another vakil. I shall always be inclined to make over to you all our cases with which you can possibly deal, and if you refuse to pay a commission to my partner, you are sure to embarrass me. As you and I have a joint establishment, your fee comes to our common purse, and I automatically get a share. But what about my partner? Supposing he gave the same case to some other barrister he would certainly get his commission from him.' I was taken in by this plea, and felt that, if I was to practise as a barrister, I could not press my principle regarding commissions in such cases. That is how I argued with myself, or to put it bluntly, how I deceived myself. Let me add, however, that I do not remember ever to have given commission in respect of any other case.

Though I thus began to make both ends meet, I got the first shock of my life about this time. I had heard what a British officer was like, but up to now had never been face to face with one.

My brother had been secretary and adviser to the late Ranasaheb of Porbandar before he was installed on his gadi*, and hanging over his head at this time was the charge of having given wrong advice when in that office. The matter had gone to the Political Agent who was prejudiced against my brother. Now I had known this officer when in England, and he may be said to have been fairly friendly to me. My brother thought that I should avail myself of the friendship and, putting in a good word on his behalf, try to disabuse the Political Agent of his prejudice. I did not at all like this idea. I should not, I thought, try to take advantage of a trifling acquaintance in England. If my brother was really at fault, what use was my recommendation? If he was innocent, he should submit a petition in the proper course and, confident of his innocence, face the result. My brother did not relish this advice. 'You do not know Kathiawad', he said, 'and you have yet to know the world. Only influence counts here. It is not proper for you, a brother, to shirk your duty, when you can clearly put in a good word about me to an officer you know.'

I could not refuse him, so I went to the officer much against my will. I knew I had no right to approach him and was fully conscious that I was compromising my self-respect. But I sought an appointment and got it. I reminded him of the old acquaintance, but I immediately saw that Kathiawad was different from England; that an officer on leave was not the same as an officer on duty. The political Agent owned the acquaintance, but the reminder seemed to stiffen him. 'Surely you have not come here to abuse that acquaintance, have you?' appeared to be the meaning of that stiffness, and seemed to be written on his brow. Nevertheless I opened my case. The sahib was impatient. 'Your brother is an intriguer. I want to hear nothing more from you. I have no time. If your brother has anything to say, let him apply through the proper channel.' The answer was enough, was perhaps deserved. But selfishness is blind. I went on with my story. The sahib got up and said: 'You must go now.'

'But please hear me out,' said I. That made him more angry. He called his peon and ordered him to show me the door. I was still hesitating when the peon came in, placed his hands on my shoulders and put me out of the room.

The sahib went away as also the peon, and I departed, fretting and fuming. I at once wrote out and sent over a note to this effect: 'You have insulted me. You have assaulted me through your peon. If you make no amends, I shall proceed against you.'

Quick came the answer through his sowar:

'You were rude to me. I asked you to go and you would not. I had no option but to order my peon to show you the door. Even after he asked you to leave the office, you did not do so. He therefore had to use just enough force to send you out. You are at liberty to proceed as you wish.'

With this answer in my pocket, I came home crest-fallen, and told my brother all that had happened. He was grieved, but was at a loss as to how to console me. He spoke to his vakil friends. For I did not know how to proceed against the sahib. Sir Pherozeshah

---

* Throne

Mehta happened to be in Rajkot at this time, having come down from Bombay for some case. But how could a junior barrister like me dare to see him? So I sent him the papers of my case, through the vakil who had engaged him, and begged for his advice. 'Tell Gandhi,' he said, 'such things are the common experience of many vakils and barristers. He is still fresh from England, and hot-blooded. He does not know British officers. If he would earn something and have an easy time here, let him tear up the note and pocket the insult. He will gain nothing by proceeding against the sahib, and on the contrary will very likely ruin himself. Tell him he has yet to know life.'

The advice was as bitter as poison to me, but I had to swallow it. I pocketed the insult, but also profited by it. 'Never again shall I place myself in such a false position, never again shall I try to exploit friendship in this way,' said I to myself, and since then I have never been guilty of a breach of that determination. This shock changed the course of my life.

Chapter 5: Preparing for South Africa

I was no doubt at fault in having gone to that officer. But his impatience and overbearing anger were out of all proportion to my mistake. It did not warrant expulsion. I can scarcely have taken up more than five minutes of his time. But he simply could not endure my talking. He could have politely asked me to go, but power had intoxicated him to an inordinate extent. Later I came to know that patience was not one of the virtues of this officer. It was usual for him to insult his visitors. The slightest unpleasantness was sure to put the sahib out.

Now most of my work would naturally be in his court. It was beyond me to conciliate him. I had no desire to curry favour with him. Indeed, having once threatened to proceed against him, I did not like to remain silent.

Meanwhile I began to learn something of the petty politics of the country. Kathiawad, being a conglomeration of small states, naturally had its rich crop of politicals. Petty intrigues between states, and intrigues of officers for power were the order of the day. Princes were always at the mercy of others and ready to lend their ears to sycophants. Even the sahib's peon had to be cajoled, and the sahib's shirastedar was more than his master, as he was his eyes, his ears and his interpreter. The shirastedar's will was law, and his income was always reputed to be more than the sahib's. This may have been an exaggeration, but he certainly lived beyond his salary.

This atmosphere appeared to me to be poisonous, and how to remain unscathed was a perpetual problem for me.

I was thoroughly depressed and my brother clearly saw it. We both felt that, if I could secure some job, I should be free from this atmosphere of intrigue. But without intrigue a ministership or judgeship was out of the question. And the quarrel with the sahib stood in the way of my practice.

Probandar was then under administration, and I had some work there in the shape of securing more powers for the prince. Also I had to see the Administrator in respect of the heavy vighoti (land rent) exacted from the Mers. This officer, though an Indian, was, I found, one better than the sahib in arrogance. He was able, but the ryots appeared to me to be none the better off for his ability. I succeeded in securing a few more powers for the Rana, but hardly any relief for the Mers. It struck me that their cause was not even carefully gone into.

So even in this mission I was comparatively disappointed. I thought justice was not done to my clients, but I had not the means to secure it. At the most I could have appealed to the Political Agent or to the Governor who would have dismissed the appeal saying, 'We decline to interfere.' If there had been any rule or regulation governing such decisions, it would have been something, but here the sahib's will was law.

I was exasperated.

In the meantime a Meman firm from Porbandar wrote to my brother making the following offer: 'We have business in South Africa. Ours is a big firm, and we have a big case there in the Court, our claim being £ 40,000. It has been going on for a long time. We have engaged the services of the best vakils and barristers. If you sent your brother there, he would be useful to us and also to himself. He would be able to instruct our counsel better than ourselves. And he would have the advantage of seeing a new part of the world, and of making new acquaintances.'

My brother discussed the proposition with me. I could not clearly make out whether I had simply to instruct the counsel or to appear in court. But I was tempted.

My brother introduced me to the late Sheth Abdul Karim Jhaveri a partner of Dada Abdulla & Co., the firm in question. 'It won't be a difficult job,' the Sheth assured me. 'We have big Europeans as our friends, whose acquaintance you will make. You can be useful to us in our shop. Much of our correspondence is in English and you can help us with that too. You will, of course, be our guest and hence will have no expense whatever.'

'How long do you require my services?' I asked. 'And what will be the payment?'

'Not more than a year. We will pay you a first class return fare and a sum of £105, all found.'

This was hardly going there as a barrister. It was going as a servant of the firm. But I wanted somehow to leave India. There was also the tempting opportunity of seeing a new country, and of having new experience. Also I could send £105 to my brother and help in the expenses of the household. I closed with the offer without any haggling, and got ready to go to South Africa.

Chapter 6: Arrival in Natal

When starting for South Africa I did not feel the wrench of separation which I had experienced when leaving for England. My mother was now no more. I had gained some knowledge of the world and of travel abroad, and going from Rajkot to Bombay was no unusual affair.

This time I only felt the pang of parting with my wife. Another baby had been born to us since my return from England. Our love could not yet be called free from lust, but it was getting gradually purer. Since my return from Europe, we had lived very little together; and as I had now become her teacher, however indifferent, and helped her to make certain reforms, we both felt the necessity of being more together, if only to continue the reforms. But the attraction of South Africa rendered the separation bearable. 'We are bound to meet again in a year,' I said to her, by way of consolation, and left Rajkot for Bombay.

Here I was to get my passage through the agent of Dada Abdulla and Co. But no berth was available on the boat, and if I did not sail then, I should be stranded in Bombay. 'We have tried our best,' said the agent, 'to secure a first-class passage, but in vain — unless you are prepared to go on deck. Your meals can be arranged for in the saloon.' Those were the days of my first class traveling, and how could a barrister travel as a deck passenger? So I refused the offer. I suspected the agent's veracity, for I could not believe that a first class passage was not available. With the agent's consent I set about securing it myself. I went on board the boat and met the chief officer. He said to me quite frankly, 'We do not usually have such a rush. But as the Governor-General of Mozambique is going by this boat, all the berths are engaged.'

'Could you not possibly squeeze me in?' I asked.

He surveyed me from top to toe and smiled. 'There is just one way', he said.

'There is an extra berth in my cabin, which is usually not available for passengers. But I am prepared to give it to you.' I thanked him and got the agent to purchase the passage. In April 1893 I set forth full of zest to try my luck in South Africa.

The first port of call was Lamu which we reached in about thirteen days. The Captain and I had become great friends by this time. He was fond of playing chess, but as he was quite a novice, he wanted one still more of a beginner for his partner, and so he invited me. I had heard a lot about the game but had never tried my hand at it. Players used to say that this was a game in which there was plenty of scope for the exercise of one's intelligence. The Captain offered to give me lessons, and he found me a good pupil as I had unlimited patience. Every time I was the loser, and that made him all the more eager to teach me. I liked the game, but never carried my liking beyond the boat or my knowledge beyond the moves of the pieces.

At Lamu the ship remained at anchor for some three to four hours, and I landed to see the port. The Captain had also gone ashore, but he had warned me that the harbour was treacherous and that I should return in good time.

It was a very small place. I went to the Post Office and was delighted to see the Indian clerks there, and had a talk with them. I also saw the Africans and tried to acquaint myself with their ways of life which interested me very much.

This took up some time.

There were some deck passengers with whom I had made acquaintance, and who had landed with a view to cooking their food on shore and having a quiet meal. I now found them preparing to return to the steamer, so we all got into the same boat. The tide was high in the harbour and our boat had more than its proper load. The high current was so strong that it was impossible to hold the boat to the ladder of the steamer. It would just touch the ladder and be drawn away again by the current. The first whistle to start had already gone. I was worried. The Captain was witnessing our plight from the bridge. He ordered the steamer to wait an extra five minutes. There was another boat near the ship which a friend hired for me for ten rupees. This boat picked me up from the overloaded one. The ladder had already been raised. I had therefore to be drawn up by means of a rope and the steamer started immediately. The other passengers were left behind. I now appreciated the Captain's warning.

After Lamu the next port was Mombassa and then Zanzibar. The halt here was a long one — eight or ten days — and we then changed to another boat.

The Captain liked me much, but the liking took an undesirable turn. He invited an English friend and me to accompany him on an outing, and we all went ashore in his boat. I had not the least notion of what the outing meant. And little did the Captain know what an ignoramus I was in such matters. We were taken to some Negro women's quarters by a tout. We were each shown into a room. I simply stood there dumb with shame. Heaven only knows what the poor woman must have thought of me. When the Captain called me I came out just as I had gone in. He saw my innocence. At first I felt very much ashamed, but as I could not think of the thing except with horror, the sense of shame wore away, and I thanked God that the sight of the woman had not moved me in the least. I was disgusted at my weakness and pitied myself for not having had the courage to refuse to go into the room.

This in my life was the third trial of its kind. Many a youth, innocent at first, must have been drawn into sin by a false sense of shame. I could claim no credit for having come out unscathed. I could have credit if I had refused to enter that room. I must entirely thank the All-merciful for having saved me.

The incident increased my faith in God and taught me, to a certain extent, to cast off false shame.

As we had to remain in this port for a week, I took rooms in the town and saw good deal by wandering about the neighbourhood. Only Malabar can give any idea of the luxuriant vegetation of Zanzibar. I was amazed at the gigantic trees and the size of the fruits. The next call was at Mozambique and thence we reached Natal towards the close of May.

Chapter 7: Some experiences

The port of Natal is Durban also known as Port Natal. Abdulla Sheth was there to receive me. As the ship arrived at the quay and I watched the people coming on board to meet their friends, I observed that the Indians were not held in much respect. I could not fail to notice a sort of snobbishness about the manner in which those who knew Abdulla Sheth behaved towards him, and it stung me. Abdulla Sheth had got used to it. Those who looked at me did so with a certain amount of curiosity. My dress marked me out from other Indians. I had a frock-coat and a turban, an imitation of the Bengal pugree.

I was taken to the firm's quarters and shown into the room set apart for me, next to Abdulla Sheth's. He did not understand me, I could not understand him. He read the papers his brother had sent through me, and felt more puzzled. He thought his brother had sent him a white elephant. My style of dress and living struck him as being expensive like that of the Europeans. There was no particular work then which could be given me. Their case was going on in the Transvaal. There was no meaning in sending me there immediately. And how far could he trust my ability and honesty? He would not be in Pretoria to watch me. The defendants were in Pretoria, and for aught he knew they might bring undue influence to bear on me. And if work in connection with the case in question was not to be entrusted to me, what work could I be given to do, as all other work could be done much better by his clerks? The clerks could be brought to book, if they did wrong. Could I be, if I also happened to err? So if no work in connection with the case could be given me, I should have to be kept for nothing.

Abdulla Sheth was practically unlettered, but he had a rich fund of experience. He had an acute intellect and was conscious of it. By practice he had picked up just sufficient English for conversational purposes, but that served him for carrying on all his business, whether it was dealing with Bank Managers and European merchants or explaining his case to his counsel. The Indians held him in very high esteem. His firm was then the biggest, or at any rate one of the biggest, of the Indian firms. With all these advantages he had one disadvantage — he was by nature suspicious.

He was proud of Islam and loved to discourse on Islamic philosophy. Though he did not know Arabic, his acquaintance with the Holy Koran and Islamic literature in general was fairly good. Illustrations he had in plenty, always ready at hand. Contact with him gave me a fair amount of practical knowledge of Islam. When we came closer to each other, we had long discussions on religious topics.

On the second or third day of my arrival, he took me to see the Durban court. There he introduced me to several people and seated me next to his attorney. The Magistrate kept staring at me and finally asked me to take off my turban.

This I refused to do and left the court.

So here too there was fighting in store for me.

Abdulla Sheth explained to me why some Indians were required to take off their turbans. Those wearing the Musalman costume might, he said, keep their turbans on, but the other Indians on entering a court had to take theirs off as a rule.

I must enter into some details to make this nice distinction intelligible. In the course of these two or three days I could see that the Indians were divided into different groups. One was that of Musalman merchants, who would call themselves 'Arabs'. Another was that of Hindu, and yet another of Parsi, clerks.

The Hindu clerks were neither here nor there, unless they cast in their lot with the 'Arabs'. The Parsi clerks would call themselves Persians. These three classes had some social relations with one another. But by far the largest class was that composed of Tamil, Telugu and North Indian indentured and freed labourers. The indentured labourers were those who went to natal on an agreement to serve for five years, and came to be known there as girmitiyas from girmit, which was the corrupt form of the English word 'agreement'. The other three classes had none but business relations with this class. Englishmen called them 'coolies' and as the majority of Indians belonged to the labouring class, all Indians were called 'coolies,' or 'samis'. Sami is a Tamil suffix occurring after many Tamil names, and it is nothing else than the Samskrit Swami, meaning a master. Whenever, therefore, an Indian resented being addressed as a sami and had enough wit in him, he would try to return the compliment in this wise: 'You may call me sami, but you forget that sami means a master. I am not your master!' Some Englishmen would wince at this, while others would get angry, swear at the Indian and, if there was a chance, would even belabour him; for sami to him was nothing better than a term of contempt. To interpret it to mean a master amounted to an insult!

I was hence known as a 'coolie barrister'. The merchants were known as 'coolie merchants'. The original meaning of the word 'coolie' was thus forgotten, and it became a common appellation for all Indians. The Musalman merchant would resent this and say: 'I am not a coolie, I am an Arab,' or 'I am a merchant', and the Englishman, if courteous, would apologize to him.

The question of wearing the turban had a great importance in this state of things. Being obliged to take off one's Indian turban would be pocketing an insult. So I thought I had better bid good-bye to the Indian turban and begin wearing an English hat, which would save me from the insult and the unpleasant controversy.

But Abdulla Sheth disapproved of the idea. He said, 'If you do anything of the kind, it will have a very bad effect. You will compromise those insisting on wearing Indian turbans. And an Indian turban sits well on your head. If you wear an English hat, you will pass for a waiter.'

There was practical wisdom, patriotism and a little bit of narrowness in this advice. The wisdom was apparent, and he would not have insisted on the Indian turban except out of patriotism; the slighting reference to the waiter betrayed a kind of narrowness. Amongst the indentured Indians there were three classes — Hindus, Musalmans and Christians. The last were the children of indentured Indians who became converts to Christanity. Even in 1893 their number was large. They wore the English costume, and the majority of them earned their living by service as waiters in hotels. Abdulla Sheth's criticism of the English hat was with reference to this class. It was considered degrading to serve as a waiter in a hotel. The belief persists even today among many.

On the whole I liked Abdulla Sheth's advice. I wrote to the press about the incident and defended the wearing of my turban in the court. The question was very much discussed in the papers, which described me as an 'unwelcome visitor'. Thus the incident gave me an unexpected advertisement in South Africa within a few days of my arrival there. Some supported me while others severely criticized my temerity.

My turban stayed with me practically until the end of my stay in South Africa. When and why I left off wearing any head-dress at all in South Africa, we shall see later.

Chapter 8: On the way to Pretoria

I soon came in contact with the Christian Indians living in Durban. The Court Interpreter, Mr. Paul, was a Roman Catholic. I made his acquaintance, as also that of the late Mr. Subhan Godfrey, then a teacher under the Protestant Mission, and father of James Godfery, who, as a member of the South African Deputation, visited India in 1924. I likewise met the late Parsi Rustomji and the late Adamji Miyakhan about the same time. All these friends, who up to then had never met one another except on business, came ultimately into close contact, as we shall see later.

Whilst I was thus widening the circle of my acquaintance, the firm received a letter from their lawyer saying that preparations should be made for the case, and that Abdulla Sheth should go to Pretoria himself or send a representative.

Abdulla Sheth gave me this letter to read, and asked me if I would go to Pretoria. 'I can only say after I have understood the case from you,' said I. 'At present I am at a loss to know what I have to do there.' He thereupon asked his clerks to explain the case to me.

As I began to study the case, I felt as though I ought to begin from the A B C of the subject. During the few days I had had at Zanzibar, I had been to the court to see the work there. A Parsi lawyer was examining a witness and asking him questions regarding credit and debit entries in account books. It was all Greek to me. Book-keeping I had learnt neither at school nor during my stay in England. And the case for which I had come to South Africa was mainly about accounts. Only one who knew accounts could understand and explain it. The clerk went on talking about this debited and that credited, and I felt more and more confused. I did not know what a P. Note meant. I failed to find the word in the dictionary. I revealed my ignorance to the clerk, and I learnt from him that a P. Note meant a promisory note. I purchased a book on book-keeping and studied it. That gave me some confidence. I understood the case. I saw that Abdulla Sheth, who did not know how to keep accounts, had so much practical knowledge that he could quickly solve intricacies of book-keeping. I told him that I was prepared to go to Pretoria.

'Where will you put up?' asked the Sheth.

'Wherever you want me to,' said I.

'Then I shall write to our lawyer. He will arrange for your lodgings. I shall also write to my Meman friends there, but I would not advise you to stay with them. The other party has great influence in Pretoria. Should any one of them manage to read our private correspondence, it might do us much harm. The more you avoid familiarity with them, the better for us.'

'I shall stay where your lawyer puts me up, or I shall find out independent lodgings. Pray don't worry. Not a soul shall know anything that is confidential between us. But I do intend cultivating the acquaintance of the other party. I should like to be friends with them. I would try, if possible, to settle the case out of court. After all Tyeb Sheth is a relative of yours.'

Sheth Tyeb Haji Khan Muhammad was a near relative of Abdulla Sheth.

The mention of a probable settlement somewhat startled the Sheth, I could see. But I had already been six or seven days in Durban, and we now knew and understood each other. I was no longer a 'white elephant.' So he said:

'Y...es, I see. There would be nothing better than a settlement out of court. But we are all relatives and know one another very well indeed. Tyeb Sheth is not a man to consent to a settlement easily. With the slightest unwariness on our part, he would screw all sorts of things out of us, and do us down in the end. So please think twice before you do anything.'

'Don't be anxious about that,' said I. 'I need not talk to Tyeb Sheth, or for that matter to anyone else, about the case. I would only suggest to him to come to an understanding, and so save a lot of unnecessary litigation.'

On the seventh or eighth day after my arrival, I left Durban. A first class seat was booked for me. It was usual there to pay five shillings extra, if one needed a bedding. Abdulla Sheth insisted that I should book one bedding but, out of obstinacy and pride and with a view to saving five shillings, I declined. Abdulla Sheth warned me. 'Look, now,' said he, 'this is a different country from India. Thank God, we have enough and to spare.

Please do not stint yourself in anything that you may need.'

I thanked him and asked him not to be anxious.

The train reached Maritzburg, the capital of Natal, at about 9 p.m. Beddings used to be provided at this station. A railway servant came and asked me if I wanted one. 'No,' said I, 'I have one with me.' He went away. But a passenger came next, and looked me up and down. He saw that I was a 'coloured' man. This disturbed him. Out he went and came in again with one or two officials. They all kept quiet, when another official came to me and said, 'Come along, you must go to the van compartment.'

'But I have a first class ticket,' said I.

'That doesn't matter,' rejoined the other. 'I tell you, you must go to the van compartment.'

'I tell you, I was permitted to travel in this compartment at Durban, and I insist on going on in it.'

'No, you won't,' said the official. 'You must leave this compartment, or else I shall have to call a police constable to push you out.'

'Yes, you may. I refuse to get out voluntarily.'

The constable came. He took me by the hand and pushed me out. My luggage was also taken out. I refused to go to the other compartment and the train steamed away. I went and sat in the waiting room, keeping my hand-bag with me, and leaving the other luggage where it was. The railway authorities had taken charge of it.

It was winter, and winter in the higher regions of South Africa is severely cold. Maritzburg being at a high altitude, the cold was extremely bitter. My over-coat was in my luggage, but I did not dare to ask for it lest I should be insulted again, so I sat and shivered. There was no light in the room. A passenger came in at about midnight and possibly wanted to talk to me. But I was in no mood to talk.

I began to think of my duty. Should I fight for my rights or go back to India, or should I go on to Pretoria without minding the insults, and return to India after finishing the case? It would be cowardice to run back to India without fulfilling my obligation. The hardship to which I was subjected was superficial — only a symptom of the deep disease of colour prejudice. I should try, if possible, to root out the disease and suffer hardships in the process. Redress for wrongs I should seek only to the extent that would be necessary for the removal of the colour prejudice.

So I decided to take the next available train to Pretoria.

The following morning I sent a long telegram to the General Manager of the Railway and also informed Abdulla Sheth, who immediately met the General Manager. The Manager justified the conduct of the railway authorities, but informed him that he had already instructed the Station Master to see that I reached my destination safely. Abdulla Sheth wired to the Indian merchants in Maritzburg and to friends in other places to meet me and look after me. The merchants came to see me at the station and tried to comfort me by narrating their own hardships and explaining that what had happened to me was nothing unusual. They also said that Indians traveling first or second class had to expect trouble from railway officials and white passengers. The day was thus spent in listening to these tales of woe. The evening train arrived. There was a reserved berth for me. I now purchased at Maritzburg the bedding ticket I had refused to book at Durban.

The train took me to Charlestown.

Chapter 9: More hardships

The train reached Charlestown in the morning. There was no railway, in those days, between Charlestown and Johannesburg, but only a stage-coach, which halted at Standerton for the night en route. I possessed a ticket for the coach, which was not cancelled by the break of the journey at Maritzburg for a day; besides, Abdulla Sheth had sent a wire to the coach agent at Charlestown.

But the agent only needed a pretext for putting me off, and so, when he discovered me to be a stranger, he said, 'Your ticket is cancelled.' I gave him the proper reply. The reason at the back of his mind was not want of accommodation, but quite another. Passengers had to be accommodated inside the coach, but as I was regarded as a 'coolie' and looked a stranger, it would be proper, thought the 'leader', as the white man in charge of the coach was called, not to seat me with the white passengers. There were seats on either side of the coachbox. The leader sat on one of these as a rule. Today he sat inside and gave me his seat. I knew it was sheer injustice and an insult, but I thought it better to pocket it. I could not have forced myself inside, and if I had raised a protest, the coach would have gone off without me. This would have meant the loss of another day, and Heaven only knows what would have happened the next day. So, much as I fretted within myself, I prudently sat next the coachman.

At about three o'clock the coach reached Pardekoph. Now the leader desired to sit where I was seated, as he wanted to smoke and possibly to have some fresh air. So he took a piece of dirty sack-cloth from the driver, spread it on the footboard and, addressing me, said, 'Sami, you sit on this, I want to sit near the driver.' The insult was more than I could bear. In fear and trembling I said to him, 'It was you who seated me here, though I should have been accommodated inside. I put up with the insult. Now that you want to sit outside and smoke, you would have me sit at your feet. I will not do so, but I am prepared to sit inside.'

As I was struggling through these sentences, the man came down upon me and began heavily to box my ears. He seized me by the arm and tried to drag me down. I clung to the brass rails of the coachbox and was determined to keep my hold even at the risk of breaking my wrist bones. The passengers were witnessing the scene—the man swearing at me, dragging and belabouring me, and I remaining still. He was strong and I was weak. Some of the passengers were moved to pity and exclaimed: 'Man, let him alone. Don't beat him. He is not to blame. He is right. If he can't stay there, let him come and sit with us.'

'No fear,' cried the man, but he seemed somewhat crestfallen and stopped beating me. He let go my arm, swore at me a little more, and asking the Hottentot servant who was sitting on the other side of the coachbox to sit on the footboard, took the seat so vacated.

The passengers took their seats and, the whistle given, the coach rattled away. My heart was beating fast within my breast, and I was wondering whether I should ever reach my destination alive. The man cast an angry look at me now and then and, pointing his finger at me, growled: 'Take care, let me once get to Standerton and I shall show you what I do.' I sat speechless and prayed to God to help me.

After dark we reached Standerton and I heaved a sigh of relief on seeing some Indian faces. As soon as I got down, these friends said: 'We are here to receive you and take you to Isa Sheth's shop. We have had a telegram from Dada Abdulla.' I was very glad, and we went to Sheth Isa Haji Sumar's shop. The Sheth and his clerks gathered round me. I told them all that I had gone through. They were very sorry to hear it and comforted me by relating to me their own bitter experiences.

I wanted to inform the agent of the Coach Company of the whole affair. So I wrote him a letter, narrating everything that had happened, and drawing his attention to the threat his man had held out. I also asked for an assurance that he would accommodate me with the other passengers inside the coach when we started the next morning. To which the agent replied to this effect: 'From Standerton we have a bigger coach with different men in charge. The man complained of will not be there tomorrow, and you will have a seat with the other passengers.' This somewhat relieved me. I had, of course, no intention of proceeding against the man who had assaulted me, and so the chapter of the assault closed there.

In the morning Isa Sheth's man took me to the coach, I got a good seat and reached Johannesburg quite safely that night.

Standerton is a small village and Johannesburg a big city. Abdulla Sheth had wired to Johannesburg also, and given me the name and address of Muhammad Kasam Kamruddin's firm there. Their man had come to receive me at the stage, but neither did I see him nor did he recognize me. So I decided to go to a hotel. I knew the names of several. Taking a cab I asked to be driven to the Grand National Hotel. I saw the Manager and asked for a room. He eyed me for a moment, and politely saying, 'I am very sorry, we are full up,' bade me good-bye. So I asked the cabman to drive to Muhammad Kasam Kamruddin's shop. Here I found Abdul Gani Sheth expecting me, and he gave me a cordial greeting. He had a hearty laugh over the story of my experience at the hotel.

'How ever did you expect to be admitted to a hotel?' he said.

'Why not?' I asked.

'You will come to know after you have stayed here a few days,' said he.

'Only we can live in a land like this, because, for making money, we do not mind pocketing insults, and here we are.' With this he narrated to me the story of the hardships of Indians in South Africa.

Of Sheth Abdul Gani we shall know more as we proceed.

He said: 'This country is not for men like you. Look now, you have to go to Pretoria tomorrow. You will have to travel third class. Conditions in the Transvaal are worse than in Natal. First and second class tickets are never issued to Indians.'

'You cannot have made persistent efforts in this direction.'

'We have sent representations, but I confess our own men too do not want as a rule to travel first or second.

I sent for the railway regulations and read them. There was a loophole. The language of the old Transvaal enactments was not very exact or precise; that of the railway regulations was even less so.

I said to the Sheth: 'I wish to go first class, and if I cannot, I shall prefer to take a cab to Pretoria, a matter of only thirty-seven miles.'

Sheth Abdul Gani drew my attention to the extra time and money this would mean, but agreed to my proposal to travel first, and accordingly we sent a note to the Station Master. I mentioned in my note that I was a barrister and that I always travelled first, I also stated in the letter that I needed to reach Pretoria as early as possible, that as there was no time to await his reply I would receive it in person at the station, and that I should expect to get a first class ticket. There was of course a purpose behind asking for the reply in person. I thought that if the Station master gave a written reply, he would certainly say 'no', especially because he would have his own notion of a 'coolie' barrister. I would therefore appear before him in faultless English dress, talk to him and possibly persuade him to issue a first class ticket. So I went to the station in a frock-coat and necktie, placed a sovereign for my fare on the counter and asked for a first class ticket.

'You sent me that note?' he asked.

'That is so. I shall be much obliged if you will give me a ticket. I must reach Pretoria today.'

He smiled and, moved to pity, said: 'I am not a Transvaaler. I am a Hollander. I appreciate your feelings, and you have my sympathy. I do want to give you a ticket — onone condition, however, that, if the guard should ask you to shift to the third class, you will not involve me in the affair, by which I mean that you should not proceed against the railway company. I wish you a safe journey.

I can see you are a gentleman.'

With these words he booked the ticket. I thanked him and gave him the necessary assurance.

Sheth Abdul Gani had come to see me off at the station. The incident gave him an agreeable surprise, but he warned me saying: 'I shall be thankful if you reach Pretoria all right. I am afraid the guard will not leave you in peace in the first class and even if he does, the passengers will not.'

I took my seat in a first class compartment and the train started. At Germiston the guard came to examine the tickets. He was angry to find me there, and signaled to me with his finger to go to the third class. I showed him my first class ticket. 'That doesn't matter,' said he, 'remove to the third class.'

There was only one English passenger in the compartment. He took the guard to task. 'What do you mena by troubling the gentleman?' he said. 'Don't you see he has a first class ticket? I do not mind in the least his travelling with me.'

Addressing me, he said, 'You should make yourself comfortable where you are.'

The guard muttered: 'If you want to travel with a coolie, what do I care?' and went away. At about eight o'clock in the evening the train reached Pretoria.

Chapter 10: First day in Pretoria

I had expected someone on behalf of Dada Abdulla's attorney to meet me at Pretoria station. I knew that no Indian would be there to receive me, since I had particularly promised not to put up at an Indian house. But the attorney had sent no one. I understood later that as I had arrived on a Sunday, he could not have sent anyone without inconvenience. I was perplexed, and wondered where to go, as I feared that no hotel would accept me.

Pretoria station in 1893 was quite different from what it was in 1914. The lights were burning dimly. The travellers were few. I let all the other passengers go and thought that, as soon as the ticket collector was fairly free, I would hand him my ticket and ask him if he could direct me to some small hotel or any other such place where I might go; otherwise I would spend the night at the station. I must confess I shrank from asking him even this, for I was afraid of being insulted.

The station became clear of all passengers. I gave my ticket to the ticket collector and began my inquiries. He replied to me courteously, but I saw that he could not be of any considerable help. But an American Negro who was standing nearby broke into the conversation.

'I see,' said he, 'that you are an utter stranger here, without any friends. If you will come with me, I will take you to a small hotel, of which the proprietor is an American who is very well known to me. I think he will accept you.'

I had my own doubts about the offer, but I thanked him and accepted his suggestion. He took me to Johnson's Family Hotel. He drew Mr. Johnson aside to speak to him, and the latter agreed to accommodate me for the night, on condition that I should have my dinner served in my room.

'I assure you,' said he, 'that I have no colour prejudice. But I have only European custom, and, if I allowed you to eat in the dining-room, my guests might be offended and even go away.'

'Thank you,' said I, 'even for accommodating me for the night. I am now more or less acquainted with the conditions here, and I understand your difficulty. I do not mind your serving the dinner in my room. I hope to be able to make some other arrangement tomorrow.'

I was shown into a room, where I now sat waiting for the dinner and musing, as I was quite alone. There were not many guests in the hotel, and I had expected the waiter to come very shortly with the dinner. Instead Mr. Johnston appeared. He said: 'I was ashamed of having asked you to have your dinner here. So I spoke to the other guests about you, and asked them if they would mind your having your dinner in the dining-room. They said they had no objection, and that they did not mind your staying here as long as you liked. Please, therefore, come to the dining-room, if you will, and stay here as long as you wish.'

I thanked him again, went to the dining-room and had a hearty dinner.

Next morning I called on the attorney, Mr. A. W. Baker. Abdulla Sheth had given me some description of him, so his cordial reception did not surprise me. He received me very warmly and made kind inquiries. I explained all about myself. Thereupon he said: 'We have no work for you here as barrister, for we have engaged the best counsel. The case is a prolonged and complicated one, so I shall take your assistance only to the extent of getting necessary information. And of course you will make communication with my client easy for me, as I shall now ask for all the information I want from him through you. That is certainly an advantage; I have not yet found rooms for you. I thought I had better do so after having seen you. There is a fearful amount of colour prejudice here, and therefore it is not easy to find lodgings for such as you. But I know a poor woman. She is the wife of a baker. I think she will take you and thus add to her income at the same time. Come, let us go to her place.'

So he took me to her house. He spoke with her privately about me, and she agreed to accept me as a boarder at 35 shilling a week.

Mr. Baker, besides being an attorney, was a staunch lay preacher, He is still alive and now engaged purely in missionary work, having given up the legal profession. He is quite well-to-do. He still corresponds with me. In his letters he always dwells on the same theme. He upholds the excellence of Christianity from various points of view, and contends that it is impossible to find eternal peace, unless one accepts Jesus as the only son of God and the Saviour of mankind.

During the very first interview Mr. Baker ascertained my religious views. I said to him:

'I am a Hindu by birth. And yet I do not know much of Hinduism, and I know less of other religions. In fact I do not know where I am, and what is and what should be my belief. I intend to make a careful study of my own religion and, as far as I can, of other religions as well.'

Mr. Baker was glad to hear all this, and said: 'I am one of the directors of the South Africa General Mission. I have built a church at my own expense, and deliver sermons in it regularly. I am free from colour prejudice. I have some co-workers, and we meet at one o'clock every day for a few minutes and pray for peace and light. I shall be glad if you will join us there. I shall introduce you to my co-workers who will be happy to meet you, and I dare say you will also like their company. I shall give you, besides, some religious books to read, though of course the book of books is the Holy Bible, which I would specially recommend to you.'

I thanked Mr. Baker and agreed to attend the one o'clock prayers as regularly as possible.

'So I shall expect you here tomorrow at one o'clock, and we shall go together to pray,' added Mr. Baker, and we said good-bye.

I had little time for reflection just yet.

I went to Mr. Johnston, paid the bill and removed to the new lodgings, where I had my lunch. The landlady was good woman. She had cooked a vegetarian meal for me. It was not long before I made myself quite at home with the family.

I next went to see the friend to whom Dada Abdulla had given me a note. From him I learnt more about the hardships of Indians in South Africa. He insisted that I should stay with him. I thanked him, and told him that I had already made arrangements. He urged me not to hesitate to ask for anything I needed.

It was now dark. I returned home, had my dinner, went to my room and lay there absorbed in deep thought. There was not any immediate work for me. I informed Abdulla Sheth of it. What, I thought, can be the meaning of Mr. Baker's interest in me? What shall I gain from his religious co-workers? How far should I undertake the study of Christianity? How was I to obtain literature about Hinduism? And how was I to understand Christianity in its proper perspective without thoroughly knowing my own religion? I could come to only one conclusion: I should make a dispassionate study of all that came to me, and deal with Mr. Baker's group as God might guide me; I should not think of embracing another religion before I had fully understood my own.

Thus musing I fell asleep...

Chapter 11 : Christian contacts

The next day at one o'clock I went to Mr. Baker's prayer-meeting. There I was introduced to Miss Harris, Miss Gabb, Mr. Coates and others. Everyone kneeled down to pray, and I followed suit. The prayers were supplications to God for various things, according to each person's desire. Thus the usual forms were for the day to be passed peacefully, or for God to open the doors of the heart.

A prayer was now added for my welfare: 'Lord, show the path to the new brother who has come amongst us. Give him, Lord, the peace that Thou hast given us. May the Lord Jesus who has saved us save him too. We ask all this in the name of Jesus.' There was no singing of hymns or other music at these meetings. After the supplication for something special every day, we dispersed, each going to his lunch, that being the hour for it. The prayer did not take more than five minutes.

The Misses Harris and Gabb were both elderly maiden ladies. Mr. Coates was a Quaker. The two ladies lived together, and they gave me a standing invitation to four o'clock tea at their house every Sunday.

When we met on Sundays, I used to give Mr. Coates my religious diary for the week, and discuss with him the books I had read and the impression they had left on me. The ladies used to narrate their sweet experiences and talk about the peace they had found.

Mr. Coates was a frank-hearted staunch young man. We went out for walks together, and he also took me to other Christian friends.

As we came closer to each other, he began to give me books of his own choice, until my shelf was filled with them. He loaded me with books, as it were. In pure faith I consented to read all those books, and as I went on reading them we discussed them.

I read a number of such books in 1893. I do not remember the names of them all, but they included the Commentary of Dr. Parker of the City Temple, Pearson's Many Infallible Proofs and Butler's Analogy. Parts of these were unintelligible to me. I liked some things in them, while I did not like others. Many Infallible Proofs were proofs in support of the religion of the Bible, as the author understood it. The book had no effect on me. Parker's Commentary was morally stimulating, but it could not be of any help to one who had no faith in the prevalent Christian beliefs. Butler's Analogy struck me to be a very profound and difficult book, which should be read four or five times to be understood properly. It seemed to me to be written with a view to converting atheists to theism. The arguments advanced in it regarding the existence of God were unnecessary for me, as I had then passed the stage of unbelief; but the arguments in proof of Jesus being the only incarnation of God and the Mediator between God and man left me unmoved.

But Mr. Coates was not the man easily to accept defeat. He had great affection for me. He saw, round my neck, the Vaishnava necklace of Tulasi-beads. He thought it to be superstition and was pained by it. 'This superstition does not become you. Come, let me break the necklace.'

'No, you will not. It is a sacred gift from my mother.'

'But do you believe in it?'

'I do not know its mysterious significance. I do not think I should come to harm if I did not wear it. But I cannot, without sufficient reason, give up a necklace that she put round my neck out of love and in the conviction that it would be conducive to my welfare. When, with the passage of time, it wears away and breaks of its own accord, I shall have no desire to get a new one. But this necklace cannot be broken.'

Mr. Coates could not appreciate my argument, as he had no regard for my religion. He was looking forward to delivering me from the abyss of ignorance. He wanted to convince me that, no matter whether there was some truth in other religions, salvation was impossible for me unless I accepted Christianity which represented the truth, and that my sins would not be washed away except by the intercession of Jesus, and that all good works were useless.

Just as he introduced me to several books, he introduced me to several friends whom he regarded as staunch Christians. One of these introductions was to a family which belonged to the Plymouth Brethren, a Christian sect.

Many of the contacts for which Mr. Coates was responsible were good. Most struck me as being God-fearing. But during my contact with this family, one of the Plymouth Brethren confronted me with an argument for which I was not prepared:

'You cannot understand the beauty of our religion. From what you say it appears that you must be brooding over your transgressions every moment of your life, always mending them and atoning for them. How can this ceaseless cycle of action bring you redemption? You can never have peace. You admit that we are all sinners. Now look at the perfection of our belief. Our attempts at improvement and atonement are futile. And yet redemption we must have. How can we bear the burden of sin? We can but throw it on Jesus. He is the only sinless Son of God. It is His word that those who believe in Him shall have everlasting life. Therein lies God's infinite mercy. And as we believe in the atonement of Jesus, our own sins do not bind us. Sin we must. It is impossible to live in this world sinless. And therefore Jesus suffered and atoned for all the sins of mankind. Only he who accepts His great redemption can have eternal peace. Think what a life of restlessness is yours, and what a promise of peace we have.'

The argument utterly failed to convince me. I humbly replied:

'If this be the Christianity acknowledged by all Christians, I cannot accept it. I do not seek redemption from the consequences of my sin. I seek to be redeemed from sin itself, or rather from the very thought of sin. Until I have attained that end, I shall be content to be restless.'

To which the Plymouth Brother rejoined: I assure you, your attempt is fruitless. Think again over what I have said.'

And the Brother proved as good as his word. he knowingly committed transgressions, and showed me that he was undisturbed by the thought of them.

But I already knew before meeting with these friends that all Christians did not believe in such a theory of atonement. Mr. Coates himself walked in the fear of God. His heart was pure, and he believed in the possibility of self-purification. The two ladies also shared this belief. Some of the books that came into my hands were full of devotion. So, although Mr. Coates was very much disturbed by this latest experience of mine, I was able to reassure him and tell him that the distorted belief of a Plymouth Brother could not prejudice me against Christianity.

My difficulties lay elsewhere. They were with regard to the Bible and its accepted interpretation.

Chapter 12: Seeking touch with Indians

Before writing further about Christian contacts, I must record other experiences of the same period.

Sheth Tyeb Haji Khan Muhammad had in Pretoria the same position as was enjoyed by Dada Abdulla in Natal. There was no public movement that could be conducted without him. I made his acquaintance the very first week and told him of my intention to get in touch with every Indian in Pretoria. I expressed a desire to study the conditions of Indians there, and asked for his help in my work, which he gladly agreed to give.

My first step was to call a meeting of all the Indians in Pretoria and to present to them a picture of their condition in the Transvaal. The meeting was held at the house of Sheth Haji Muhammad Haji Joosab, to whom I had a letter of introduction. It was principally attended by Meman merchants, though there was a sprinkling of Hindus as well. The Hindu population in Pretoria was, as a matter of fact, very small.

My speech at this meeting may be said to have been the first public speech in my life. I went fairly prepared with my subject, which was about observing truthfulness in business. I had always heard the merchants say that truth was not possible in business. I did not think so then, nor do I now. Even today there are merchant friends who contend that truth is inconsistent with business. Business, they say, is a very practical affair, and truth a matter of religion; and they argue that practical affairs are one thing, while religion is quite another. Pure truth, they hold, is out of the question in business, one can speak it only so far as is suitable. I strongly contested the position in my speech and awakened the merchants to a sense of their duty, which was two-fold. Their responsibility to be truthful was all the greater in a foreign land, because the conduct of a few Indians was the measure of that of the millions of their fellow-countrymen.

I had found our peoples' habits to be insanitary, as compared with those of the Englishmen around them, and drew their attention to it. I laid stress on the necessity of forgetting all distinctions such as Hindus, Musalmans, Parsis, Christians, Gujaratis,

Madrasis, Punjabis, Sindhis, Kachchhis, Surtis and so on.

I suggested, in conclusion, the formation of an association to make representations to the authorities concerned in respect of the hardships of the Indian settlers, and offered to place at its disposal as much of my time and service as was possible.

I saw that I made a considerable impression on the meeting.

My speech was followed by discussion. Some offered to supply me with facts. I felt encouraged. I saw that very few amongst my audience knew English. As I felt that knowledge of English would be useful in that country, I advised those who had leisure to learn English. I told them that it was possible to learn a language even at an advanced age, and cited cases of people who had done so. I undertook, besides, to teach a class, if one was started, or personally to instruct individuals desiring to learn the language.

The class was not started, but three young men expressed their readiness to learn at their convenience, and on condition that I went to their places to teach them. Of these, two were Musalmans — one of them a barber and the other a clerk — and the third was a Hindu, a petty shopkeeper. I agreed to suit them all. I had no misgivings regarding my capacity to teach. My pupils might become tired, but not I. Sometimes it happened that I would go to their places only to find them engaged in their business. But I did not lose patience. None of the three desired a deep study of English, but two may be said to have made fairly good progress in about eight months. Two learnt enough to keep accounts and write ordinary business letters. The barber's ambition was confined to acquiring just enough English for dealing with his customers. As a result of their studies, two of the pupils were equipped for making a fair income.

I was satisfied with the result of the meeting. It was decided to hold such meetings, as far as I remember, once a week or, maybe, once a month. These were held more or less regularly, and on these occasions there was a free exchange of ideas. The result was that there was now in Pretoria no Indian I did not know, or whose condition I was not acquainted with. This prompted me in turn to make the acquaintance of the British Agent in Pretoria, Mr. Jacobus de Wet. He had sympathy for the Indians, but he had very little influence. However, he agreed to help us as best he could, and invited me to meet him whenever I wished.

I now communicated with the railway authorities and told them that, even under their own regulations, the disabilities about travelling under which the Indians laboured could not be justified. I got a letter in reply to the effect that first and second class tickets would be issued to Indians who were properly dressed. This was far from giving adequate relief, as it rested with the station master to decide who was 'properly dressed'.

The British Agent showed me some papers dealing with Indian affairs. Tyeb Sheth had also given me similar papers. I learnt from them how cruelly the Indians were hounded out from the Orange Free State.

In short, my stay in Pretoria enabled me to make a deep study of the social, economic and political condition of the Indians in the Transvaal and the Orange Free State. I had no idea that this study was to be of invaluable service to me in the future. For I had thought of returning home by the end of the year, or even earlier, if the case was finished before the year was out.

But God disposed otherwise.

Chapter 13: What it is to be a 'coolie'

It would be out of place here to describe fully the condition of Indians in the Transvaal and the Orange Free State. I would suggest that those who wish to have a full idea of it may turn to my History of Satyagraha in South Africa. It is, however, necessary to give here a brief outline.

In the Orange Free State the Indians were deprived of all their rights by a special law enacted in 1888 or even earlier. If they chose to stay there, they could do so only to serve as waiters in hotels or to pursue some other such menial calling. The traders were driven away with a nominal compensation.

They made representations and petitions, but in vain.

A very stringent enactment was passed in the Transvaal in 1885. It was slightly amended in 1886, and it was provided under the amended law that all Indians should pay a poll tax of £3 as fee for entry into the Transvaal. They might not own land except in locations set apart for them, and in practice even that was not to be ownership. They had no franchise. All this was under the special law for Asiatics, to whom the laws for the coloured people were also applied. Under these latter, Indians might not walk on public footpaths, and might not move out of doors after 9 p.m. without a permit. The enforcement of this last regulation was elastic so far as the Indians were concerned. Those who passed as 'Arabs' were, as a matter of favour, exempted from it. The exemption thus naturally depended on the sweet will of the police.

I had to experience the effect of both these regulations. I often went out at night for a walk with Mr. Coates, and we rarely got back home much before ten o'clock. What if the police arrested me? Mr. Coates was more concerned about this than I. He had to issue passes to his Negro servants. But how could he give one to me? Only a master might issue a permit to a servant. If I had wanted one, and even if Mr. Coates had been ready to give it, he could not have done so, for it would have been fraud.

So Mr. Coates or some friend of his took me to the State Attorney, Dr. Krause. We turned out to be barristers of the same Inn. The fact that I needed a pass to enable me to be out of doors after 9 p.m. was too much for him. He expressed sympathy for me. Instead of ordering for me a pass, he gave me a letter authorizing me to be out of doors at all hours without police interference. I always kept this letter on me whenever I went out. The fact that I never had to make use of it was a mere accident.

Dr. Krause invited me to his place, and we may be said to have become friends. I occasionally called on him, and it was through him that I was introduced to his more famous brother, who was public Prosecutor in Johannesburg. During the Boer War he was court-martialled for conspiring to murder an English officer, and was sentenced to imprisonment for seven years. He was also disbarred by the Benchers. On the termination of hostilities he was released and being honourably readmitted to the Transvaal bar, resumed practice.

These connections were useful to me later on in my public life, and simplified much of my work.

The consequences of the regulation regarding the use of footpaths were rather serious for me. I always went out for a walk through President Street to an open plain. President Kruger's house was in this street — a very modest, unostentatious building, without a garden, and not distinguishable from other houses in its neighbourhood. The houses of many of the millionaires in Pretoria were far more pretentious, and were surrounded by gardens. Indeed President Kruger's simplicity was proverbial. Only the presence of a police patrol before the house indicated that it belonged to some official. I nearly always went along the footpath past this patrol without the slightest hitch or hindrance.

Now the man on duty used to be changed from time to time. Once one of these men, without giving me the slightest warning, without even asking me to leave the footpath, pushed and kicked me into the street. I was dismayed. Before I could question him as to his behaviour, Mr. Coates, who happened to be passing the spot on horseback, hailed me and said:

'Gandhi, I have seen everything. I shall gladly be your witness in court if you proceed against the man. I am very sorry you have been so rudely assaulted.'

'You need not be sorry', I said. 'What does the poor man know? All coloured people are the same to him. He no doubt treats Negroes just as he has treated me. I have made it a rule not go to court in respect of any personal grievance.

So I do not intend to proceed against him.'

'That is just like you,' said Mr. Coates, but do think it over again. We must teach such men a lesson.' He then spoke to the policeman and reprimanded him. I could not follow their talk, as it was in Dutch, the policeman being a Boer. But he apologized to me, for which there was no need. I had already forgiven him.

But I never again went through this street. There would be other men coming in this man's place and, ignorant of the incident, they would behave likewise. Why should I unnecessarily court another kick? I therefore selected a different walk.

The incident deepened my feeling for the Indian settlers. I discussed with them the advisability of making a test case, if it were found necessary to do so, after having seen the British Agent in the matter of these regulations.

I thus made an intimate study of the hard condition of the Indian settlers, not only by reading and hearing about it, but by personal experience. I saw that South Africa was no country for a self-respecting Indian, and my mind became more and more occupied with the question as to how this state of thing might be improved.

But my principal duty for the moment was to attend to the case of Dada Abdulla.

Chapter 14: Preparation for the case

The year's stay in Pretoria was a most valuable experience in my life. Here it was that I had opportunities of learning public work and acquired some measure of my capacity for it. Here it was that the religious spirit within me became a living force, and here too I acquired a true knowledge of legal practice. Here I learnt the things that a junior barrister learns in a senior barrister's chamber, and here I also gained confidence that I should not after all fail as a lawyer. It was likewise here that I learnt the secret of success as a lawyer.

Dada Abdulla's was no small case. The suit was for £40,000. Arising out of business transactions, it was full of intricacies of accounts. Part of the claim was based on promissory notes, and part on the specific performance of promise to deliver promissory notes. The defence was that the promissory notes were fraudulently taken and lacked sufficient consideration. There were numerous points of fact and law in this intricate case.

Both parties had engaged the best attorneys and counsel. I thus had a fine opportunity of studying their work. The preparation of the plaintiff's case for the attorney and the sorting of facts in support of his case had been entrusted to me. It was an education to see how much the attorney accepted, and how much he rejected from my preparation, as also to see how much use the counsel made of the brief prepared by the attorney. I saw that this preparation for the case would give me a fair measure of my powers of comprehension and my capacity for marshalling evidence.

I took the keenest interest in the case. Indeed I threw myself into it. I read all the papers pertaining to the transactions. My client was a man of great ability and reposed absolute confidence in me, and this rendered my work easy. I made a fair study of book-keeping. My capacity for translation was improved by having to translate the correspondence, which was for the most part in Gujarati.

Although, as I have said before, I took a keen interest in religious communion and in public work and always gave some of my time to them, they were not then my primary interest. The preparation of the case was my primary interest. Reading of law and looking up law cases, when necessary, had always a prior claim on my time. As a result, I acquired such a grasp of the facts of the case as perhaps was not possessed even by the parties themselves, inasmuch as I had with me the papers of both the parties.

I recalled the late Mr. Pincutt's advice — facts are three-fourths of the law. At a later date it was amply borne out by that famous barrister of South Africa, the late Mr. Leonard. In a certain case in my charge I saw that, though justice was on the side of my client, the law seemed to be against him. In despair I approached Mr. Leonard for help. He also felt that the facts of the case were very strong. He exclaimed, 'Gandhi, I have learnt one thing, and it is this, that if we take care of the facts of a case, the law will take care of itself. Let us dive deeper into the facts of this case.' With these words he asked me to study the case further and then see him again. On a re-examination of the facts I saw them in an entirely new light, and I also hit upon an old South African case bearing on the point. I was delighted and went to Mr. Leonard and told him everything, 'Right,' he said, 'we shall win the case. Only we must bear in mind which of the judges takes it.'

When I was making preparation for Dada Abdulla's case, I had not fully realized this paramount importance of facts. Facts mean truth, and once we adhere to truth, the law comes to our aid naturally. I saw that the facts of Dada Abdulla's case made it very strong indeed, and that the law was bound to be on his side.

But I also saw that the litigation, if it were persisted in, would ruin the plaintiff and the defendant, who were relatives and both belonged to the same city. No one knew how long the case might go on. Should it be allowed to continue to be fought out in court, it might go on indefinitely and to no advantage of either party. Both, therefore, desired an immediate termination of the case, if possible.

I approached Tyeb Sheth and requested and advised him to go to arbitration. I recommended him to see his counsel. I suggested to him that, if an arbitrator commanding the confidence of both parties could appointed, the case would be quickly finished. The lawyers' fees were so rapidly mounting up that they were enough to devour all the resources of the clients, big merchants as they were. The case occupied so much of their attention that they had no time left for any other work. In the meantime mutual ill-will was steadily increasing. I became disgusted with the profession. As lawyers the counsel on both sides were bound to rake up points of law in support of their own clients. I also saw for the first time that the winning party never recovers all the costs incurred. Under the Court Fees Regulation there was a fixed scale of costs to be allowed as between party and party, the actual costs as between attorney and client being very much higher. This was more than I could bear. I felt that my duty was to befriend both parties and bring them together. I strained every nerve to bring about a compromise. At last Tyeb Sheth agreed. An arbitrator was appointed, the case was argued before him, and Dada Abdulla won.

But that did not satisfy me. If my client were to seek immediate execution of the award, it would be impossible for Tyeb Sheth to meet the whole of the awarded amount, and there was an unwritten law among the Porbandar Memans living in South Africa that death should be preferred to bankruptcy. It was impossible for Tyeb Sheth to pay down the whole sum of about £37,000 and costs. He meant to pay not a pie less than the amount, and he did not want to be declared bankrupt. There was only one way. Dada Abdulla should allow him to pay in moderate installments. He was equal to the occasion, and granted Tyeb Sheth installments spread over a very long period. It was more difficult for me to secure this concession of payment by installments than to get the parties to agree to arbitration. But both were happy over the result, and both rose in the public estimation. My joy was boundless. I had learnt the true practice of law. I had learnt to find out the better side of human nature and to enter men's hearts. I realized that the true function of a lawyer was to unite parties riven asunder. The lesson was so indelibly burnt into me that a large part of my time during the twenty years of my practice as a lawyer was occupied in bringing about private compromises of hundreds of cases. I lost nothing thereby — not even money, certainly not my soul.

Chapter 15: Religious ferment

It is now time to turn again to my experiences with Christian friends.

Mr. Baker was getting anxious about my future. He took me to the Wellington Convention. The Protestant Christians organize such gatherings every few years for religious enlightenment or, in other words, self-purification. One may call this religious restoration or revival. The Wellington Convention was of this type. The chairman was the famous divine of the place, the Rev. Andrew Murray. Mr. Baker had hoped that the atmosphere of religious exaltation at the Convention, and the enthusiasm and earnestness of the people attending it, would inevitably lead me to embrace Christianity.

But his final hope was the efficacy of prayer. He had an abiding faith in prayer. It was his firm conviction that God could not but listen to prayer fervently offered. He would cite the instances of men like George Muller of Bristol, who depended entirely on prayer even for his temporal needs. I listened to his discourse on the efficacy of prayer with unbiased attention, and assured him that nothing could prevent me from embracing Christianity, should I feel the call. I had no hesitation in giving him this assurance, as I had long since taught myself to follow the inner voice. I delighted in submitting to it. To act against it would be difficult and painful to me.

So we went to Wellington. Mr. Baker was hard put to it in having a 'coloured man' like me for his companion. He had to suffer inconveniences on many occasions entirely on account of me. We had to break the journey on the way, as one of the days happened to be a Sunday, and Mr. Baker and his party would not travel on the Sabbath. Though the manager of the station hotel agreed to take me in after much altercation, he absolutely refused to admit me to the dining-room. Mr. Baker was not the man to give in easily. He stood by the rights of the guests of a hotel. But I could see his difficulty. At Wellington also I stayed with Mr. Baker. In spite of his best efforts to conceal the little inconveniences that he was put to, I could see them all.

This Convention was an assemblage of devout Christians. I was delighted at their faith. I met the Rev. Murray. I saw that many were praying for me. I liked some of their hymns, they were very sweet.

The Convention lasted for three days. I could understand and appreciate the devoutness of those who attended it. But I saw no reason for changing my belief — my religion. It was impossible for me to believe that I could go to heaven or attain salvation only by becoming a Christian. When I frankly said so to some good Christian friends, they were shocked. But there was no help for it.

My difficulties lay deeper. It was more than I could believe that Jesus was the only incarnate son of God, and that only he who believed in Him, would have everlasting life. If God could have sons, all of us were His sons. If Jesus was like God, or God Himself, then all men were like God and could be God Himself. My reason was not ready to believe literally that Jesus by his death and by his blood redeemed the sins of the world. Metaphorically there might be some truth in it. Again, according to Christianity only human beings had souls, and not other living beings, for whom death meant complete extinction; while I held a contrary belief. I could accept Jesus as a martyr, an embodiment of sacrifice, and a divine teacher, but not as the most perfect man ever born. His death on the Cross was a great example to the world, but that there was anything like a mysterious or miraculous virtue in it my heart could not accept. The pious lives of Christians did not give me anything that the lives of men of other faiths had failed to give. I had seen in other lives just the same reformation that I had heard of among Christians. Philosophically there was nothing extraordinary in Christian principles. From the point of view of sacrifice, it seemed to me that the Hindus greatly surpassed the Christians. It was impossible for me to regard Christianity as a perfect religion or the greatest of all religions.

I shared this mental churning with my Christian friends whenever there was an opportunity, but their answers could not satisfy me.

Thus if I could not accept Christianity either as a perfect, or the greatest religion, neither was I then convinced of Hinduism being such. Hindu defects were pressingly visible to me. If untouchability could be a part of Hinduism, it could but be a rotten part or an excrescence. I could not understand the raison d'être of a multitude of sects and castes. What was the meaning of saying that the Vedas were the inspired Word of God? If they were inspired, why not also the Bible and the Koran?

As Christian friends were endeavouring to convert me, even so were Musalman friends.

Abdulla Sheth had kept on inducing me to study Islam, and of course he had always something to say regarding its beauty.

I expressed my difficulties in a letter to Raychandbhai. I also corresponded with other religious authorities in India and received answers from them. Raychandbhai's letter somewhat pacified me. He asked me to be patient and to study Hinduism more deeply. One of his sentences was to this effect: 'On a dispassionate view of the question I am convinced that no other religion has the subtle and profound thought of Hinduism, its vision of the soul, or its charity.'

I purchased Sale's translation of the Koran and began reading it. I also obtained other books on Islam. I communicated with Christian friends in England. One of them introduced me to Edward Maitland, with whom I opened correspondence. He sent me The Perfect Way, a book he had written in collaboration with Anna Kingsford. The book was a repudiation of the current Christian belief. He also sent me another book, The New Interpretation of the Bible. I liked both. They seemed to support Hinduism. Tolstoy's The Kingdom of God is Within You overwhelmed me. It left an abiding impression on me. Before the independent thinking, profound morality, and the truthfulness of this book, all the books given me by Mr. Coates seemed to pale into insignificance.

My studies thus carried me in a direction unthought of by the Christian friends. My correspondence with Edward Maitland was fairly prolonged, and that with Raychandbhai continued until his death. I read some of the books he sent me. These included Panchikaran, Maniratnamala, Mumukshu Prakaran of Yogavasishtha, Haribhadra Suri's Shaddarshana Samuchchaya and others.

Though I took a path my Christian friends had not intended for me, I have remained for ever indebted to them for the religious quest that they awakened in me. I shall always cherish the memory of their contact. The years that followed had more, not less, of such sweet and sacred contacts in store for me.

Chapter 16: Man proposes, God disposes

The case having been concluded, I had no reason for staying in Pretoria. So I went back to Durban and began to make preparations for my return home. But Abdulla Sheth was not the man to let me sail without a send-off. He gave a farewell party in my honour at Sydenham.

It was proposed to spend the whole day there. Whilst I was turning over the sheets of some of the newspapers I found there, I chanced to see a paragraph in a corner of one of them under the caption 'Indian Franchise'. It was with reference to the bill then before the House of Legislature, which sought to deprive the

Indians of their right to elect members of the Natal Legislative Assembly. I was ignorant of the bill, and so were the rest of the guests who had assembled there.

I inquired of Abdulla Sheth about it. He said: 'What can we understand in these matters? We can only understand things that affect our trade. As you know all our trade in the Orange Free State has been swept away. We agitated about it, but in vain. We are after all lame men, being unlettered. We generally take in newspapers simply to ascertain the daily market rates, etc. What can we know of legislation? Our eyes and ears are the European attorneys here.'

'But', said I, 'there are so many young Indians born and educated here, Do they not help you?'

'They!' exclaimed Abdulla Sheth in despair. 'They never care to come to us, and to tell you the truth, we care less to recognize them. Being Christians, they are under the thumb of the white clergymen, who in their turn are subject to the Government.'

This opened my eyes. I felt that this class should be claimed as our own. Was this the meaning of Christianity? Did they cease to be Indians because they had become Christians?

But I was on the point of returning home and hesitated to express what was passing through my mind in this matter. I simply said to Abdulla Sheth: 'This bill, if it passes into law, will make our lot extremely difficult. It is the first nail into our coffin. It strikes at the root of our self-respect.'

'It may', echoed Sheth Abdulla. 'I will tell you the genesis of the franchise question. We knew nothing about it. But Mr. Escombe, one of our best attorneys, whom you know, put the idea into our heads. It happened thus. He is a great fighter, and there being no love lost between him and the Wharf Engineer, he feared that the Engineer might deprive him of his votes and defeat him at the election. So he acquainted us with our position, and at his instance we all registered ourselves as voters, and voted for him. You will now see how the franchise has not for us the value that you attach to it. But we understand what you say. Well, then, what is your advice?'

The other guests were listening to this conversation with attention. One of them said: 'Shall I tell you what should be done? You cancel your passage by this boat, stay here a month longer, and we will fight as you direct us.'

All the others chimed in: 'Indeed, indeed. Abdulla Sheth, you must detain Gandhibhai.'

The Sheth was a shrewd man. He said: 'I may not detain him now. Or rather, you have as much right as I to do so. But you are quite right. Let us all persuade him to stay on. But you should remember that he is a barrister. What about his fees?'

The mention of fees pained me, and I broke in: 'Abdulla Sheth, fees are out of the question. There can be no fees for public work. I can stay, if at all, as a servant. And as you know, I am not acquainted with all these friends. But if you believe that they will co-operate, I am prepared to stay a month longer. There is one thing, however. Though you need not pay me anything, work of the nature we contemplate cannot be done without some funds to start with. Thus we may have to send telegrams, we may have to print some literature, some touring may have to be done, the local attorneys may have to be consulted, and as I am ignorant of your laws, I may need some law-books for reference. All this cannot be done without money. And it is clear that one man is not enough for this work. Many must come forward to help him.'

And a chorus of voices was heard: 'Allah is great and merciful. Money will come in. Men there are, as many as you may need. You please consent to stay, and all will be well.'

The farewell party was thus turned into a working committee. I suggested finishing dinner etc. quickly and getting back home. I worked out in my own mind an outline of the campaign. I ascertained the names of those who were on the list of voters, and made up my mind to stay on for a month.

Thus God laid the foundations of my life in South Africa and sowed the seed of the fight for national self-respect.

Chapter 17: Settled in Natal

Sheth Haji Muhammad Haji Dada was regarded as the foremost leader of the Indian community in Natal in 1893. Financially Sheth Abdulla Haji Adam was the chief among them, but he and others always gave the first place to Sheth Haji Muhammad in public affairs. A meeting was, therefore, held under his presidentship at the house of Abdulla Sheth, at which it was resolved to offer opposition to the Franchise Bill.

Volunteers were enrolled. Natal-born Indians, that is, mostly Christian Indian youths, had been invited to attend this meeting. Mr. Paul, the Durban court interpreter, and Mr. Subhan Godfrey, headmaster of a mission school, were present, and it was they who were responsible for bringing together at the meeting a good number of Christian youths. All these enrolled themselves as volunteers.

Many of the local merchants were of course enrolled, noteworthy among them Sheths Dawud Muhammad, Muhammad Kasam Kamruddin, Adamji Miyakhan, A. Kolandavellu Pillai, C. Lachhiram, Rangasami Padiachi, and Amod Jiva. Parsi Rustomji was of course there. From among the clerks were Messrs Manekji, Joshi, Narsinhram and others, employees of Dada Abdulla and Co. and other big firms. They were all agreeably surprised to find themselves taking a share in public work. To be invited thus to take part was a new experience in their lives. In face of the calamity that had overtaken the community, all distinctions such as high and low, small and great, master and servant, Hindus, Musalmans, Parsis, Christians, Gujaratis, Madrasis, Sindhis, etc., were forgotten. All were alike the children and servants of the motherland.

The bill had already passed, or was about to pass, its second reading. In the speeches on the occasion the fact that Indians had expressed no opposition the stringent bill was urged as proof of their unfitness for the franchise.

I explained the situation to the meeting. The first thing we did was to despatch a telegram to the Speaker of the Assembly requesting him to postpone further discussion of the bill. A similar telegram was sent to the premier, Sir John Robinson, and another to Mr. Escombe, as a friend of Dada Abdulla's. The Speaker promptly replied that discussion of the bill would be postponed for two days. This gladdened our hearts.

The petition to be presented to the Legislative Assembly was drawn up. Three copies had to be prepared and one extra was needed for the press. It was also proposed to obtain as many signatures to it as possible, and all this work had to be done in the course of a night. The volunteers with a knowledge of English and several others sat up the whole night. Mr. Arthur, an old man, who was known for his calligraphy, wrote the principal copy. The rest were written by others to someone's dictation. Five copies were thus got ready simultaneously. Merchant volunteers went out in their own carriages, or carriages whose hire they had paid, to obtain signatures to the petition. This was accomplished in quick time and the petition was despatched. The newspapers published it with favourable comments. It likewise created an impression on the Assembly. It was discussed in the House. Partisans of the Bill offered a defence — an admittedly lame one — in reply to the arguments advanced in the petition. The ill, however, was passed.

We all knew that this was a foregone conclusion, but the agitation had infused new life into the community and had brought home to them the conviction that the community was one and indivisible, and that it was as much their duty to fight for its political rights as for its trading rights.

Lord Ripon was at this time Secretary of State for the Colonies. It was decided to submit to him a monster petition. This was no small task and could not be done in a day. Volunteers were enlisted, and all did their due share of the work.

I took considerable pains over drawing up this petition. I read all the literature available on the subject. My argument centred round a principle and on expedience. I argued that we had a right to the franchise in Natal, as we had a kind of franchise in India. I urged that it was expedient to retain it, as the Indian population capable of using the franchise was very small.

Ten thousand signatures were obtained in the course of a fortnight. To secure this number of signatures from the whole of the province was no light task, especially when we consider that the men were perfect strangers to the work. Specially competent volunteers had to be selected for the work, as it had been decided not to take a single signature without the signatory fully understanding the petition. The villages were scattered at long distances. The work could be done promptly only if a number of workers put their whole heart into it. And this they did. All carried out their allotted task with enthusiasm. But as I am writing these lines, figures of Sheth Dawud Muhammad, Rustomji, Adamji Miyakhan, and Amod Jiva rise clearly before my mind. They brought in the largest number of signatures. Dawud Sheth kept going about in his carriage the whole day. And it was all a labour of love, not one of them asking for even his out-of-pocket expenses. Dada Abdulla's house became at once a caravanserai and a public office. A number of educated fiends who helped me and many others had their food there. Thus every helper was put to considerable expense.

The petition was at last submitted. A thousand copies had been printed for circulation and distribution. It acquainted the Indian public for the first time with conditions in Natal. I sent copies to all the newspapers and publicists I knew.

The Times of India, in a leading article on the petition, strongly supported the Indian demands. Copies were sent to journals and publicists in England representing different parties. The London Times supported our claims, and we began to entertain hopes of the bill being vetoed.

It was now impossible for me to leave Natal. The Indian friends surrounded me on all sides and importuned me to remain there permanently. I expressed my difficulties. I had made up my mind not to stay at public expense. I felt it necessary to set up an independent household. I thought that the house should be good and situated in a good locality. I also had the idea that I could not add to the credit of the community, unless I lived in a style usual for barristers. And it seemed to me to be impossible to run such a household with anything less than £300 a year. I therefore decided that I could stay only if the members of the community guaranteed legal work to the extent of that minimum, and I communicated my decision to them.

'But,' said they, 'we should like you to draw that amount for public work, and we can easily collect it. Of course, this is apart from the fees you must charge for private legal work.'

'No, I could not thus charge you for public work,' said I. 'The work would not involve the exercise on my part of much skill as barrister. My work would be mainly to make you all work. And how could I charge you for that? And then I should have to appeal to you frequently for funds for the work, and if I were to draw my maintenance from you, I should find myself at a disadvantage in making an appeal for large amounts, and we should ultimately find ourselves at a standstill. Besides I want the community to find more than £300 annually for public work.'

'But we have now known you for some time, and are sure you would not draw anything you do not need. And if we wanted you to stay here, should we not find your expenses?'

'It is your love and present enthusiasm that make you talk like this. How can we be sure that this love and enthusiasm will endure for ever? And as your friend and servant, I should occasionally have to say hard things to you. Heaven only knows whether I should then retain your affection. But the fact is that I must not accept any salary for public work. It is enough for me that you should all agree to entrust me with your legal work. Even that may be hard for you. For one thing I am not a white barrister. How can I be sure that the court will respond to me? Nor can I be sure how I shall fare as a lawyer. So even in giving me retainers you may be running some risk. I should regard even the fact of your giving them to me as the reward of my public work.'

The upshot of this discussion was that about twenty merchants gave me retainers for one year for their legal work. Besides this, Dada Abdulla purchased me the necessary furniture in lieu of a purse he had intended to give me on my departure.

Thus I settled in Natal.

Chapter 18: Colour Bar

The symbol of a Court of justice is pair of scales held evenly by an impartial and blind but sagacious woman. Fate has purposely made her blind, in order that she may not judge a person from his exterior but from his intrinsic worth. But the Law Society of Natal set out to persuade the Supreme Court to act in contravention of this principle and to belie its symbol.

I applied for admission as an advocate of the Supreme Court. I held a certificate of admission from the Bombay High Court. The English certificate I had to deposit with the Bombay High Court when I was enrolled there. It was necessary to attach two certificates of character to the application for admission, and thinking that these would carry more weight if given by Europeans, I secured them from two well-known European merchants whom I knew through Sheth Abdulla. The application had to be presented through a member of the bar, and as a rule the Attorney General presented such applications without fees. Mr. Escombe, who, as we have seen, was legal adviser to Messrs. Dada Abdulla & Co, was the Attorney General. I called on him, and he willingly consented to present my application.

The Law Society now sprang a surprise on me by serving me with a notice opposing my application for admission. One of their objections was that the original English certificate was not attached to my application. But the main objection was that, when the regulations regarding admission of advocates were made, the possibility of a coloured man applying could not have been contemplated. Natal owed its growth to European enterprise, and therefore it was necessary that the European element should predominate in the bar. If coloured people were admitted, they might gradually outnumber the Europeans, and the bulwark of their protection would break down.

The Law Society had engaged a distinguished lawyer to support their opposition. As he too was connected with Dada Abdulla & Co., he sent me word through Sheth Abdulla to go and see him. He talked with me quite frankly, and inquired about my antecedents, which I gave. Then he said:

'I have nothing to say against you. I was only afraid lest you should be some colonial-born adventurer. And the fact that your application was unaccompanied by the original certificate supported my suspicion. There have been men who have made use of diplomas which did not belong to them. The certificates of character from European traders you have submitted have no value for me. What do they know about you? What can be the extent of their acquaintance with you?'

'But,' said I, 'everyone here is a stranger to me. Even Sheth Abdulla first came to know me here.'

'But then you say he belongs to the same place as you? It your father was Prime Minister there, Sheth Abdulla is bound to know your family. if you were to produce his affidavit, I should have absolutely no objection. I would then gladly communicate to the Law Society my inability to oppose your application.'

This talk enraged me, but I restrained my feelings. 'If I had attached Dada Abdulla's certificate,' said I to myself, 'it would have been rejected, and they would have asked for Europeans' certificates. And what has my admission as advocate to do with my birth and my antecedents? How could my birth, whether humble or objectionable, be used against me?' But I contained myself and quietly replied:

'Though I do not admit that the Law Society has any authority to require all these details, I am quite prepared to present the affidavit you desire.'

Sheth Abdulla's affidavit was prepared and duly submitted to the counsel for the Law Society. He said he was satisfied. But not so the Law Society. it opposed my application before the Supreme Court, which ruled out the opposition without even calling upon Mr. Escombe to reply. The Chief justice said in effect:

'The objection that the applicant has not attached the original certificate has no substance. If he has made a false affifavit, he can be prosecuted, and his name can then be struck off the roll, if he is proved guilty. The law makes no distinction between white and coloured people. The court has therefore no authority to prevent Mr. Gandhi from being enrolled as an advocate. We admit his application. Mr. Gandhi, you can now take the oath.'

I stood up and took the oath before the Registar. As soon as I was sworn in, the Chief Justice, addressing me, said:

'You must now take off your turban, Mr. Gandhi. you must submit to the rules of the court with regard to the dress to be worn by practising barristers.'

I saw my limitations. The turban that I had insisted on wearing in the District Magistrate's Court I took off in obedience to the order of the Supreme Court. Not that, if I had resisted the order, the resistance could not have been justified. But I wanted to reserve my strength for fighting bigger battles. I should not exhaust my skill as a fighter in insisting on retaining my turban. It was worthy of a better cause.

Sheth Abdulla and other friends did not like my submission (or was it weakness?). They felt that I should have stood by my right to wear the turban while practising in the Court. I tried to reason with them. I tried to press home to them the truth of the maxim, 'When at Rome do as the Romans do.' 'It would be right', I said, 'to refuse to obey, if in India an English officer or judge ordered you to take off your turban; but as an officer of the court, it would have ill become me to disregard a custom of the court in the province of Natal.'

I pacified the friends somewhat with these and similar arguments, but I do not think I convinced them completely, in this instance, of the applicability of the principle of looking at a thing from a different standpoint in different circumstances. But all my life through, the very insistence on truth has taught me to appreciate the beauty of compromise. I saw in later life that this spirit was an essential part of Satyagraha. It has often meant endangering my life and incurring the displeasure of friends. But truth is hard as adamant and tender as a blossom.

The opposition of the Law Society gave me another advertisement in South Africa. Most of the newspapers condemned the opposition and accused the Law Society of jealousy. The advertisement, to some extent, simplified my work.

Chapter 19: Natal Indian Congress

Practice as a lawyer was and remained for me a subordinate occupation. It was necessary that I should concentrate on public work to justify my stay in Natal. The despatch of the petition regarding the disfranchising bill was not sufficient in itself. Sustained agitation was essential for making an impression on the Secretary of State for the Colonies. For this purpose it was thought necessary to bring into being a permanent organization. So I consulted Sheth Abdulla and other friends, and we all decided to have a public organization of a permanent character.

To find out a name to be given to the new organization perplexed me sorely. It was not to identify itself with any particular party. The name 'Congress', I knew, was in bad odour with the Conservatives in England, and yet the Congress was the very life of India. I wanted to popularize it in Natal. It savoured of cowardice to hesitate to adopt the name. Therefore, with full explanation of my reasons, I recommended that the organization should be called the Natal Indian Congress, and on the 22nd May the Natal Indian Congress came into being.

Dada Abdulla's spacious room was packed to the full on that day. The Congress received the enthusiastic approval of all present. Its constitution was simple, the subscription was heavy. Only he who paid five shillings monthly could be a member. The well-to-do classes were persuaded to subscribe as much as they could. Abdulla Sheth headed the list with £2 per month. Two other friends also put down the same. I thought I should not stint my subscription, and put down a pound per month. This was for me no small amount. But I thought that I would not be beyond my means, if I was to pay my way at all. And God helped me. We thus got a considerable number of members who subscribed £1 per month. The number of those who put down 10s. was even larger. Besides this, there were donations which were gratefully accepted.

Experience showed that no one paid his subscription for the mere asking. It was impossible to call frequently on members outside Durban. The enthusiasm of one moment seemed to wear away the next. Even the members in Durban had to be considerably dunned before they would pay in their subscriptions.

The task of collecting subscriptions lay with me, I being the secretary. And we came to a stage when I had to keep my clerk engaged all day long in the work of collection. The man got tired of the job, and I felt that, if the situation was to be improved, the subscriptions should be made payable annually and not monthly and that too strictly in advance. So I called a meeting of the Congress. Everyone welcomed the proposal for making the subscription annual instead of monthly and for fixing the minimum at £3. Thus the work of collection was considerably facilitated.

I had learnt at the outset not to carry on public work with borrowed money. One could rely on people's promises in most matters except in respect of money. I had never found people quick to pay the amounts they had undertaken to subscribe, and the Natal Indians were no exception to the rule. As, therefore, no work was done unless there were funds on hand, the Natal Indian Congress has never been in debt.

My co-workers evinced extraordinary enthusiasm in canvassing members. It was work which interested them and was at the same time an invaluable experience. Large numbers of people gladly came forward with cash subscriptions. Work in the distant villages of the interior was rather difficult. People did not know the nature of public work. And yet we had invitations to visit faraway places, leading merchants of every place extending their hospitality.

On one occasion during this tour the situation was rather difficult. We expected our host to contribute £6, but he refused to give anything more than £3. If we had accepted that amount from him, others would have followed suit, and our collections would have been spoiled. It was a late hour of the night, and we were all hungry. But how could we dine without having first obtained the amount we were bent on getting? All persuasion was useless. The host seemed to be adamant. Other merchants in the town reasoned with him, and we all sat up throughout the night, he as well as we determined not to budge one inch. Most of my co-workers were burning with rage, but they contained themselves. At last, when day was already breaking, the host yielded, paid down £6 and feasted us. This happened at Tongaat, but the repercussion of the incident was felt as far as Stanger on the North Coast and Charlestown in the interior. It also hastened our work of collection.

But collecting funds was not the only thing to do. In fact I had long learnt the principle of never having more money at one's disposal than necessary.

Meetings used to be held once a month or even once a week if required. Minutes of the proceedings of the preceding meeting would be read, and all sorts of questions would be discussed. People had no experience of taking part in public discussion or of speaking briefly and to the point. Everyone hesitated to stand up to speak. I explained to them the rules of procedure at meetings and they respected them. They realized that it was an education for them, and many who had never been accustomed to speaking before an audience soon acquired the habit of thinking and speaking publicly about matters of public interest.

Knowing that in public work minor expenses at times absorbed large accounts, I had decided not to have even the receipt books printed in the beginning. I had a cyclostyle machine in my office, on which I took copies of receipts and reports. Such things I began to get printed only when the Congress coffers were full, and when the number of members and work had increased. Such economy is essential for every organization, and yet I know that it is not always exercised. That is why I have thought it proper to enter into these little details of the beginnings of a small but growing organization.

People never cared to have receipts for the amounts they paid, but we always insisted on the receipts being given. Every pie was thus clearly accounted for, and I dare say the account books for the year 1894 can be found intact even today in the records of Natal Indian Congress. Carefully kept accounts are a sine qua non for any organization. Without them it falls into disrepute. Without properly kept accounts it is impossible to maintain truth in its pristine purity.

Another feature of the Congress was service of colonial-born educated Indians. The Colonial-born Indian Educational Association was founded under the auspices of the Congress. The members consisted mostly of these educated youths. They had to pay a nominal subscription. The Association served to ventilate their needs and grievances, to stimulate thought amongst them, to bring them into touch with Indian merchants and also to afford them scope for service of the community. It was a sort of debating society. The members met regularly and spoke or read papers on different subjects. A small library was also opened in connection with the Association.

The third feature of the Congress was propaganda. This consisted in acquainting the English in South Africa and England and people in India with the real state of things in Natal. With that end in view I wrote two pamphlets.

The first was An Appeal to Every Briton in South Africa. It contained a statement, supported by evidence, of the general condition of Natal Indians. The other was entitled The Indian Franchise — An Appeal. It contained a brief history of the Indian franchise in

Natal with facts and figures. I had devoted considerable labour and study to the preparation of these pamphlets, and the result was quite commensurate with the trouble taken. They were widely circulated.

All this activity resulted in winning the Indians numerous friends in South Africa and in obtaining the active sympathy of all parties in India. It also opened out and placed before the South African Indians a definite line of action.

Chapter 20: Balasundaram

The heart's earnest and pure desire is always fulfilled. In my own experience I have often seen this rule verified. Service of the poor has been my heart's desire, and it has always thrown me amongst the poor and enabled me to identify myself with them.

Although the members of the Natal Indian Congress included the colonial-born Indians and the clerical class, the unskilled wage-earners, the indentured labourers were still outside its pale. The Congress was not yet theirs. They could not afford to belong to it by paying the subscription and becoming its members. The Congress could win their attachment only by serving them. An opportunity offered itself when neither the Congress nor I was really ready for it. I had put in scarcely three or four month's practice, and the Congress also was still in its infancy, when a Tamil man in tattered clothes, head-gear in hand, two front teeth broken and his mouth bleeding, stood before me trembling and weeping. He had been heavily belaboured by his master. I learnt all about him from my clerk, who was a Tamilian. Balasundaram — as that was the visitor's name — was serving his indenture under a well-known European resident of Durban. The master, getting angry with him, had lost self-control, and had beaten Balasundaram severely, breaking two of his teeth.

I sent him to a doctor. In those days only white doctors were available. I wanted a certificate from the doctor about the nature of the injury Balasundaram had sustained. I secured the certificate, and straightway took the injured man to the magistrate, to whom I submitted his affidavit. The magistrate was indignant when he read it and issued a summons against the employer.

It was far from my desire to get the employer punished. I simply wanted Balasundaram to be released from him. I read the law about indentured labour. If an ordinary servant left service without giving notice, he was liable to be sued by his master in a civil court. With the indentured labourer the case was entirely different. He was liable, in similar circumstances, to be proceeded against in a criminal court and to be imprisoned on conviction. That is why Sir William Hunter called the indenture system almost as bad as slavery. Like the slave the indentured labourer was the property of his master.

There were only two ways of releasing Balasundaram: either by getting the Protector of Indentured Labourers to cancel his indenture or transfer him to someone else, or by getting Balasundaram's employer to release him. I called on the latter and said to him: 'I do not want to proceed against you and get you punished. I think you realize that you have severely beaten the man. I shall be satisfied if you will transfer the indenture to someone else.' To this he readily agreed. I next saw the Protector. He also agreed, on condition that I found a new employer.

So I went off in search of an employer. He had to be a European, as no Indians could employ indentured labour. At that time I knew very few Europeans. I met one of them. He very kindly agreed to take on Balasundaram. I gratefully acknowledged his kindness. The magistrate convicted Balasundaram's employer, and recorded that he had undertaken to transfer the indenture to someone else.

Balasundaram's case reached the ears of every indentured labourer, and I came to be regarded as their friend. I hailed this connection with delight. A regular stream of indentured labourers began to pour into my office, and I got the best opportunity of learning their joys and sorrows.

The echoes of Balasundaram's case were heard in far off Madras. Labourers from different parts of the province, who went to Natal on indenture, came to know of this case through their indentured brethren.

There was nothing extraordinary in the case itself, but the fact that there was someone in Natal to espouse their cause and publicly work for them gave the indentured labourer a joyful surprise and inspired him with hope.

I have said that Balasundaram entered my office, head-gear in hand. There was a peculiar pathos about the circumstance which also showed our humiliation. I have already narrated the incident when I was asked to take off my turban. A practice had been forced upon every indentured labourer and every Indian stranger to take off his head-gear, when visiting a European, whether the head-gear were a cap, turban or a scarf wrapped round the head. A salute even with both hands was not sufficient. Balasundaram thought that he should follow the practice even with me. This was the first case in my experience. I felt humiliated and asked him to tie up his scarf. He did so, not without a certain hesitation, but I could perceive the pleasure on his face.

It has always been a mystery to me how men can feel themselves honoured by the humiliation of their fellow beings.

Chapter 21: The £3 tax

Balasundaram's case brought me into touch with the indentured Indians. What impelled me, however, to make a deep study of their condition was the campaign for bringing them under special heavy taxation.

In the same year, 1894, the Natal Government sought to impose an annual tax of £25 on the indentured Indians. The proposal astonished me. I put the matter before the Congress for discussion, and it was immediately resolved to organize the necessary opposition.

At the outset I must explain briefly the genesis of the tax.

About the year 1860 the Europeans in Natal, finding that there was considerable scope for sugarcane cultivation, felt themselves in need of labour. Without outside labour the cultivation of cane and the manufacture of sugar were impossible, as the Natal Zulus were not suited to this form of work. The Natal Government therefore corresponded with the Indian Government, and secured their permission to recruit Indian labour. These recruits were to sign an indenture to work in Natal for five years, and at the end of the term they were to be at liberty to settle there and to have full rights of ownership of land. Those were the inducements held out to them for the whites then had looked forward to improving their agriculture by the industry of the Indian labourers after the term of their indentures had expired.

But the Indians gave more than had been expected of them. They grew large quantities of vegetables. They introduced a number of Indian varieties and made it possible to grow the local varieties cheaper. They also introduced the mango. Nor did their enterprise stop at agriculture. They entered trade. They purchased land for building, and many raised themselves from the status of labourers to that of owners of land and houses. Merchants from India followed them and settled there for trade. The late Sheth Abubakar Amod was first among them. He soon built up an extensive business.

The white traders were alarmed. When they first welcomed the Indian labourers, they had not reckoned with their business skill. They might be tolerated as independent agriculturists, but their competition in trade could not be brooked.

This sowed the seed of the antagonism to Indians. Many other factors contributed to its growth. Our different ways of living, our simplicity, our contentment with small gains, our indifference to the laws of hygiene and sanitation, our slowness in keeping our surroundings clean and tidy, and our stinginess in keeping our houses in goodrepair — all these combined with the difference in religion, contributed to fan the flame of antagonism. Through legislation this antagonism found its expression in the disfranchising bill and the bill to impose a tax on the indentured Indians. Independent of legislation a number of pinpricks had already been started.

The first suggestion was that the Indian labourers should be forcibly repatriated, so that the term of their indentures might expire in India. The Government of India was not likely to accept the suggestion. Another proposal was therefore made to the effect that:

1. The indentured labourer should return to India on the expiry of his indenture; or that

2. he should sign a fresh indenture every two years, an increment being given at each renewal; and that
3. in the case of his refusal to return to India or renew the indenture he should pay an annual tax of £25.

A deputation composed of Sir Henry Binns and Mr. Mason was sent to India to get the proposal approved by the Government there. The Viceroy at that time was Lord Elgin. He disapproved of the £25 tax, but agreed to a poll tax of £3. I thought then, as I do even now, that this was a serious blunder on the part of the Viceroy. In giving his approval he had in no way thought of the interests of India. It was no part of his duty thus to accommodate the Natal Europeans. In the course of three or four years an indentured labourer with his wife and each male child over 16 and female child over 13 came under the impost. To levy a yearly tax of £12 from a family of four — husband, wife and two children — when the average income of the husband was never more than 14s. a month, was atrocious and unknown anywhere else in the world.

We organized a fierce campaign against this tax. If the Natal Indian Congress had remained silent on the subject, the Viceroy might have approved of even the £25 tax. The reduction from £25 to £3 was probably due solely to the Congress agitation. But I may be mistaken in thinking so. It may be possible that the Indian Government had disapproved of the £25 tax from the beginning and reduced it to £3, irrespective of the opposition from the Congress. In any case it was a breach of trust on the part of the Indian Government. As trustee of the welfare of India, the Viceroy ought never to have approved of this inhuman tax.

The Congress could not regard it as any great achievement to have succeeded in getting the tax reduced from £25 to £3. The regret was still there that it had not completely safeguarded the interests of the indentured Indians. It ever remained its determination to get the tax remitted, but it was twenty years before the determination was realized. And when it was realized, it came as a result of the labours of not only the Natal Indians but of all the Indians in South Africa. The breach of faith with the late Mr. Gokhale became the occasion of the final campaign, in which the indentured Indians took their full share, some of them losing their lives as a result of the firing that was resorted to, and over ten thousand suffering imprisonment.

But truth triumphed in the end. The sufferings of the Indians were the expression of that truth. Yet it would not have triumphed except for unflinching faith, great patience, and incessant effort. Had the community given up the struggle, had the Congress abandoned the campaign and submitted to the tax as inevitable, the hated impost would have continued to be levied from the indentured Indians until this day, to the eternal shame of the Indians in South Africa and of the whole of India.

Chapter 22: Comparative study of religions

If I found myself entirely absorbed in the service of the community, the reason behind it was my desire for self-realization. I had made the religion of service my own, as I felt that God could be realized only through service. And service for me was the service of India, because it came to me without my seeking, because I had an aptitude for it. I had gone to South Africa for travel, for finding an escape from Kathiawad intrigues and for gaining my own livelihood. But as I have said, I found myself in search of God and striving for self-realization.

Christian friends had whetted my appetite for knowledge, which had become almost insatiable, and they would not leave me in peace, even if I desired to be indifferent. In Durban Mr. Spencer Walton, the head of the South Africa General Mission, found me out. I became almost a member of his family. At the back of this acquaintance was of course my contact with Christians in Pretoria. Mr. Walton had a manner all his own. I do not recollect his ever having invited me to embrace Christianity. But he placed his life as an open book before me, and let me watch all his movements. Mrs. Walton was a very gentle and talented woman. I liked the attitude of this couple. We knew the fundamental differences between us. Any amount of discussion could not efface them. Yet even differences prove helpful, where there is tolerance, charity and truth. I liked Mr. and Mrs. Walton's humility, perseverance and devotion to work, and we met very frequently.

This friendship kept alive my interest in religion. It was impossible now to get the leisure that I used to have in Pretoria for my religious studies. But what little time I could spare I turned to good account. My religious correspondence continued. Raychandbhai was guiding me. Some friend sent me Narmadashanker's book Dharma Vichar. Its preface proved very helpful. I had heard about the Bohemian way in which the poet had lived, and a description in the preface of the revolution effected in his life by his religious studies captivated me. I came to like the book, and read it from cover to cover with attention. I read with interest Max Muller's book, India — WhatCan It Teach Us? and the translation of the Upanishads published by the Theosophical Society. All this enhanced my regard for Hinduism, and its beauties began to grow upon me. It did not, however, prejudice me against other religions. I read Washington Irving's Life of Mahomet and His Successors and Carlyle's panegyric on the Prophet. These books raised Muhammad in my estimation. I also read a book called The Sayings of Zarathustra.

Thus I gained more knowledge of the different religions. The study stimulated my self-introspection and fostered in me the habit of putting into practice whatever appealed to me in my studies. Thus I began some of the Yogic practices, as well as I could understand them from a reading of the Hindu books. But I could not get on very far, and decided to follow them with the help of some expert when I returned to India. The desire has never been fulfilled.

I made too an intensive study of Tolstoy's books. The Gospels in Brief, What to Do? and other books made a deep impression on me. I began to realize more and more the infinite possibilities of universal love.

About the same time I came in contact with another Christian family. At their suggestion I attended the Wesleyan church every Sunday. For these days I also had their standing invitation to dinner. The church did not make a favourable impression on me. The sermons seemed to be uninspiring. The congregation did not strike me as being particularly religious. They were not an assembly of devout souls; they appeared rather to be worldly-minded people, going to church for recreation and in conformity to custom. Here, at times, I would involuntarily doze. I was ashamed, but some of my neighbours, who were in no better case, lightened the shame. I could not go on long like this, and soon gave up attending the service.

My connection with the family I used to visit every Sunday was abruptly broken. In fact it may be said that I was warned to visit it no more. It happened thus. My hostess was a good and simple woman, but somewhat narrow-minded. We always discussed religious subjects. I was then re-reading Arnold's Light of Asia. Once we began to compare the life of Jesus with that of Buddha. 'Look at Gautama's compassion!' said I. 'It was not confined to mankind, it was extended to all living beings. Does not one's heart overflow with love to think of the lamb joyously perched on his shoulders? One fails to notice this love for all living beings in the life of Jesus.' The comparison pained the good lady. I could understand her feelings. I cut the matter short, and we went to the dining room. Her son, a cherub aged scarcely five, was also with us. I am happiest when in the midst of children, and this youngster and I had long been friends. I spoke derisively of the piece of meat on his plate and in high praise of the apple on mine. The innocent boy was carried away and joined in my praise of the fruit.

But the mother? she was dismayed.

I was warned. I checked myself and changed the subject. The following week I visited the family as usual, but not without trepidation. I did not see that I should stop going there, I did not think it proper either. But the good lady made my way easy.

'Mr. Gandhi,' she said, 'please don't take it ill if I feel obliged to tell you that my boy is none the better for your company. Every day he hesitates to eat meat and asks for fruit, reminding me of your argument. This is too much. If he gives up meat, he is bound to get weak, if not ill. How could I bear it? Your discussion should henceforth be only with us elders. They are sure to react badly on children.'

'Mrs — —,' I replied, 'I am sorry. I can understand your feelings as a parent, for I too have children. We can very easily end this unpleasant state of things. What I eat and omit to eat is bound to have a greater effect on the child than what I say. The best way, therefore, is for me to stop these visits. That certainly need not affect our friendship.'

'I thank you,' she said with evident relief.

Chapter 23: As a householder

To set up a household was no new experience for me. But the establishment in Natal was different from the ones that I had had in Bombay and London. This time part of the expense was solely for the sake of prestige. I thought it necessary to have a household in keeping with my position as an Indian barrister in Natal and as a representative. So I had a nice little house in a prominent locality. It was also suitably furnished. Food was simple, but as I used to invite English friends and Indian co-workers, the housekeeping bills were always fairly high.

A good servant is essential in every household. But I have never known how to keep anyone as a servant.

I had a friend as companion and help, and a cook who had become a member of the family. I also had office clerks boarding and lodging with me.

I think I had a fair amount of success in this experiment, but it was not without its modicum of the bitter experiences of life.

The companion was very clever and, I thought, faithful to me. But in this I was deceived. He became jealous of an office clerk who was staying with me, and wove such a tangled web that I suspected the clerk. This clerical friend had a temper of his own. Immediately he saw that he had been the object of my suspicion, he left both the house and the office. I was pained. I felt that perhaps I had been unjust to him, and my conscience always stung me.

In the meanwhile, the cook needed a few days' leave, or for some other cause was away. It was necessary to procure another during his absence. Of this new man I learnt later that he was a perfect scamp. But for me he proved a godsend. Within two or three days of his arrival, he discovered certain irregularities that were going on under my roof without my knowledge, and he made up his mind to warn me. I had the reputation of being a credulous but straight man. The discovery was to him, therefore, all the more shocking. Every day at one o'clock I used to go home from office for lunch. At about twelve o'clock one day the cook came panting to the office, and said, 'Please come home at once. There is a surprise for you.'

'Now, what is this?' I asked. 'You must tell me what it is. How can I leave the office at this hour to go and see it?'

'You will regret it, if you don't come. That is all I can say.'

I felt an appeal in his persistence. I went home accompanied by a clerk and the cook who walked ahead of us. He took me straight to the upper floor, pointed at my companion's room, and said, 'Open this door and see for yourself.'

I saw it all. I knocked at the door. No reply! I knocked heavily so as to make the very walls shake. The door was opened. I saw a prostitute inside. I asked her to leave the house, never to return.

To the companion I said, 'From this moment I cease to have anything to do with you. I have been thoroughly deceived and have made a fool of myself. That is how you have requited my trust in you?'

Instead of coming to his senses, he threatened to expose me.

'I have nothing to conceal,' said I, 'Expose whatever I may have done. But you must leave me this moment.'

This made him worse. There was no help for it. So I said to the clerk standing downstairs: 'Please go and inform the police superintendent, with my compliments, that a person living with me has misbehaved himself. I do not want to keep him in my house, but he refuses to leave. I shall be much obliged if police help can be sent me.'

This showed him that I was in earnest. His guilt unnerved him. He apologized to me, entreated me not to inform the police, and agreed to leave the house immediately, which he did.

The incident came as a timely warning in my life. Only now could I see clearly how thoroughly I had been beguiled by this evil genius. In harbouring him I had chosen a bad means for a good end. I had expected to 'gather figs of thistles'. I had known that the companion was a bad character, and yet I believed in his faithfulness to me. In the attempt to reform him I was near ruining myself. I had disregarded the warning of kind friends. Infatuation had completely blinded me.

But for the new cook I should never have discovered the truth and being under the influence of the companion, I should probably have been unable to lead the life of detachment that I then began. I should always have been wasting time on him. He had the power to keep me in the dark and to mislead me.

But God came to the rescue as before. My intentions were pure, and so I was saved in spite of my mistakes, and this early experience thoroughly forewarned me for the future.

The cook had been almost a messenger sent from Heaven. He did not know cooking, and as a cook he could not have remained at my place. But no one else could have opened my eyes. This was not the first time, as I subsequently learnt, that the woman had been brought into my house. She had come often before, but no one had the courage of this cook. For everyone knew how blindly I trusted the companion. The cook had, as it were, been sent to me just to do this service, for he begged leave of me that very moment.

'I cannot stay in your house,' he said. 'You are so easily misled. This is no place for me.'

I let him go.

I soon discovered that the man who had poisoned my ears against the clerk was no other than this companion. I tried very hard to make amends to the clerk for the injustice I had done him. It has, however, been my eternal regret that I could never satisfy him fully. Howsoever you may repair it, a rift is a rift.

Chapter 24: Homeward

By now I had been three years in South Africa. I had got to know the people and they had got to know me. In 1896 I asked permission to go home for six months, for I saw that I was in for a long stay there. I had established a fairly good practice, and could see that people felt the need of my presence. So I made up my mind to go home, fetch my wife and children, and then return and settle out there. I also saw that, if I went home, I might be able to do there some public work by educating public opinion and creating more interest in the Indians of South Africa. The £3 tax was an open sore. There could be no peace until it was abolished.

But who was to take charge of the Congress work and Education Society in my absence? I could think of two men — Adamji Miyakhan and Parsi Rustomji. There were many workers now available from the commercial class. But the foremost among those who could fulfill the duties of the secretary by regular work, and who also commanded the regard of the Indian community, were these two. The secretary certainly needed a working knowledge of English. I recommended the late Adamji Miyakhan's name to the Congress, and it approved of his appointment as secretary. Experience showed that the choice was a very happy one. Adamji Miyakhan satisfied all with his perseverance, liberality, amiability and courtesy, and proved to everyone that the secretary's work did not require a man with a barrister's degree or high English education.

About the middle of 1896 I sailed for home in the s. s. Pongola which was bound for Calcutta.

There were very few passengers on board. Among them were two English officers, with whom I came in close contact. With one of them I used to play chess for an hour daily. The ship's doctor gave me a Tamil Self-Teacher which I began to study. My experience in Natal had shown me that I should acquire a knowledge of Urdu to get into closer contact with the Musalmans, and of Tamil to get into closer touch with the Madras Indians.

At the request of the English friend, who read Urdu with me, I found out a good Urdu Munshi from among the deck passengers, and we made excellent progress in our studies. The officer had a better memory than I. He would never forget a word after once he had seen it; I often found it difficult to decipher Urdu letters. I brought more perseverance to bear, but could never overtake the officer.

With Tamil I made fair progress. There was no help available, but the Tamil Self-Teacher was a well-written book, and I did not feel in need of much outside help.

I had hoped to continue these studies even after reaching India, but it was impossible. Most of my reading since 1893 has been done in jail. I did make some progress in Tamil and Urdu, in jails — Tamil in South African jails, and Urdu in Yeravda jail. But I never learnt to speak Tamil, and the little I could do by way of reading is now rusting away for want of practice.

I still feel what a handicap this ignorance of Tamil or Telugu has been. The affection that the Dravidians in South Africa showered on me has remained a cherished memory. Whenever I see a Tamil or Telugu friend, I cannot but recall the faith, perseverance and selfless sacrifice of many of his compatriots in South Africa. And they were mostly illiterate, the men no less than the women. The fight in South Africa was for such, and it was fought by illiterate soldiers; it was for the poor and the poor took their full share in it. Ignorance of their language, however, was never a handicap to me in stealing the hearts of these simple and good countrymen. They spoke broken Hindustani or broken English, and we found no difficulty in getting on with our work. But I wanted to requite their affection by learning Tamil and Telugu. In Tamil, as I have said, I made some little progress, but in Telugu, which I tried to learn in India, I did not get beyond the alphabet. I fear now I can never learn these languages, and am therefore hoping that the Dravidians will learn Hindustani. The non-English-speaking among them in South Africa do speak Hindi or Hindustani, however indifferently. It is only the English-speaking ones who will not learn it, as though a knowledge of English were an obstacle to learning our own languages.

But I have digressed. Let me finish the narrative of my voyage. I have to introduce to my readers the captain of the S.S. Poongola. We had become friends. The good captain was a Plymouth Brother. Our talks were more about spiritual subjects than nautical. He drew a line between morality and faith. The teaching of the Bible was to him child's play. Its beauty lay in its simplicity. Let all, men, women and children, he would say, have faith in Jesus and his sacrifice, and their sins were sure to be redeemed. This friend revived my memory of the Plymouth Brother of Pretoria. The religion that imposed any moral restrictions was to him no good. My vegetarian food had been the occasion of the whole of this discussion. Why should I not eat meat, or for that matter beef? Had not God created all the lower animals for the enjoyment of mankind as, for instance, He had created the vegetable kingdom? These questions inevitably drew us into religious discussion.

We could not convince each other. I was confirmed in my opinion that religion and morality were synonymous. The captain had no doubt about the correctness of his opposite conviction.

At the end of twenty-four days the pleasant voyage came to a close, and admiring the beauty of the Hooghly, I landed at Calcutta. The same day I took the train for Bombay.

Chapter 25: In India

On my way to Bombay the train stopped at Allahabad for forty-five minutes. I decided to utilize the interval for a drive through the town. I also had to purchase some medicine at a chemist's shop. The chemist was half asleep, and took an unconscionable time in dispensing the medicine, with the result that when I reached the station, the train had just started. The station master had kindly detained the train one minute for my sake, but not seeing me coming, had carefully ordered my luggage to be taken out of the train.

I took a room at Kellner's, and decided to start work there and then. I had heard a good deal about The Pioneer published from Allahabad, and I had understood it to be an opponent of Indian aspirations. I have an impression that Mr. Chesney Jr. was the editor at that time. I wanted to secure the help of every party, so I wrote a note to Mr. Chesney, telling him how I had missed the train, and asking for an appointment so as to enable me to leave the next day. He immediately gave me one, at which I was very happy especially when I found that he gave me a patient hearing. He promised to notice in his paper anything that I might write, but added that he could not promise to endorse all the Indian demands, inasmuch as he was bound to understand and give due weight to the viewpoint of the Colonials as well.

'It is enough,' I said, 'that you should study the question and discuss it in your paper. I ask and desire nothing but the barest justice that is due to us.'

The rest of the day was spent in having a look round admiring the magnificent confluence of the three rivers, the 'Triveni', and planning the work before me.

This unexpected interview with the editor of The Pioneer laid the foundation of the series of incidents which ultimately led to my being lynched in Natal.

I went straight to Rajkot without halting at Bombay and began to make preparations for writing a pamphlet on the situation in South Africa. The writing and publication of the pamphlet took about a month. It had a green cover and came to be known afterwards as the Green Pamphlet. In it I drew a purposely subdued picture of the conditions of Indians in South Africa. The language I used was more moderate than that of the two pamphlets which I have referred to before, as I knew that things heard of from a distance appear bigger than they are.

Ten thousand copies were printed and sent to all the papers and leaders of every party in India. The Pioneer was the first to notice it editorially. A summary of the article was cabled by Reuter to England, and a summary of that summary was cabled to Natal by Reuter's London office. This cable was not longer than three lines in print. It was a miniature, but exaggerated, edition of the picture I had drawn of the treatment accorded to the Indians in Natal, and it was not in my words. We shall see later on the effect this had in Natal. In the meanwhile every paper of note commented at length on the question.

To get these pamphlets ready for posting was no small matter. It would have been expensive too, if I had employed paid help for preparing wrappers, etc. But I hit upon a much simpler plan. I gathered together all the children in my locality and asked them to volunteer two or three hours' labour of a morning, when they had no school. This they willingly agreed to do. I promised to bless them and give them, as a reward, used postage stamps which I had collected. They got through the work in no time. That was my first experiment of having little children as volunteers. Two of those little friends are my co-workers today.

Plague broke out in Bombay about this time, and there was panic all around. There was fear of an outbreak in Rajkot. As I felt that I could be of some help in the sanitation department, I offered my services to the State. They were accepted, and I was put on the committee which was appointed to look into the question. I laid especial emphasis on the cleanliness of latrines, and the committee decided to inspect these in every street. The poor people had no objection to their latrines being inspected, and what is more, they carried out the improvements suggested to them. But when we went to inspect the houses of the upper ten, some of them even refused us admission, not to talk of listening to our suggestions. It was our common experience that the latrines of the rich were more unclean. They were dark and stinking and reeking with filth and worms. The improvements we suggested were quite simple, e.g., to have buckets for excrement instead of allowing it to drop on the ground; to see that urine also was collected in buckets, instead of allowing it to soak into the ground, and to demolish the partitions between the outer walls and the latrines, so as to give the latrines more light and air and enable the scavenger to clean them properly. The upper classes raised numerous objections to this last improvement, and in most cases it was not carried out.

The committee had to inspect untouchables' quarters also. Only one member of the committee was ready to accompany me there. To the rest it was something preposterous to visit those quarters, still more so to inspect their latrines. But for me those quarters were an agreeable surprise. That was the first visit in my life to such a locality. The men and women there were surprised to see us. I asked them to let us inspect their latrines.

'Latrines for us!' they exclaimed in astonishment. 'We go and perform our functions out in the open. Latrines are for you big people.'

'Well, then, you won't mind if we inspect your houses?' I asked.

'You are perfectly welcome, sir. You may see every nook and corner of our houses. Ours are no houses, they are holes.'

I went in and was delighted to see that the insides were as clean as the outsides. The entrances were well swept, the floors were beautifully smeared with cow-dung, and the few pots and pans were clean and shining. There was no fear of an outbreak in those quarters.

In the upper class quarters we came across a latrine which I cannot help describing in some detail. Every room had its gutter, which was used both for water and urine, which meant that the whole house would stink. But one of the houses had a storeyed bedroom with a gutter which was being used both as a urinal and a latrine. The gutter had a pipe discending to the ground floor. It was not possible to stand the foul smell in this room. How the occupant could sleep there I leave the readers to imagine.

The committee also visited the Vaishnava Haveli. The priest in charge of the Haveli was very friendly with my family. So he agreed to let us inspect everything and suggest whatever improvements we liked. There was a part of the Haveli premises that he himself had never seen. It was the place where refuse and leaves used as dinner-plates used to be thrown over the wall. It was the haunt of crows and kites. The latrines were of course dirty. I was not long enough in Rajkot to see how many of our suggestions the priest carried out.

It pained me to see so much uncleanliness about a place of worship. One would expect a careful observance of the rules of sanitation and hygiene in a place which is regarded as holy. The authors of the Smritis, as I knew even then, have laid the greatest emphasis on cleanliness both inward and outward.

Chapter 26: Two passions

Hardly ever have I know anybody to cherish such loyalty as I did to the British Constitution. I can see now that my love of truth was at the root of this loyalty. It has never been possible for me to simulate loyalty or, for that matter, any other virtue. The National Anthem used to be sung at every meeting that I attended in Natal. I then felt that I must also join in the singing. Not that I was unaware of the defects in British rule, but I thought it was on the whole acceptable. In those days I believed that British rule was on the whole beneficial to the ruled.

The colour prejudice that I saw in South Africa was, I thought, quite contrary to British traditions, and I believed that it was only temporary and local. I therefore vied with Englishmen in loyalty to the throne. With careful perseverance I learnt the tune of the National Anthem and joined in the singing whenever it was sung. Whenever there was an occasion for the expression of loyalty without fuss or ostentation, I readily took part in it.

Never in my life did I exploit this loyalty, never did I seek to gain a selfish end by its means. It was for me more in the nature of an obligation, and I rendered it without expecting a reward.

Preparations were going on for the celebration of Queen Victoria's Diamond Jubilee when I reached India. I was invited to join the committee appointed for the purpose in Rajkot. I accepted the offer, but had a suspicion that the celebrations would be largely a matter of show. I discovered much humbug about them and was considerably pained. I began to ask myself whether I should remain on the committee or not, but ultimately decided to rest content with doing my part of the business.

One of the proposals was to plant trees. I saw that many did it merely for show and for pleasing the officials. I tried to plead with them that tree-planting was not compulsory, but merely a suggestion. It should be done seriously or not at all. I have an impression that they laughed at my ideas. I remember that I was in earnest when I planted the tree allotted to me and that I carefully watered and tended it.

I likewise taught the National Anthem to the children of my family. I recollect having taught it to students of the local Training College, but I forget whether it was on the occasion of the jubilee or of King Edward VII's coronation as Emperor of India. Later on the text began to jar on me. As my conception of Ahimsa went on maturing, I became more vigilant about my thought and speech. The lines in the Anthem:

> *Scatter her enemies, And make them fall; Confound their politics, Frustrate their knavish tricks.*

particularly jarred upon my sentiment of Ahimsa. I shared my feelings with Dr. Booth who agreed that it ill became a believer in Ahimsa to sing those lines. How could we assume that the so-called 'enemies' were 'knavish'? And because they were enemies, were they bound to be in the wrong? From God we could only ask for justice. Dr. Booth entirely endorsed my sentiments, and composed a new anthem for his congregation. But of Dr. Booth more later.

Like loyalty an aptitude for nursing was also deeply rooted in my nature. I was fond of nursing people, whether friends or strangers.

Whilst busy in Rajkot with the pamphlet on South Africa, I had an occasion to pay a flying visit to Bombay. It was my intention to educate public opinion in cities on this question by organizing meetings, and Bombay was the first city I chose. First of all I met Justice Ranade, who listened to me with attention, and advised me to meet Sir Pherozeshah Mehta. Justice Badruddin Tyabji, whom I met next, also gave the same advice. 'Justice Ranade and I can guide you but little,' he said. 'You know our position. We cannot take an active part in public affairs, but our sympathies are with you. The man who can effectively guide you is Sir Pherozeshah Mehta.'

I certainly wanted to see Sir Pherozeshah Mehta, but the fact that these senior men advised me to act according to his advice gave me a better idea of the immense influence that Sir Pherozeshah had on the public. In due course I met him. I was prepared to be awed by his presence. I had heard of the popular titles that he had earned, and knew that I was to see the 'Lion of Bombay', the 'Uncrowned King of the Presidency.' But the king did not overpower me. He met me as a loving father would meet his grown up son. Our meeting took place at his chamber. He was surrounded by a circle of friends and followers. Amongst them were Mr. D. E. Wacha and Mr. Cama, to whom I was introduced. I had already heard of Mr. Wacha. He was regarded as the right-hand man of Sir Pherozeshah, and Sjt. Virchand Gandhi had described him to me as a great statistician. Mr. Wacha said, 'Gandhi, we must meet again.'

These introductions could scarcely have taken two minutes. Sir Pherozeshah carefully listened to me. I told him that I had seen Justices Ranade and Tyabji.

'Gandhi,' said he, 'I see that I must help you. I must call a public meeting here.' With this he turned to Mr. Munshi, the secretary, and told him to fix up the date of the meeting. The date was settled, and he made me good-bye, asking me to see him again on the day previous to the meeting. The interview removed my fears, and I went home delighted.

During this stay in Bombay I called on my brother-in-law, who was staying there and lying ill. He was not a man of means, and my sister (his wife) was not equal to nursing him. The illness was serious, and I offered to take him to Rajkot. He agreed, and so I returned home with my sister and her husband. The illness was much more prolonged than I had expected. I put my brother-in-law in my room and remained with him night and day. I was obliged to keep awake part of the night and had to get through some of my South African work whilst I was nursing him. Ultimately, however, the patient died, but it was a great consolation to me that I had had an opportunity to nurse him during his last days.

My aptitude for nursing gradually developed into a passion, so much so that it often led me to neglect my work, and on occasions I engaged not only my wife but the whole household in such service.

Such service can have no meaning unless one takes pleasure in it. When it is done for show or for fear of public opinion, it stunts the man and crushes his spirit. Service which is rendered without joy helps neither the servant nor the served. But all other pleasures and possessions pale into nothingness before service which is rendered in a spirit of joy.

Chapter 27 : The Bombay meeting

On the very day after my brother-in-law's death I had to go to Bombay for the public meeting. There had hardly been time for me to think out my speech. I was feeling exhausted after days and nights of anxious vigil, and my voice had become husky. However, I went to Bombay trusting entirely to God. I had never dreamt of writing out my speech.

In accordance with Sir Pherozeshah's instructions I reported myself at his office at 5 P. M. on the eve of the meeting.

'Is your speech ready, Gandhi?' he asked.

'No, sir,' said I, trembling with fear, 'I think of speaking *ex tempore.*'

'That will not do in Bombay. Reporting here is bad, and if we would benefit by this meeting, you should write out your speech, and it should be printed before daybreak tomorrow. I hope you can manage this?'

I felt rather nervous, but I said I would try.

'Then, tell me, what time should Mr. Munshi come to you for the manuscript?'

'Eleven o'clock tonight,' said I.

On going to the meeting the next day, I saw the wisdom of Sir Pherozeshah's advice.

The meeting was held in the hall of the Sir Cowasji Jehangir Institute. I had heard that when Sir Pherozeshah Mehta addressed meetings the hall was always packed — chiefly by the students intent on hearing him — leaving not an inch of room. This was the first meeting of the kind in my experience. I saw that my voice could reach only a few. I was trembling as I began to read my speech. Sir Pherozeshah cheered me up continually by asking me to speak louder and still louder. I have a feeling that, far from encouraging me, it made my voice sink lower and lower.

My old friend Sjt. Keshavrao Deshpande came to my rescue. I handed my speech to him. His was just the proper voice. But the audience refused to listen. The hall rang with the cries of 'Wacha,' 'Wacha.' So Mr. Wacha stood up and read the speech, with wonderful results. The audience became perfectly quiet, and listened to the speech to the end, punctuating it with applause and cries of 'shame' where necessary. This gladdened my heart.

Sir Pherozeshah liked the speech. I was supremely happy.

The meeting won me the active sympathy of Sjt. Deshpande and a Parsi friend, whose name I hesitate to mention, as he is a high-placed Government official today. Both expressed their resolve to accompany me to South Africa. Mr. C. M. Cursetji, who was then Small Causes Court Judge, however, moved the Parsi friend from his resolve as he had plotted his marriage. He had to choose between marriage and going to South Africa, and he chose the former. But Parsi Rustomji made amends for the broken resolve, and a number of Parsi sisters are now making amends for the lady who helped in the breach, by dedicating themselves to khadi work. I have therefore gladly forgiven that couple. Sjt. Deshpande had no temptations of marriage, but he too could not come. Today he is himself doing enough reparation for the broken pledge. On my way back to South Africa I met one of the Tyabjis at Zanzibar. He also promised to come and help me, but never came. Mr. Abbas Tyabji is atoning for that offence. Thus none of my three attempts to induce barristers to go to South Africa bore any fruit.

In this connection I remember Mr. Pestonji Padshah. I had been on friendly terms with him ever since my stay in England. I first met him in a vegetarian restaurant in London. I knew of his brother Mr. Barjorji Padshah by his reputation as a 'crank'. I had never met him, but friends said that he was eccentric. Out of pity for the horses he would not ride in tramcars, he refused to take degrees in spite of a prodigious memory, he had developed an independent spirit, and he was a vegetarian, though a Parsi. Pestonji had not quite this reputation, but he was famous for his erudition even in London. The common factor between us, however, was vegetarianism, and not scholarship, in which it was beyond my power to approach him.

I found him out again in Bombay. He was Protonotary in the High Court. When I met him he was engaged on his contribution to a Higher Gujarati Dictonary. There was not a friend I had not approached for help in my South African work. Pestonji Padshah, however, not only refused to aid me, but even advised me not to return to South Africa.

'It is impossible to help you,' he said. 'But I tell you I do not like even your going to South Africa. Is there lack of work in our country? Look, now, there is not a little to do for our language. I have to find out scientific words. But this is only one branch of the work. Think of the poverty of the land. Our people in South Africa are no doubt in difficulty, but I do not want a man like you to be sacrificed for that work. Let us win self-government here, and we shall automatically help our countrymen there. I know I cannot prevail upon you, but I will not encourage anyone of your type to throw in his lot with you.'

I did not like this advice, but it increased my regard for Mr. Pestonji Padshah. I was struck with his love for the country and for the mother tongue. The incident brought us closer to each other. I could understand his point of view. But far from giving up my work in South Africa, I became firmer in my resolve. A patriot cannot afford to ignore any branch of service to the motherland. And for me the text of the Gita was clear and emphatic:

> Finally, this is better, that one do
> His own task as he may, even though he fail,
> Then take tasks not his own, though they seem good
> To die performing duty is no ill:
> But who seeks other roads shall wander still.

Chapter 28: Poona and Madras

Sir Pherozeshah had made my way easy. So from Bombay I went to Poona. Here there were two parties. I wanted the help of people of every shade of opinion.

First I met Lokamanya Tilak. He said:

'You are quite right in seeking the help of all parties. There can be no difference of opinion on the South African question. But you must have a non-party man for your president. Meet Professor Bhandarkar. He has been taking no part of late in any public movement. But this question might possibly draw him out. See him and let me know what he says. I want to help you to the fullest extent. Of course you will meet me whenever you like. I am at your disposal.'

This was my first meeting with the Lokamanya. It revealed to me the secret of his unique popularity.

Next I met Gokhale. I found him on the Fergusson College grounds. He gave me an affectionate welcome, and his manner immediately won my heart. With him too this was my first meeting, and yet it seemed as though we were renewing an old friendship. Sir Pherozeshah had seemed to me like the Himalaya, the Lokamanya like the ocean.

But Gokhale was as the Ganges. One could have a refreshing bath in the holy river. The Himalaya was unscaleable, and one could not easily launch forth on the sea, but the Ganges invited one to its bosom. It was a joy to be on it with a boat and an oar. Gokhale closely examined me, as a schoolmaster would examine a candidate seeking admission to a school. He told me whom to approach and how to approach them. He asked to have a look at my speech. He showed me over the college, assured me that he was always at my disposal, asked me to let him know the result of the interview with Dr. Bhandarkar, and sent me away exultantly happy. In the sphere of politics the place that Gokhale occupied in my heart during his lifetime and occupies even now was and is absolutely unique.

Dr. Bhandarkar received me with the warmth of a father. It was noon when I called on him. The very fact that I was busy seeing people at that hour appealed greatly to this indefatigable savant, and my insistence on a non-party man for the president of the meeting had his ready approval, which was expressed in the spontaneous exclamation, 'That's it,' 'that's it.'

After he had heard me out he said: 'Anyone will tell you that I do not take part in politics. But I cannot refuse you. Your case is so strong and your industry is so admirable that I cannot decline to take part in your meeting. You did well in consulting Tilak and Gokhale. Please tell them that I shall be glad to preside over the meeting to be held under the joint auspices of the two Sabhas. You need not have the time of the meeting from me. Any time that suits them will suit me.' With this he bade me good-bye with congratulations and blessings.

Without any ado this erudite and selfless band of workers in Poona held a meeting in an unostentatious little place, and sent me away rejoicing and more confident of my mission.

I next proceeded to Madras. It was wild with enthusiasm. The Balasundaram incident made a profound impression on the meeting. My speech was printed and was, for me, fairly long. But the audience listened to every word with attention. At the close of the meeting there was a regular run on the 'Green Pamphlet.' I brought out a second and revised edition of 10,000 copies. They sold like hot cakes, but I saw that it was not necessary to print such a large number. In my enthusiasm I had overcalculated the demand. It was the English-speaking public to which my speech had been addressed, and in Madras that class alone could not take the whole ten thousand.

The greatest help here came to me from the late Sjt. G. Parameshvaran Pillay, the editor of The Madras Standard. He had made a careful study of the question, and he often invited me to his office and gave me guidance. Sjt. G. Subrahmaniam of The Hindu and Dr. Subrahmaniam also were very sympathetic. But Sjt. G. Parameshvaran Pillay placed the columns of The Madras Standard entirely at my disposal, and I freely availed myself of the offer. The meeting in Pachaiappa's Hall, so far as I can recollect, was with Dr. Subrahmaniam in the chair.

The affection showered on me by most of the friends I met and their enthusiasm for the cause were so great that, in spite of my having to communicate with them in English, I felt myself entirely at home. What barrier is there that love cannot break?

Chapter 29: 'Return soon'

From Madras I proceeded to Calcutta where I found myself hemmed by difficulties. I knew no one there. So I took a room in the Great Eastern Hotel. Here I became acquainted with Mr. Ellerthorpe, a representative of The Daily Telegraph. He invited me to the Bengal Club, where he was staying. He did not then realize that an Indian could not be taken to the drawing-room of the club. Having discovered the restriction, he took me to his room. He expressed his sorrow regarding this prejudice of the local Englishmen and apologized to me for not having been able to take me to the drawing-room.

I had of course to see Surendranath Banerji, the 'Idol of Bengal'. When I met him, he was surrounded by a number of friends. He said:

'I am afraid people will not take interest in your work. As you know, our difficulties here are by no means few. But you must try as best you can. You will have to enlist the sympathy of Maharajas. Mind you meet the representatives of the British Indian Association. You should meet Raja Sir Pyarimohan Mukarji and Maharaja Tagore. Both are liberal-minded and take a fair share in public work.'

I met these gentlemen, but without success. Both gave me a cold reception and said it was no easy thing to call a public in Calcutta, and if anything could be done, it would practically all depend on Surendranath Banerji.

I saw that my task was becoming more and more difficult. I called at the office of The Amrita Bazar Patrika. The gentleman whom I met there took me to be a wandering Jew. The Bangabasi went even one better. The editor kept me waiting for an hour. He had evidently many interviewers, but he would not so much as look at me, even when he had disposed of the rest. On my venturing to broach my subject after the long wait, he said: 'Don't you see our hands are full? There is no end to the number of visitors like you. You had better go. I am not disposed to listen to you.' For a moment I felt offended, but I quickly understood the editor's position. I had heard of the fame of The Bangabasi. I could see that there was a regular stream of visitors there. And they were all people acquainted with him. His paper had no lack of topics to discuss, and South Africa was hardly known at that time.

However serious a grievance may be in the eyes of the man who suffers from it, he will be but one of the numerous people invading the editor's office, each with a grievance of his own. How is the editor to meet them all? Moreover, the aggrieved party imagines that the editor is a power in the land. Only he knows that his powers can hardly travel beyond the threshold of his office. But I was not discouraged. I kept on seeing editors of other papers. As usual I met the Anglo-Indian editors also. The Statesman and The Englishman realized the importance of the question. I gave them long interviews, and they published them in full.

Mr. Saunders, editor of The Englishman, claimed me as his own. He placed his office and paper at my disposal. He even allowed me the liberty of making whatever changes I liked in the leading article he had written on the situation, the proof of which he sent me in advance. It is no exaggeration to say that a friendship grew up between us. He promised to render me all the help he could, carried out the promise to the letter, and kept on his correspondence with me until the time when he was seriously ill.

Throughout my life I have had the privilege of many such friendships, which have sprung up quite unexpectedly. What Mr. Saunders liked in me was my freedom from exaggeration and my devotion to truth. He subjected me to a searching cross-examination before he began to sympathize with my cause, and he saw that I had spared neither will nor pains to place before him an impartial statement of the case even of the white man in South Africa and also to appreciate it.

My experience has shown me that we win justice quickest by rendering justice to the other party.

The unexpected help of Mr. Saunders had begun to encourage me to think that I might succeed after all in holding a public meeting in Calcutta, when I received the following cable from Durban: 'Parliament opens January. Return soon.'

So I addressed a letter to the press, in which I explained why I had to leave Calcutta so abruptly, and set off for Bombay. Before starting I wired to the Bombay agent of Dada Abdulla & Co., to arrange for my passage by the first possible boat to South Africa. Dada Abdulla had just then purchased the steamship Courland and insisted on my travelling on that boat, offering to take me and my family free of charge. I gratefully accepted the offer, and in the beginning of December set sail a second time for South Africa, now with my wife and two sons and the only son of my widowed sister. Another steamship Naderi also sailed for Durban at the same time. The agents of the Company were Dada Abdulla & Co. The total number of passengers these boats carried must have been about eight hundred, half of whom were bound for the Transvaal.

PART III

Chapter 1 : Rumblings of the storm

This was my first voyage with my wife and children. I have often observed in the course of this narrative that, on account of child marriages amongst middle class Hindus, the husband will be literate whilst the wife remains practically unlettered. A wide gulf thus separates them, and the husband has to become his wife's teacher. So I had to think out the details of the dress to be adopted by my wife and children, the food they were to eat, and the manners which would be suited to their new surroundings. Some of the recollections of those days are amusing to look back upon.

A Hindu wife regards implicit obedience to her husband as the highest religion. A Hindu husband regards himself as lord and master of his wife, who must ever dance attendance upon him.

I believed, at the time of which I am writing, that in order to look civilized, our dress and manners had, as far as possible, to approximate to the European standard. Because, I thought, only thus could we have some influence, and without influence it would not be possible to serve the community.

I therefore determined the style of dress for my wife and children. How could I like them to be known as Kathiawad Banias? The Parsis used then to be regarded as the most civilized people amongst Indians, and so, when the complete European style seemed to be unsuited, we adopted the Parsi style. Accordingly my wife wore the Parsisari, and the boys the Parsi coat and trousers. Of course no one could be without shoes and stockings. It was long before my wife and children could get used to them. The shoes cramped their feet and the stockings stank with perspiration. The toes often got sore. I always had my answers ready to all these objections. But I have an impression that it was not so much the answers as the force of authority that carried conviction.

They agreed to the changes in dress as there was no alternative. In the same spirit and with even more reluctance they adopted the use of knives and forks. When my infatuation for these signs of civilization wore away, they gave up the knives and forks. After having become long accustomed to the new style, it was perhaps no less irksome for me to return to the original mode. But I can see today that we feel all the freer and lighter for having cast off the tinsel of 'civilization'.

On board the same steamer with us were some relatives and acquaintances. These and other deck passengers I frequently met, because, the boat belonging to my client's friends, I was free to move about anywhere and every where I liked.

Since the steamer was making straight for Natal, without calling at intermediate ports, our voyage was of only eighteen days. But as though to warn us of the coming real storm on land, a terrible gale overtook us, whilst we were only four days from Natal. December is a summer month of monsoon in the southern hemisphere, and gales, great and small, are, therefore, quite common in the southern seas at that season. The gale in which we were caught was so violent and prolonged that the passengers became alarmed. It was a solemn scene. All became one in face of the common danger. They forgot their differences and began to think of the one and only God — Musalmans, Hindus, Christians and all. Some took various vows. The captain also joined the passengers in their prayers. He assured them that, though the storm was not without danger, he had had experience of many worse ones, and explained to them that a well-built ship could stand almost any weather. But they were inconsolable. Every minute were heard sounds and crashes which foreboded breaches and leaks. The ship rocked and rolled to such an extent that it seemed as though she would capsize at any moment. It was out of the question for anyone to remain on deck. 'His will be done' was the only cry on every lip. So far as I can recollect, we must have been in this plight for about twenty-four hours. At last the sky cleared, the sun made its appearance, and the captain said that the storm had blown over. People's faces beamed with gladness, and with the disappearance of danger disappeared also the name of God from their lips, Eating and drinking, singing and merry-making again became the order of the day. The fear of death was gone, and the momentary mood of earnest prayer gave place to maya[*]. There were of course the usual namaz[†] and the prayers, yet they had none of the solemnity of that dread hour.

But the storm had made me one with the passengers. I had little fear of the storm, for I had had experience of similar ones. I am a good sailor and do not get sea-sick. So I could fearlessly move amongst the passengers, bringing them comfort and good cheer, and conveying to them hourly reports of the captain.

The friendship I thus formed stood me, as we shall see, in very good stead.

The ship cast anchor in the port of Durban on the 18th or 19th of December. The Naderi also reached the same day.

But the real storm was still to come.

Chapter 2: The storm

We have seen that the two ships cast anchor in the port of Durban on or about the 18th of December. No passengers are allowed to land at any of the South African ports before being subjected to a thorough medical examination. If the ship has any passenger suffering from a contagious disease, she has to undergo a period of quarantine. As there had been plague in Bombay when we met sail, we feared that we might have to go through a brief quarantine. Before the examination every ship has to fly a yellow flag, which is

---

[*] The famous word in Hindu philosophy which is nearly untranslatable, but has been frequently translated in English as 'delusion', 'illusion'.

[†] The prayer prescribed by the Koran.

lowered only when the doctor has certified her to be healthy. Relatives and friends of passengers are allowed to come on board only after the yellow flag has been lowered.

Accordingly our ship was flying the yellow flag, when the doctor came and examined us. He ordered a five days' quarantine because, in his opinion, plague germs took twenty-three days at the most to develop. Our ship was therefore ordered to be put in quarantine until the twenty-third day of our sailing from Bombay. But this quarantine order had more than health reasons behind it.

The white residents of Durban had been agitating for our repatriation, and the agitation was one of the reasons for the order. Dada Abdulla and Co. kept us regularly informed about the daily happenings in the town. The whites were holding monster meetings every day. They were addressing all kinds of threats and at times offering even inducements to Dada Abdulla and Co. They were ready to indemnify the Company if both the ships should be sent back. But Dada Abdulla and Co. were not the people to be afraid of threats. Sheth Abdul Karim Haji Adam was then the managing partner of the firm. He was determined to moor the ships at the wharf and disembark the passengers at any cost. He was daily sending me detailed letters. Fortunately the Sjt. Mansukhlal Naazar was then in Durban, having gone there to meet me. He was capable and fearless and guided the Indian community. Their advocate Mr. Laughton was an equally fearless man. He condemned the conduct of the white residents and advised the community, not merely as their paid advocate, but also as their true friend.

Thus Durban had become the scene of an unequal duel. On one side there was a handful of poor Indians and a few of their English friends, and on the other were ranged the white men, strong in arms, in numbers, in education and in wealth. They had also the backing of the State, for the Natal Government openly helped them. Mr.Harry Escombe, who was the most influential of the members of the Cabinet, openly took part in their meetings.

The real object of the quarantine was thus to coerce the passengers into returning to India by somehow intimidating them or the Agent Company. For now threats began to be addressed to us also: 'If you do not go back, you will surely be pushed into the sea. But if you consent to return, you may even get your passage money back.' I constantly moved amongst my fellow-passengers cheering them up. I also sent messages of comfort to the passengers of the s.s.Naderi. All of them kept calm and courageous.

We arranged all sorts of games on the ship for the entertainment of the passengers. On Christmas Day the captain invited the saloon passengers to dinner. The principal among these were my family and I. In the speeches after dinner I spoke on Western civilization. I knew that this was not an occasion for a serious speech. But mine could not be otherwise. I took part in the merriment, but my heart was in the combat that was going on in Durban. For I was the real target. There were two charges against me:

1. That whilst in India I had indulged in unmerited condemnation of the Natal whites;
2. That with a view to swamping Natal with Indians I had specially brought the two

shiploads of passengers to settle there.

I was conscious of my responsibility. I knew that Dada Abdulla and Co. had incurred grave risks on my account, the lives of the passengers were in danger, and by bringing my family with me I had put them likewise in jeopardy.

But I was absolutely innocent. I had induced no one to go to Natal. I did not know the passengers when they embarked. And with the exception of a couple of relatives, I did not know the name and address of even one of the hundreds of passengers on board. Neither had I said, whilst in India, a word about the whites in Natal that I had not already said in Natal itself. And I had ample evidence in support of all that I had said.

I therefore deplored the civilization of which the Natal whites were the fruit, and which they represented and championed. This civilization had all along been on my mind, and I therefore offered my views concerning it in my speech before that little meeting. The captain and other friends gave me a patient hearing, and received my speech in the spirit in which it was made. I do not know that it in any way affected the course of their lives, but afterwards I had long talks with the captain and other officers regarding the civilization of the West. I had in my speech described Western civilization as being, unlike the Eastern, predominantly based on force. The questioners pinned me to my faith, and one of them the captain, so far as I can recollect — said to me:

'Supposing the whites carry out their threats, how will you stand by your principle of non-violence?' To which I replied: 'I hope God will give me the courage and the sense to forgive them and to refrain from bringing them to law. I have no anger against them. I am only sorry for their ignorance and their narrowness. I know that they sincerely believe that what they are doing today is right and proper. I have no reason therefore to be angry with them.'

The questioner smiled, possibly distrustfully.

Thus the days dragged on their weary length. When the quarantine would terminate was still uncertain. The Quarantine Officer said that the matter had passed out of his hands and that, as soon as he had orders from the Government, he would permit us to land.

At last ultimatums were served on the passengers and me. We were asked to submit, if we would escape with our lives. In our reply the passengers and I both maintained our right to land at Port Natal, and intimated our determination to enter Natal at any risk.

At the end of twenty-three days the ships were permitted to enter the harbour, and orders permitting the passengers to land were passed.

Chapter 3: The test

So the ships were brought into the dock and the passengers began to go ashore. But Mr.

Escombe had sent word to the captain that, as the whites were highly enraged against me and my life was in danger, my family and I should be advised to land at dusk, when the port superintendent Mr. Tatum would escort us home. The captain communicated the message to me, and I agreed to act accordingly. But scarcely half an hour after this, Mr. Laughton came to the captain. He said: 'I would like to take Mr. Gandhi with me, should he have no objection. As the legal adviser of the Agent Company I tell you that you are not bound to carry out the message you have received from Mr. Escombe.' After this he came to me and said somewhat to this effect: 'If you are not afraid, I suggest that Mrs. Gandhi and the children should drive to Mr. Rustomji's house, whilst you and I follow them on foot. I do not at all like the idea of your entering the city like a thief in the night. I do not think there is any fear of anyone hurting you. Everything is quiet now. The whites have all dispersed. But in any case I am convinced that you ought not to enter the city stealthily.' I readily agreed. My wife and children drove safely to Mr. Rustomji's place. With the captain's permission I went ashore with Mr. Laughton. Mr Rustomji's house was about two miles from the dock.

As soon as we landed, some youngsters recognized me and shouted 'Gandhi, Gandhi.' About half a dozen men rushed to the spot and joined in the shouting. Mr. Laughton feared that the crowd might swell and hailed a rickshaw. I had never liked the idea of being in a rickshaw. This was to be my first experience. But the youngsters would not let me get into it. They frightened the rickshaw boy out of his life, and he took to his heels. As we went ahead, the crowd continued to swell, until it became impossible to proceed further. They first caught hold of Mr. Laughton and separated us. Then they pelted me with stones, brickbats and rotten eggs. Someone snatched away my turban, whilst others began to batter and kick me. I fainted and caught hold of the front railings of a house and stood there to get my breath. But it was impossible. They came upon me boxing and battering. The wife of the police superintendent, who knew me, happened to be passing by. The brave lady came up, opened her parasol though there was no sun then, and stood between the crowd and me. This checked the fury of the mob, as it was difficult for them to deliver blows on me without harming Mrs. Alexander.

Meanwhile an Indian youth who witnessed the incident had run to the police station. The police superintendent Mr. Alexander, sent a posse of men to ring me round and escort me safely to my destination. They arrived in time. The police station lay on our way. As we reached there, the superintendent asked me to take refuge in the station, but I gratefully declined the offer, 'They are sure to quiet down when they realize their mistake,' I said. 'I have trust in their sense of fairness.' Escorted by the police, I arrived without further harm at Mr. Rustomji's place. I had bruises all over, but no abrasions except in one place. Dr. Dadibarjor, the ship's doctor, who was on the spot, rendered the best possible help.

There was quiet inside, but outside the whites surrounded the house. Night was coming on, and the yelling crowd was shouting, 'We must have Gandhi.' The quick-sighted police superintendent was already there trying to keep the crowds under control, not by threats, but by humouring them. But he was not entirely free from anxiety. He sent me a message to this effect: 'If you would save your friend's house and property and also your family, you should escape from the house in disguise, as I suggest.'

Thus on one and the same day I was faced with two contradictory positions. When danger to life had been no more than imaginary, Mr. Laughton advised me to launch forth openly. I accepted the advice. When the danger was quite real, another friend gave me the contrary advice, and I accepted that too. Who can say whether I did so because I saw that my life was in jeopardy, or because I did not want to put my friend's life and property or the lives of my wife and children in danger? Who can say for certain that I was right both when I faced the crowd in the first instance bravely, as it was said, and when I escaped from it in disguise?

It is idle to adjudicate upon the right and wrong of incidents that have already happened. It is useful to understand them and, if possible, to learn a lesson from them for the future. It is difficult to say for certain how a particular man would act in a particular set of circumstances. We can also see that judging a man from his outward act is no more than a doubtful inference, inasmuch as it is not based on sufficient data.

Be that as it may, the preparations for escape made me forget my injuries. As suggested by the superintendent, I put on an Indian constable's uniform and wore on my head a Madrasi scarf, wrapped round a plate to serve as a helmet. Two detectives accompanied me, one of them disguised as an Indian merchant and with his face painted to resemble that of an Indian. I forget the disguise of the other. We reached a neighbouring shop by a by-lane, and making our way through the gunny bags piled in the godown, escaped by the gate of the shop and threaded our way through the crowd to a carriage that had been kept for me at the end of the street. In this we drove off to the same police station where Mr. Alexander had offered me refuge a short time before, and I thanked him and the detective officers.

Whilst I had been thus effecting my escape, Mr. Alexander had kept the crowd amused by singing the tune:

'Hang old Gandhi

On the sour apple tree.'

When he was informed of my safe arrival at the police station, he thus broke the news to the crowd: 'Well, your victim had made good his escape through a neighbouring shop. You had better go home now.' Some of them were angry, others laughed, some refused to believe the story.

'Well then,' said the superintendent, 'If you do not believe me, you may appoint one or two representatives, whom I am ready to take inside the house. If they succeed in finding out Gandhi, I will gladly deliver him to you. But if they fail, you must disperse.

I am sure that you have no intention of destroying Mr. Rustomji's house or of harming Mr. Gandhi's wife and children.'

The crowed sent their representatives to search the house. They soon returned with disappointing news, and the crowd broke up at last, most of them admiring the superintendent's tactful handling of the situation, and a few fretting and fuming.

The late Mr. Chamberlain, who was then Secretary of State for the Colonies, cabled asking the Natal Government to prosecute my assailants. Mr. Escombe sent for me, expressed his regret for the injuries I had sustained, and said:

'Believe me, I cannot feel happy over the least little injury done to your person. You had a right to accept Mr. Laughton's advice and to face the worst, but I am sure that, if you had considered my suggestion, these sad occurrences would not have happened. If you can identify the assailants, I am prepared to arrest and prosecute them. Mr. Chamberlain also desires me to do so.'

To which I gave the following reply:

'I do not want to prosecute anyone. It is possible that I may be able to identify one or two of them, but what is the use of getting them punished? Besides, I do not hold the assailants to blame. They were given to understand that I had made exaggerated statements in India about the whites in Natal and calumniated them. If they believed these reports, it is no wonder that they were enraged. The leaders and, if you will permit me to say so, you are to blame. You could have guided the people properly, but you also believed Reuter and assumed that I must have indulged in exaggeration. I do not want to bring anyone to book. I am sure that, when the truth becomes known, they will be sorry for their conduct.'

'Would you mind giving me this in writing?' said Mr. Escombe. 'Because I shall have to cable to Mr. Chamberlain to that effect. I do not want you to make any statement in haste. You may, if you like, consult Mr. Laughton and your other friends, before you come to a final decision. I may confess, however, that, if you waive the right of bringing your assailants to book, you will considerably help me in restoring quiet, besides enhancing your own reputation.'

'Thank you,' said I. 'I need not consult anyone. I had made my decision in the matter before I came to you. It is my conviction that I should not prosecute the assailants, and I am prepared this moment to reduce my decision to writing.'

With this I gave him the necessary statement.

Chapter 4: The calm after the storm

I had not yet left the police station, when, after two days, I was taken to see Mr. Escombe.

Two constables were sent to protect me, though no such precaution was then needed.

On the day of landing, as soon as the yellow flag was lowered, a representative of The Natal Advertiser had come to interview me. He had asked me a number of questions, and in reply I had been able to refute everyone of the charges that had been leveled against me. Thanks to Sir Pherozeshah Mehta, I had delivered only written speeches in India, and I had copies of them all, as well as of my other writings. I had given the interviewer all this literature and showed him that in India I had said nothing which I had not already said in South Africa in stronger language. I had also shown him that I had had no hand in bringing the passengers of the Courlandand Naderi to South Africa. Many of them were old residents, and most of them, far from wanting to stay in Natal, meant to go to the Transvaal. In those days the Transvaal offered better prospects than Natal to those coming in search of wealth, and most Indians, therefore, preferred to go there.

This interview and my refusal to prosecute the assailants produced such a profound impression that the Europeans of Durban were ashamed of their conduct. The press declared me to be innocent and condemned the mob. Thus the lynching ultimately proved to be a blessing for me, that is, for the cause. It enhanced the prestige of the Indian community in South Africa and made my work easier.

In three or four days I went to my house, and it was not long before I settled down again. The incident added also to my professional practice.

But if it enhanced the prestige of the community, it also fanned the flame of prejudice against it. As soon as it was proved that the Indian could put up a manly fight, he came to be regarded as a danger. Two bills were introduced in the Natal Legislative Assembly, one of them calculated to affect the Indian trader adversely, and the other to impose a stringent restriction on Indian immigration. Fortunately the fight for the franchise had resulted in a decision to the effect that no enactment might be passed against the Indians as such, that is say, that the law should make no distinctions of colour or race. The language of the bills above mentioned made them applicable to all, but their object undoubtedly was to impose further restrictions on the Indian residents of Natal.

The bills considerably increased my public work and made the community more alive then ever to their sense of duty. They were translated into Indian languages and fully explained, so as to bring home to the community their subtle implications. We appealed to the Colonial Secretary, but he refused to interfere and the bills became law.

Public work now began to absorb most of my time. Sjt. Mansukhlal Naazar, who, as I have said, was already in Durban, came to stay with me, and as he gave his time to public work, he lightened my burden to some extent.

Sheth Adamji Miyakhan had, in my absence, discharged his duty with great credit. He had increased the membership and added about £1,000 to the coffers of the Natal Indian Congress. The awakening caused by the bills and the demonstration against the passengers I turned to good account by making an appeal for membership and funds, which now amounted to £5,000. My desire was to secure for the Congress a permanent fund, so that it might procure property of its own and then carry on its work out of the rent of the property.

This was my first experience of managing a public institution. I placed my proposal before my co-workers, and they welcomed it. The property that was purchased was leased out, and the rent was enough to meet the current expenses of the Congress. The property was vested in a strong body of trustees and is still there today, but it has become the source of much internecine quarrelling with the result that the rent of the property now accumulates in the court.

This sad situation developed after my departure from South Africa, but my idea of having permanent funds for public institutions underwent a change long before this difference arose. And now after considerable experience with the many public institutions which I have managed, it has become my firm conviction that it is not good to run public institutions on permanent funds. A permanent fund carries in itself the seed of the moral fall of the institution. A public institution means an institution conducted with the approval, and from the funds, of the public. When such an institution ceases to have public support, it forfeits its right to exist. Institutions maintained on permanent funds are often found to ignore public opinion, and are frequently responsible for acts contrary to it. In our country we experience this at every step. Some of the so-called religious trusts have ceased to render any accounts. The trustees have become the owners and are responsible to none. I have no doubt that the ideal is for public institutions to live, like nature, from day to day. The institution that fails to win public support has no right to exist as such. The subscriptions that an institution annually receives are a test of its popularity and the honesty of its management; and I am of opinion that every institution should submit to that test. But let no one misunderstand me. My remarks do not apply to the bodies which cannot, by their very nature, be conducted without permanent buildings. What I mean to say is that the current expenditure should be found from subscriptions voluntarily received from year to year.

These views were confirmed during the days of the Satyagraha in South Africa. That magnificent campaign extending over six years was carried on without permanent funds, though lakhs of rupees were necessary for it. I can recollect times when I did not know what would happen the next day if no subscriptions came in. But I shall not anticipate future events. The reader will find the opinion expressed above amply borne out in the coming narrative.

Chapter 5: Education of children

When I landed at Durban in January 1897, I had three children with me, my sister's son ten years old, and my own sons nine and five years of age. Where was I to educate them?

I could have sent them to the schools for European children, but only as a matter of favour and exception. No other Indian children were allowed to attend them. For these there were schools established by Christian missions, but I was not prepared to send my children there, as I did not like the education imparted in those schools. For one thing, the medium of instruction would be only English, or perhaps incorrect Tamil or Hindi; this too could only have been arranged with difficulty. I could not possibly put up with this and other disadvantages. In the meantime I was making my own attempt to teach them. But that was at best irregular, and I could not get hold of a suitable Gujarati teacher.

I was at my wits' end. I advertised for an English teacher who should teach the children under my direction. Some regular instruction was to be given them by this teacher, and for the rest they should be satisfied with what little I could give them irregularly. So I engaged an English governess at £7 pounds a month. This went on for some time, but not to my satisfaction. The boys acquired some knowledge of Gujarati through my conversation and intercourse with them, which was strictly in the mother-tongue. I was loath to send them back to India, for I believed even then that young children should not be separated from their parents. The education that children naturally imbibe in a well-ordered household is impossible to obtain in hostels. I therefore kept my children with me. I did send my nephew and elder son to be educated at residential schools in India for a few months, but I soon had to recall them. Later, the eldest son, long after he had come of age, broke away from me, and went to India to join a high school in Ahmedabad. I have an impression that the nephew was satisfied with what I could give him. Unfortunately he died in the prime of youth after a brief illness. The other three of my sons have never been at a public school, though they did get some regular schooling in an improvised school which I started for the children of Satyagrahi parents in South Africa.

These experiments were all inadequate. I could not devote to the children all the time I had wanted to give them. My inability to give them enough attention and other unavoidable causes prevented me from providing them with the literary education I had desired, and all my sons have had complaints to make against me in this matter. Whenever they come across an M.A. or a B.A., or even a matriculate, they seem to feel the handicap of a want of school education.

Nevertheless I am of opinion that, if I had insisted on their being educated somehow at public schools, they would have been deprived of the training that can be had only at the school of experience, or from constant contact with the parents. I should never have been free, as I am today, from anxiety on their score, and the artificial education that they could have had in England or South Africa, torn from me, would never have taught them the simplicity and the spirit of service that they show in their lives today, while their artificial ways of living might have been a serious handicap in my public work. Therefore, though I have not been able to give them a literary education either to their or to my satisfaction, I am not quite sure, as I look back on my past years, that I have not done my duty by them to the best of my capacity. Nor do I regret not having sent them to public schools. I have always felt that the undesirable traits I see today in my eldest son are an echo of my own undisciplined and unformulated early life. I regard that time as a period of half-baked knowledge and indulgence. It coincided with the most impressionable years of my eldest son, and naturally he has refused to regard it as my time of indulgence and inexperience. He has on the contrary believed that that was the brightest period of my life, and the changes, effected later, have been due to delusion miscalled enlightenment. And well he might. Why should he not think that my earlier years represented a period of awakening, and the later years of radical change, years of delusion and egotism? Often have I been confronted with various posers from friends: What harm had there been, if I had given my boys an academical education? What right had I thus to clip their wings? Why should I have come in the way of their taking degrees and choosing their own careers?

I do not think that there is much point in these questions. I have come in contact with numerous students. I have tried myself or through others to impose my educational 'fads' on other children too and have seen the results thereof. There are within my knowledge a number of young men today contemporaneous with my sons. I do not think that man to man they are any better that my sons, or that my sons have much to learn from them.

But the ultimate result of my experiments is in the womb of the future. My object in discussing this subject here is that a student of the history of civilization may have some measure of the difference between disciplined home education and school education, and so of the effect produced on children through changes introduced by parents in their lives. The purpose of this chapter is also to show the lengths to which a votary of truth is driven by his experiments with truth as also to show the votary of liberty how many are the sacrifices demanded by that stern goddess. Had I been without a sense of self-respect and satisfied myself with having for my children the education that other children could not get, I should have deprived them of the object-lesson in liberty and self-respect that I gave them at the cost of the literary training. And where a choice has to be made between liberty and learning, who will not say that the former has to be preferred a thousand times to the latter?

The youths whom I called out in 1920 from those citadels of slavery — their schools and colleges — and whom I advised that it was far better to remain unlettered and break stones for the sake of liberty than to go in for a literary education in the chains of slaves will probably be able now to trace my advice to its source.

Chapter 6: Spirit of service

My profession progressed satisfactorily, but that was far from satisfying me. The question of further simplifying my life and of doing some concrete act of service to my fellowmen had been constantly agitating me, when a leper came to my door. I had not the heart to dismiss him with a meal. So I offered him shelter, dressed his wounds, and began to look after him. But I could not go on like that indefinitely. I could not afford, I lacked the will, to keep him always with me. So I sent him to the government hospital for indentured labourers.

But I was still ill at ease. I longed for some humanitarian work of a permanent nature. Dr. Booth was the head of the St. Aidan's Mission. He was a kind-hearted man and treated his patients free. Thanks to a Parsi Rustomji's charities, it was possible to open a small charitable hospital under Dr. Booth's charge. I felt strongly inclined to serve as a nurse in this hospital. The work of dispensing medicines took from one to two hours daily, and I made up my mind to find time from my office-work, so as to be able to fill the place of a compounder in the dispensary attached to the hospital. Most of my professional work was chamber work, conveyancing and arbitration. I of course used to have a few cases in the magistrate's court, but most of them were of a non-controversial character, and Mr. Khan, who had followed me to South Africa and was then living with me, undertook to take them if I was absent. So I found time to serve in the small hospital. This meant two hours every morning, including the time taken in going to and from the hospital. This work brought me some peace. It consisted in ascertaining the patient's complaints, laying the facts before the doctor and dispensing the prescriptions. It brought me in close touch with suffering Indians, most of them indentured Tamil, Telugu or North Indian men.

The experience stood me in good stead, when during the Boer War I offered my services for nursing the sick and wounded soldiers.

The question of the rearing of children had been ever before me. I had two sons born in South Africa, and my service in the hospital was useful in solving the question of their upbringing. My independent spirit was a constant source of trial. My wife and I had decided to have the best medical aid at the time of her delivery, but if the doctor and the nurse were to leave us in the lurch at the right moment, what was I to do? Then the nurse had to be an Indian. And the difficulty of getting a trained Indian nurse in South Africa can be easily imagined from the similar difficulty in India. So I studied the things necessary for safe labour. I read Dr. Tribhuvandas' book, Ma-ne Shikhaman — Advice to a mother — and I nursed both my children according to the instructions given in the book, tempered here and there by experiences as I had gained elsewhere. The services of a nurse were utilized — not for more than two months each time — chiefly for helping my wife, and not for taking care of the babies, which I did myself.

The birth of the last child put me to the severest test. The travail came on suddenly. The doctor was not immediately available, and some time was lost in fetching the midwife. Even if she had been on the spot, she could not have helped delivery. I had to see through the safe delivery of the baby. My careful study of the subject in Dr. Tribhuvandas' work was of inestimable help. I was not nervous.

I am convinced that for the proper upbringing of children the parents ought to have a general knowledge of the care and nursing of babies. At every step I have seen the advantages of my careful study of the subject. My children would not have enjoyed the general health that they do today, had I not studied the subject and turned my knowledge to account. We labour under a sort of superstition that a child has nothing to learn during the first five years of its life. On the contrary the fact is that the child never learns in after life what it does in its first five years. The education of the child begins with conception. The physical and mental states of the parents at the moment of conception are reproduced in the baby. Then during the period of pregnancy it continues to be affected by the mother's moods, desires and temperament, as also by her ways of life. After birth the child imitates the parents, and for a considerable number of years entirely depends on them for its growth.

The couple who realize these things will never have sexual union for the fulfillment of their lust, but only when they desire issue. I think it is the height of ignorance to believe that the sexual act is an independent function necessary like sleeping or eating. The world depends for its existence on the act of generation, and as the world is the play-ground of God and a reflection of His glory, the act of generation should be controlled for the ordered growth of the world. He who realizes this will control his lust at any cost, equip himself with the knowledge necessary for the physical, mental and spiritual well-being of his progeny, and give the benefit of that knowledge to posterity.

Chapter 7 : Brahmacharya — I

We now reach the stage in this story when I began seriously to think of taking the brahmacharya vow. I had been wedded to a monogamous ideal ever since my marriage, faithfulness to my wife being part of the love of truth. But it was in South Africa that I came to realize the importance of observing brahmacharya even with respect to my wife. I cannot definitely say what circumstance or what book it was, that set my thoughts in that direction, but I have a recollection that the predominant factor was the influence of Raychandbhai, of whom I have already written, I can still recall a conversation that I had with him. On one occasion I spoke to him in high praise of Mrs. Gladstone's devotion to her husband. I had read some where that Mrs. Gladstone insisted on preparing tea for Mr. Gladstone even in the House of Commons, and that this had become a rule in the life of this illustrious couple, whose actions were governed by regularity. I spoke of this to the poet, and incidentally eulogized conjugal love. 'Which of the two do you prize more,' asked Raychandbhai, 'the love of Mrs. Gladstone for her husband as his wife, or her devoted service irrespective of her relation to Mr. Gladstone? Supposing she had been his sister, or his devoted servant, and ministered to him with the same attention, what would you have said? Do we not have instances of such devoted sisters or servants? Supposing you had found the same loving devotion in a male servant, would you have been pleased in the same way as in Mrs. Gladstone's case? Just examine the view-point suggested by me.'

Raychandbhai was himself married. I have an impression that at the moment his words sounded harsh, but they gripped me irresistibly. The devotion of a servant was, I felt, a thousand times more praiseworthy than that of a wife to her husband. There was nothing surprising in the wife's devotion to her husband, as there was an indissoluble bond between them. The devotion was perfectly natural. But it required a special effort to cultivate equal devotion between master and servant. The poet's point of view began gradually to grow upon me.

What then, I asked myself, should be my relation with my wife? Did my faithfulness consist in making my wife the instrument of my lust? So long as I was the slave of lust, my faithfulness was worth nothing. To be fair to my wife, I must say that she was never the temptress. It was therefore the easiest thing for me to take the vow of brahmacharya, if only I willed it. It was my weak will or lustful attachment that was the obstacle.

Even after my conscience had been roused in the matter, I failed twice. I failed because the motive that actuated the effort was none the highest. My main object was to escape having more children. Whilst in England I had read something about contraceptives. I have already referred to Dr. Allinson's birth control propaganda in the chapter on Vegetarianism. If it had some temporary effect on me, Mr. Hill's opposition to those methods and his advocacy of internal efforts as opposed to outward means, in a word, of self-control, had a far greater effect, which in due time came to be abiding. Seeing, therefore, that I did not desire more children I began to strive after self-control. There was endless difficulty in the task. We began to sleep in separate beds. I decided to retire to bed only after the day's work had left me completely exhausted. All these efforts did not seem to bear much fruit, but when I look back upon the past, I feel that the final resolution was the cumulative effect of those unsuccessful strivings.

The final resolution could only be made as late as 1906. Satyagraha had not then been started. I had not the least notion of its coming. I was practising in Johannesburg at the time of the Zulu 'Rebellion' in Natal, which came soon after the Boer War. I felt that I must offer my services to the Natal Government on that occasion. The offer was accepted, as we shall see in another chapter. But the work set me furiously thinking in the direction of self-control, and according to my wont I discussed my thoughts with my co-workers. It became my conviction that procreation and the consequent care of children were inconsistent with public service. I had to break up my household at Johannesburg to be able to serve during the 'Rebellion'. Within one month of offering my services, I had to give up the house I had so carefully furnished. I took my wife and children to Phoenix and led the Indian ambulance corps attached to the Natal forces. During the difficult marches that had then to be performed, the idea flashed upon me that, if I wanted to devote myself to the service of the community in this manner I must relinquish the desire for children and wealth and live the life of a vanaprastha — of one retired from household cares.

The 'Rebellion' did not occupy me for more than six weeks, but this brief period proved to be a very important epoch in my life. The importance of vows grew upon me more clearly than ever before. I realized that a vow, far from closing the door to real freedom, opened it. Up to this time I had not met with success because the will had been lacking, because I had had no faith in myself, no faith in the grace of God, and therefore my mind had been tossed on the boisterous sea of doubt. I realized that in refusing to take a vow man was drawn into temptation, and that to be bound by a vow was like a passage from libertinism to a real monogamous marriage. 'I believe in effort, I do not want to bind myself with vows' is the mentality of weakness and betrays a subtle desire for the thing to be avoided. Or where can be the difficulty in making a final decision? I vow to flee from the serpent which I know will bite me, I do not simply make an effort to flee from him. I know that mere effort may mean certain death. Mere effort means ignorance of the certain fact that the serpent is bound to kill me. The fact, therefore, that I could rest content with an effort only means that I have not yet clearly realized the necessity of definite action.

'But supposing my views are changed in the future, how can I bind myself by a vow?' Such a doubt often deters us. But that doubt also betrays a lack of clear perception that a particular thing must be renounced. That is why Nishkulanand has sung:

'Renunciation without aversion is not lasting.'
Where therefore the desire is gone, a vow of renunciation is the natural and inevitable fruit.

Chapter 8: Brahmacharya — II

After full discussion and mature deliberation I took the vow in 1906. I had not shared my thoughts with my wife until then, but only consulted her at the time of taking the vow. She had no objection. But I had great difficulty in making the final resolve. I had not the necessary strength. How was I to control my passions? The elimination of carnal relationship with one's wife seemed then a strange thing. But I launched forth with faith in the sustaining power of God.

As I look back upon the twenty years of the vow, I am filled with pleasure and wonderment. The more or less successful practice of self-control had been going on since 1901. But the freedom and joy that came to me after taking the vow had never been experienced before 1906. Before the vow I had been open to being overcome by temptation at any moment. Now the vow was a sure shield against temptation. The great potentiality of brahmacharya daily became more an more patent to me. The vow was taken when I was in Phoenix. As soon as I was free from ambulance work, I went to Phoenix, whence I had to return to Johannesburg. In about a month of my returning there, the foundation of Satyagraha was laid. As though unknown to me, the brahmacharya vow had been preparing me for it. Satyagraha had not been a preconceived plan. It came on spontaneously, without my having willed it. But I could see that all my previous steps had led up to that goal. I had cut down my heavy household expenses at Johannesburg and gone to Phoenix to take, as it were, the brahmacharya vow.

The knowledge that a perfect observance of brahmacharya means realization of brahman, I did not owe to a study of the Shastras. It slowly grew upon me with experience. The shastric texts on the subject I read only later in life. Every day of the vow has taken me nearer the knowledge that in brahmacharya lies the protection of the body, the mind and the soul.

For brahmacharya was now no process of hard penance, it was a matter of consolation and joy. Every day revealed a fresh beauty in it.

But if it was a matter of ever-increasing joy, let no one believe that it was an easy thing for me. Even when I am past fifty-six years, I realize how hard a thing it is. Every day I realize more and more that it is like walking on the sword's edge, and I see every moment the necessity for eternal vigilance.

Control of the palate is the first essential in the observance of the vow. I found that complete control of the palate made the observance very easy, and so I now pursued my dietetic experiments not merely from the vegetarian's but also from the brahmachari's point of view. As the result of these experiments I saw that thebrahmachari's food should be limited, simple, spiceless, and, if possible, uncooked.

Six years of experiment have showed me that the brahmachari's ideal food is fresh fruit and nuts. The immunity from passion that I enjoyed when I lived on this food was unknown to me after I changed that diet. Brahmacharya needed no effort on my part in South Africa when I lived on fruits and nuts alone. It has been a matter of very great effort ever since I began to take milk. How I had to go back to milk from a fruit diet will be considered in its proper place. It is enough to observe here that I have not the least doubt that milk diet makes the brahmacharya vow difficult to observe. Let no one deduce from this that all brahmacharis must give up milk. The effect onbrahmacharya of different kinds of food can be determined only after numerous experiments. I have yet to find a fruit-substitute for milk which is an equally good muscle-builder and easily digestible. The doctors, vaidyas and hakims have alike failed to enlighten me. Therefore, though I know milk to be partly a stimulant, I cannot, for the time being, advise anyone to give it up.

As an external aid to brahmacharya, fasting is as necessary as selection and restriction in diet. So overpowering are the senses that they can be kept under control only when they are completely hedged in on all sides, from above and from beneath. It is common knowledge that they are powerless without food, and so fasting undertaken with a view to control of the senses is, I have no doubt, very helpful. With some, fasting is of no avail, because assuming that mechanical fasting alone will make them immune, they keep their bodies without food, but feast their minds upon all sorts of delicacies, thinking all the while what they will eat and what they will drink after the fast terminates. Such fasting helps them in controlling neither palate nor lust. Fasting is useful, when mind co-operates with starving body, that is to say, when it cultivates a distaste for the objects that are denied to the body. Mind is at the root of all sensuality. Fasting, therefore, has a limited use, for a fasting man may continue to be swayed by passion. But it may be said that extinction of the sexual passion is as a rule impossible without fasting, which may be said to be indispensable for the observance of brahmacharya. Many aspirants after brahmacharya fail because in the use of their other senses they want to carry on like those who are not brahmacharis. Their effort is, therefore, identical with the effort to experience the bracing cold of winter in the scorching summer months. There should be a clear line between the life of a brahmachari and of one who is not. The resemblance that there is between the two is only apparent. The distinction ought to be clear as daylight. Both use their eyesight, but whereas the brahmachari uses it to see the glories of God, the other uses it to see the frivolity around him. Both use their ears, but whereas the one hears nothing but praises of God, the other feasts his ears upon ribaldry. Both often keep late hours, but whereas the one devotes them to prayer, the other fritters them away in wild and wasteful mirth. Both feed the inner man, but the one only to keep the temple of God in good repair, while the other gorges himself and makes the sacred vessel a stinking gutter. Thus both live as the poles apart, and the distance between them will grow and not diminish with the passage of time.

Brahmacharya means control of the senses in thought, word and deed. Every day I have been realizing more and more the necessity for restraints of the kind I have detailed above. There is no limit to the possibilities of renunciation, even as there is none to those of brahmacharya. Such brahmacharya is impossible of attainment by limited effort. For many it must remain only as an ideal. An aspirant after brahmacharya will always be conscious of his shortcomings, will seek out the passions lingering in the innermost recesses of his heart and will incessantly strive to get rid of them. So long as thought is not under complete control of the will, brahmacharya in its fullness is absent.

Involuntary thought is an affection of the mind, and curbing of thought, therefore, means curbing of the mind which is even more difficult to curb than the wind. Nevertheless the existence of God within makes even control of the mind possible. Let no one think that it is impossible because it is difficult. It is the highest goal, and it is no wonder that the highest effort should be necessary to attain it.

But it was after coming to India that I realized that such brahmacharya was impossible to attain by mere human effort. Until then I had been labouring under the delusion that fruit diet alone would enable me to eradicate all passions, and I had flattered myself with the belief that I had nothing more to do.

But I must not anticipate the chapter of my struggles. Meanwhile let me make it clear that those who desire to observe brahmacharya with a view to realizing God need not despair, provided their faith in God is equal to their confidence in their own effort. 'The sense-objects turn away from an abstemious soul, leaving the relish behind. The relish also disappears with the realization of the Highest.'* Therefore His name and His grace are the last resources of the aspirant after moksha. This truth came to me only after my return to India.

Chapter 9: Simple life

I had started on a life of ease and comfort, but the experiment was short-lived. Although I had furnished the house with care, yet it failed to have any hold on me. So no sooner had I launched forth on that life, than I began to cut down expenses. The washerman's bill was heavy, and as he was besides by no means noted for his punctuality, even two to three dozen shirts and collars proved insufficient for me. Collars had to be changed daily and shirts, if not daily, at least every alternate day. This meant a double expense, which appeared to me unnecessary. So I equipped myself with a washing outfit to save it. I bought a book on washing, studied the art and taught it also to my wife. This no doubt added to my work, but its novelty made it a pleasure.

I shall never forget the first collar that I washed myself. I had used more starch than necessary, the iron had not been made hot enough, and for fear of burning the collar I had not pressed it sufficiently. The result was that, though the collar was fairly stiff, the superfluous starch continually dropped off it. I went to court with the collar on, thus inviting the ridicule of brother barristers, but even in those days I could be impervious to ridicule.

'Well,' said I, 'this is my first experiment at washing my own collars and hence the loose starch. But it does not trouble me, and then there is the advantage of providing

---

* The Bhagavad Gita, 2-59.

you with so much fun.'

'But surely there is no lack of laundries here?' asked a friend.

'The laundry bill is very heavy,' said I. 'The charge for washing a collar is almost as much as its price, and even then there is the eternal dependence on the washerman. I prefer by far to wash my things myself.'

But I could not make my friends appreciate the beauty of self-help. In course of time I became an expert washerman so far as my own work went, and my washing was by no means inferior to laundry washing. My collars were no less stiff or shiny than others.

When Gokhale came to South Africa, he had with him a scarf which was a gift from Mahadeo Govind Ranade. He treasured the memento with the utmost care and used it only on special occasions. One such occasion was the banquet given in his honour by the Johannesburg Indians. The scarf was creased and needed ironing. It was not possible to send it to the laundry and get it back in time. I offered to try my art.

'I can trust to your capacity as a lawyer, but not as a washerman,' said Gokhale; 'What if you should soil it? Do you know what it means to me?'

With this he narrated, with much joy, the story of the gift. I still insisted, guaranteed good work, got his permission to iron it, and won his certificate.

After that I did not mind if the rest of the world refused me its certificate.

In the same way, as I freed myself from slavery to the washerman, I threw off dependence on the barber. All people who go to England learn there at least the art of shaving, but none, to my knowledge, learn to cut their own hair. I had to learn that too. I once went to an English hair-cutter in Pretoria. He contemptuously refused to cut my hair. I certainly felt hurt, but immediately purchased a pair of clippers and cut my hair before the mirror. I succeeded more or less in cutting the front hair, but I spoiled the back. The friends in the court shook with laughter.

'What's wrong with your hair, Gandhi? Rats have been at it?'

'No. The white barber would not condescend to touch my black hair,' said I, 'so I preferred to cut it myself, no matter how badly.'

The reply did not surprise the friends.

The barber was not at fault in having refused to cut my hair. There was every chance of his losing his custom, if he should serve black men. We do not allow our barbers to serve our untouchable brethren. I got the reward of this in South Africa, not once, but many times, and the conviction that it was the punishment for our own sins saved me from becoming angry.

The extreme forms in which my passion for self-help and simplicity ultimately expressed itself will be described in their proper place. The seed had been long sown. It only needed watering to take root, to flower and to fructify, and the watering came in due course.

Chapter 10: The Boer War

I must skip many other experiences of the period between 1897 and 1899 and come straight to the Boer War.

When the war was declared, my personal sympathies were all with the Boers, but I believed then that I had yet no right, in such cases, to enforce my individual convictions. I have minutely dealt with the inner struggle regarding this in my history of the Satyagraha in South Africa, and I must not repeat the argument here. I invite the curious to turn to those pages. Suffice it to say that my loyalty to the British rule drove me to participation with the British in that war. I felt that, if I demanded rights as a British citizen, it was also my duty, as such, to participate in the defence of the British Empire. I held then that India could achieve her complete emancipation only within and through the British Empire. So I collected together as many comrades as possible, and with very great difficulty got their services accepted as an ambulance corps.

The average Englishman believed that the Indian was a coward, incapable of taking risks or looking beyond his immediate self-interest. Many English friends, therefore, threw cold water on my plan. But Dr. Booth supported it whole-heartedly. He trained us in ambulance work. We secured medical certificates of fitness for service. Mr. Laughton and the late Mr. Escombe enthusiastically supported the plan, and we applied at last for service at the front. The Government thankfully acknowledged our application, but said that our services were not then needed.

I would not rest satisfied, however, with this refusal. Through the introduction of Dr. Booth, I called on the Bishop of Natal. There were many Christian Indians in our corps. The Bishop was delighted with my proposal and promised to help us in getting our services accepted.

Time too was working with us. The Boer had shown more pluck, determination and bravery than had been expected; and our services were ultimately needed.

Our corps was 1,100 strong, with nearly 40 leaders, About three hundred were free Indians, and the rest indentured. Dr. Booth was also with us. The corps acquitted itself well. Though our work was to be outside the firing line, and though we had the protection of the Red Cross, we were asked at a critical moment to serve within the firing line. The reservation had not been of our seeking. The authorities did not want us to be within the range of fire. The situation, however, was changed after the repulse at Spion Kop, and General Buller sent the message that, though we were not bound to take the risk, Government would be thankful if we would do so and fetch the wounded from the field. We had no hesitation, and so the action at Spion Kop found us working within the firing line. During these days we had to march from twenty to twenty-five miles a day, bearing the wounded on stretchers. Amongst the wounded we had the honour of carrying soldiers like General Woodgate.

The corps was disbanded after six weeks' service. After the reverses at Spion Kop and Vaalkranz, the British Commander-in-Chief abandoned the attempt to relieve Ladysmith and other places by summary procedure, and decided to proceed slowly, awaiting reinforcements from England and India.

Our humble work was at the moment much applauded, and the Indians' prestige was enhanced. The newspapers published laudatory rhymes with the refrain, 'We are sons of Empire after all.'

General Buller mentioned with appreciation the work of the corps in his despatch, and the leaders were awarded the War Medal.

The Indian community became better organized. I got into closer touch with the indentured Indians. There came a greater awakening amongst them, and the feeling that Hindus, Musalmans, Christians, Tamilians, Gujaratis and Sindhis were all Indians and children of the same motherland took deep root amongst them. Everyone believed that the Indians' grievances were now sure to be redressed. At the moment the white man's attitude seemed to be distinctly changed. The relations formed with the whites during the war were of the sweetest. We had come in contact with thousands of tommies. They were friendly with us and thankful for being there to serve them.

I cannot forbear from recording a sweet reminiscence of how human nature shows itself at its best in moments of trial. We were marching towards Chievely Camp where Lieutenant Roberts, the son of Lord Roberts, had received a mortal wound. Our corps had the honour of carrying the body from the field. It was a sultry day — the day of our march. Everyone was thirsting for water. There was a tiny brook on the way where we could slake our thirst. But who was to drink first? We had proposed to come in after the tommies had finished. But they would not begin first and urged us to do so, and for a while a pleasant competition went on for giving precedence to one another.

Chapter 11 : Sanitary reform and famine relief

It has always been impossible for me to reconcile myself to any one member of the body politic remaining out of use. I have always been loath to hide or connive at the weak points of the community or to press for its rights without having purged it of its blemishes. Therefore, ever since my settlement in Natal, I had been endeavouring to clear the community of a charge that had been leveled against it, not without a certain amount of truth. The charge had often been made that the Indian was slovenly in his habits and did not keep his house and surroundings clean. The principal men of the community had, therefore, already begun to put their houses in order, but house-to-house inspection was undertaken only when plague was reported to be imminent in Durban. This was done after consulting, and gaining the approval of, the city fathers, who had desired our co-operation. Our co-operation made work easier for them and at the same time lessened our hardships. For whenever there is an outbreak of epidemics, the executive, as a general rule, get impatient, take excessive measures and behave to such as may have incurred their displeasure with a heavy hand. The community saved itself from this oppression by voluntarily taking sanitary measures.

But I had some bitter experiences. I saw that I could not so easily count on the help of the community in getting it to do its own duty, as I could in claiming for it rights. At some places I met with insults, at others with polite indifference. It was too much for people to bestir themselves to keep their surroundings clean. To expect them to find money for the work was out of the question. These experiences taught me, better than ever before, that without infinite patience it was impossible to get the people to do any work. It is the reformer who is anxious for the reform, and not society, from which he should expect nothing better than opposition, abhorrence and even mortal persecution. Why may not society regard as retrogression what the reformer holds dear as life itself?

Nevertheless the result of this agitation was that the Indian community learnt to recognize more or less the necessity for keeping their houses and environments clean. I gained the esteem of the authorities. They saw that, though I had made it my business to ventilate grievances and press for rights, I was no less keen and insistent upon self-purification.

There was one thing, however, which still remained to be done, namely, the awakening in the Indian settler of a sense of duty to the motherland. India was poor, the Indian settler went to South Africa in search of wealth, and he was bound to contribute part of his earnings for the benefit of his countrymen in the hour of their adversity. This the settler did during the terrible famines of 1897 and 1899. They contributed handsomely for famine relief, and more so in

1899 than in 1897. We had appealed to Englishmen also for funds, and they had responded well. Even the indentured Indians gave their share to the contribution, and the system inaugurated at the time of these famines has been continued ever since, and we know that Indians in South Africa never fail to send handsome contributions to India in times of national calamity.

Thus service of the Indians in South Africa ever revealed to me new implications of Truth at every stage. Truth is like a vast tree, which yields more and more fruit, the more you nurture it. The deeper the search in the mine of Truth, the richer the discovery of the gems buried there, in the shape of openings for an ever greater variety of service.

Chapter 12: Return to India

On my relief from war-duty I felt that my work was no longer in South Africa but in India. Not that there was nothing to be done in South Africa, but I was afraid that my main business might become merely money-making.

Friends at home were also pressing me to return, and I felt that I should be of more service in India. And for the work in South Africa, there were, of course, Messrs Khan and Mansukhlal Naazar. So I requested my co-workers to relieve me. After very great difficulty my request was conditionally accepted, the condition being that I should be ready to go back to South Africa if, within a year, the community should need me. I thought it was a difficult condition but the love that bound me to the community made me accept it.

The Lord has bound me With the cotton-thread of love, I am His bondslave, sang Mirabai. And for me, too, the cotton-thread of love that bound me to the community was too strong to break. The voice of the people is the voice of God, and here the voice of friends was too real to be rejected. I accepted the condition and got their permission to go.

At this time I was intimately connected only with Natal. The Natal Indians bathed me with the nectar of love. Farewell meetings were arranged at every place, and costly gifts were presented to me.

Gifts had been bestowed on me before when I returned to India in 1899, but this time the farewell was overwhelming. The gifts of course included things in gold and silver, but there were articles of costly diamond as well.

What right had I to accept all these gifts? Accepting them, how could I persuade myself that I was serving the community without remuneration? All the gifts, excepting a few from my clients, were purely for my service to the community, and I could make no difference between my clients and co-workers; for the clients also helped me in my public work.

One of the gifts was a gold necklace worth fifty guineas, meant for my wife. But even that gift was given because of my public work, and so it could not be separated from the rest.

The evening I was presented with the bulk of these things I had a sleepless night. I walked up and down my room deeply agitated, but could find no solution. It was difficult for me to forego gifts worth hundreds, it was more difficult to keep them.

And even if I could keep them, what about my children? What about my wife? They were being trained to a life of service and to an understanding that service was its own reward.

I had no costly ornaments in the house. We had been fast simplifying our life How then could we afford to have gold watches? How could we afford to wear gold chains and diamond rings? Even then I was exhorting people to conquer the infatuation for jewellery. What was I now to do with the jewellery that had come upon me?

I decided that I could not keep these things. I drafted a letter, creating a trust of them in favour of the community and appointing Parsi Rustomji and other trustees. In the morning I held a consultation with my wife and children and finally go rid of the heavy incubus.

I knew that I should have some difficulty in persuading my wife, and I was sure that I should have none so far as the children were concerned. So I decided to constitute them my attorneys.

The children readily agreed to my proposal. 'We do not need these costly presents, we must return them to the community, and should we ever need them, we could easily purchase them,' they said. I was delighted. 'Then you will plead with mother won't you?' I asked them.

'Certainly', said they. 'That is our business. She does not need to wear the ornaments. She would want to keep them for us, and if we don't want them, why should she not agree to part with them?'

But it was easier said than done.

'You may not need them', said my wife. 'Your children may not need them. Cajoled, they will dance to your tune. I can understand your not permitting me to wear them. But what about my daughters-in-law? They will be sure to need them. And who knows what will happen tomorrow? I would be the last person to part with gifts so lovingly given.'

And thus the torrent of argument went on, reinforced, in the end, by tears. But the children were adamant. And I was unmoved.

I mildly put in: 'The children have yet to get married. We do not want to see them married young. When they are grown up, they can take care of themselves. And surely we shall not have, for our sons, brides who are fond of ornaments. And if after all, we need to provide them with ornaments, I am there. You will ask me then.'

'Ask you? I know you by this time. You deprived me of my ornaments, you would not leave me in peace with them. Fancy you offering to get ornaments for the daughters-in-law! You who are trying to make sadhus of my boys from today! No, the ornaments will not be returned. And pray what right have you to my necklace?'

'But', I rejoined, 'is the necklace given you for your service or for my service?'

'I agree. But service rendered by you is as good as rendered by me. I have toiled and moiled for you day and night. Is that no service? You forced all and sundry on me, making me weep bitter tears, and I slaved for them!'

These were pointed thrusts, and some of them went home. But I was determined to return the ornaments. I somehow succeeded in extorting a consent from her. The gifts received in 1896 and 1901 were all returned. A trust-deed was prepared, and they were deposited with a bank, to be used for the service of the community, according to my wishes or to those of the trustees.

Often, when I was in need of funds for public purposes, and felt that I must draw upon the trust, I have been able to raise the requisite amount, leaving the trust money intact.

The fund is still there, being operated upon in times of need, and it has regularly accumulated.

I have never since regretted the step, and as the years have gone by, my wife has also seen its wisdom. It has saved us from many temptations.

I am definitely of opinion that a public worker should accept no costly gifts.

Chapter 13: In India again

So I sailed for home. Mauritius was one of the ports of call, and as the boat made a long halt there, I went ashore and acquainted myself fairly well with the local conditions. For one night I was the guest of Sir Charles Bruce, the Governor of the Colony.

After reaching India I spent some time in going about the country. It was the year 1901 when the Congress met at Calcutta under the presidentship of Mr. (later Sir) Dinshaw Wacha. And I of course attended it. It was my first experience of the Congress.

From Bombay I traveled in the same train as Sir Pherozeshah Mehta, as I had to speak to him about conditions in South Africa. I knew the kingly style in which he lived. He had engaged a special saloon for himself, and I had orders to take my opportunity of speaking to him by traveling in his saloon for one stage. I, therefore, went to the saloon and reported myself at the appointed station. With him were Mr. Wacha, and Mr. (now Sir) Chimanlal Setalvad. They were discussing politics. As soon as Sir Pherozeshah saw me, he said, 'Gandhi, it seems nothing can be done for you. Of course we will pass the resolution you want. But what rights have we in our own country? I believe that, so long as we have no power in our own land, you cannot fare better in the colonies.'

I was taken aback. Mr. Setalvad seemed to concur in the view; Mr. Wacha cast a pathetic look at me.

I tried to plead with Sir Pherozeshah, but it was out of the question for one like me to prevail upon the uncrowned king of Bombay. I contented myself with the fact that I should be allowed to move my resolution.

'You will of course show me the resolution,' said Mr. Wacha, to cheer me up. I thanked him and left them at the next stop.

So we reached Calcutta. The President was taken to his camp with great éclat by the Reception Committee. I asked a volunteer where I was to go. He took me to the Ripon College, where a number of delegates were being put up. Fortune favoured me. Lokamanya was put up in the same block as I. I have a recollection that he came a day later.

And as was natural, Lokamanya would never be without his darbar. Were I a painter, I could paint him as I saw him seated on his bed — so vivid is the whole scene in my memory. Of the numberless people that called on him, I can recollect today only one, namely, the late Babu Motilal Ghose, editor of the Amrita Bazar Patrika. Their loud laughter and their talks about the wrong-doings of the ruling race cannot be forgotten.

But I propose to examine in some detail the appointments in this camp. The volunteers were clashing against one another. You asked one of them to do something. He delegated it to another, and he in his turn to a third, and so on; and as for the delegates, they were neither here nor there.

I made friends with a few volunteers. I told them some things about South Africa, and they felt somewhat ashamed. I tried to bring home to them the secret of service. They seemed to understand, but service is no mushroom growth. It presupposes the will first, and then experience. There was no lack of will on the part of those good simple-hearted young men, but their experience was nil. The Congress would meet three days every year and then go to sleep. What training could one have out of a three days' show once a year? And the delegates were of a piece with the volunteers. They had no better or longer training. They would do nothing themselves. 'Volunteer, do this', 'Volunteer, do that', were their constant orders.

Even here I was face to face with untouchability in a fair measure. The Tamilian kitchen was far away from the rest. To the Tamil delegates even the sight of others, whilst they were dining, meant pollution. So a special kitchen had to be made for them in the college compound, walled in by wicker-work. It was full of smoke which choked you. It was a kitchen, dining room, washroom, all in one — a close safe with no outlet. To me this looked like a travesty of Varnadharma.* If, I said to myself, there was such untouchability between the delegates of the Congress, one could well imagine the extent to which it existed amongst their constituents. I heaved a sigh at the thought.

There was no limit to insanitation. Pools of water were everywhere. There were only a few latrines, and the recollection of their stink still oppresses me. I pointed it out to the volunteers. They said pointblank: 'That is not our work, it is the scavenger's work.' I asked for a broom. The man stared at me in wonder. I procured one and cleaned the latrine. But that was for myself. The rush was so great, and the latrines were so few, that they needed frequent cleaning; but that was more than I could do. So I had to content myself with simply ministering to myself. And the others did not seem to mind the stench and the dirt.

But that was not all. Some of the delegates did not scruple to use the verandahs outside their rooms for calls of nature at night. In the morning I pointed out the spots to the volunteers. No one was ready to undertake the cleaning, and I found no one to share the honour with me of doing it. Conditions have since considerably improved, but even today thoughtless delegates are not wanting who disfigure the Congress camp by committing nuisances wherever they choose, and all the volunteers are not always ready to clean up after them.

---

* Duties of the four fundamental divisions of Hindu society.

I saw that, if the Congress session were to be prolonged, conditions would be quite favourable for the outbreak of an epidemic.

Chapter 14: Clerk and bearer

There were yet two days for the Congress session to begin. I had made up my mind to offer my services to the Congress office in order to gain some experience. So as soon as I had finished the daily ablutions on arrival at Calcutta, I proceeded to the Congress office.

Babu Bhupendranath Basu and Sjt. Ghosal were the secretaries. I went to Bhupenbabu and offered my services. He looked at me, and said: 'I have no work, but possibly Ghosalbabu might have something to give you. Please go to him.'

So I went to him. He scanned me and said with a smile: 'I can give you only clerical work. Will you do it?'

'Certainly', said I. 'I am here to do anything that is not beyond my capacity.'

'That is the right spirit, young man', he said. Addressing the volunteers who surrounded him, he added, 'Do you hear what this young man says?'

Then turning to me he proceeded: 'Well then, here is a heap of letters for disposal. Take that chair and begin. As you see, hundreds of people come to see me. What am I to do? Am I to meet them, or am I to answer these busybodies inundating me with letters? I have no clerks to whom I can entrust this work. Most of these letters have nothing in them, but you will please look them through. Acknowledge those that are worth it, and refer to me those that need a considered reply.'

I was delighted at the confidence reposed in me.

Sjt. Ghosal did not know me when he gave me the work. Only later did he enquire about my credentials.

I found my work very easy — the disposal of that heap of correspondence. I had done with it in no time, and Sjt. Ghosal was very glad. He was talkative. He would talk away for hours together. When he learnt something from me about my history, he felt rather sorry to have given me clerical work. But I reassured him: 'Please don't worry. What am I before you? You have grown gray in the service of the Congress, and are as an elder to me. I am but an inexperienced youth. You have put me under a debt of obligation by entrusting me with this work. For I want to do Congress work, and you have given me the rare opportunity of understanding the details.'

'To tell you the truth,' said Sjt. Ghosal, 'that is the proper spirit. But young men of to-day do not realize it. Of course I have known the Congress since its birth. In fact I may claim a certain share with Mr. Hume in bringing the Congress into being.'

And thus we became good friends. He insisted on my having lunch with him.

Sjt. Ghosal used to get his shirt buttoned by his bearer. I volunteered to do the bearer's duty, and I loved to do it, as my regard for elders was always great. When he came to know this, he did not mind my doing little acts of personal service for him. In fact he was delighted. Asking me to button his shirt, he would say, 'You see, now, the Congress secretary has no time even to button his shirt. He has always some work to do.' Sjt. Ghosal's naiveté amused me, but did not create any dislike in me for service of that nature. The benefit I received from this service in incalculable.

In a few days I came to know the working of the Congress. I met most of the leaders, I observed the movements of stalwarts like Gokhale and Surendranath. I also noticed the huge waste of time there. I observed too, with sorrow even then, the prominent place that the English language occupied in our affairs. There was little regard for economy of energy. More than one did the work of one, and many an important thing was no one's business at all.

Critical as my mind was in observing these things, there was enough charity in me, and so I always thought that it might, after all, be impossible to do better in the circumstances, and that saved me from undervaluing any work.

Chapter 15: In the Congress

In the Congress at last. The immense pavilion and the volunteers in stately array, as also the elders seated on the dais, overwhelmed me. I wondered where I should be in that vast assemblage.

The presidential address was a book by itself. To read it from cover to cover was out of the question. Only a few passages were therefore read.

After this came the election of the Subjects Committee. Gokhale took me to the Committee meetings.

Sir Pherozeshah had of course agreed to admit my resolution, but I was wondering who would put it before the Subjects Committee, and when. For there were lengthy speeches to every resolution, all in English to boot, and every resolution had some well-known leader to back it. Mine was but a feeble pipe amongst those veteran drums, and as the night was closing in, my heart beat fast. The resolutions coming at the fag-end were, so far as I can recollect, rushed through at lighting speed. Everyone was hurrying to go. It was eleven o'clock. I had not the courage to speak. I had already met Gokhale, who had looked at my resolution. So I drew near his chair and whispered to him: 'Please do something for me.' He said: 'Your resolution is not out of my mind. You see the way they are rushing through the resolutions. But I will not allow yours to be passed over.'

'So we have done?' said Sir Pherozeshah Mehta.

'No, no there is still the resolution on South Africa. Mr. Gandhi has been waiting long,' cried out Gokhale.

'Have you seen the resolution?' asked Sir Pherozeshah.

'Of course.'

'Do you like it?'

'It is quite good.'

'Well then, let us have it, Gandhi.' I read it trembling. Gokhale supported it.

'Unanimously passed,' cried out everyone.

'You will have five minutes to speak on it, Gandhi,' said Mr. Wacha.

The procedure was far from pleasing to me. No one had troubled to understand the resolution, everyone was in a hurry to go and, because Gokhale had seen the resolution, it was not thought necessary for the rest to see it or understand it!

The morning found me worrying about my speech. What was I to say in five minutes? I had prepared myself fairly well, but the words would not come to me. I had decided not to read my speech but to speak ex tempore. But the faculty for speaking that I had acquired in South Africa seemed to have left me for the moment.

As soon as it was time for my resolution, Mr. Wacha called out my name. I stood up. My head was reeling. I read the resolution somehow. Someone had printed and distributed amongst the delegates copies of a poem he had written in praise of foreign emigration. I read the poem and referred to the grievances of the settlers in South Africa. Just at this moment Mr. Wacha rang the bell. I was sure I had not yet spoken for five minutes. I did not know that the bell was rung in order to warn me to finish in two minutes more. I had heard others speak for half an hour or three quarters of an hour, and yet no bell was rung for them. I felt hurt and sat down as soon as the bell was rung. But my child-like intellect thought then that the poem contained an answer to Sir Pherozeshah.* There was no question about the passing of the resolution. In those days there was hardly any difference between visitors and delegates. Everyone raised his hand and all resolutions passed unanimously. My resolution also fared in this wise and so lost all its importance for me. And yet the very fact that it was passed by the Congress was enough to delight my heart. The knowledge that the imprimatur of the Congress meant that of the whole country was enough to delight anyone.

Chapter 16: Lord Curzon's Darbar

The Congress was over, but as I had to meet the Chamber of Commerce and various

---

* See Chapter 67, paragraph three.

people in connection with work in South Africa, I stayed in Calcutta for a month. Rather than stay this time in a hotel, I arranged to get the required introduction for a room in the India Club. Among its members were some prominent Indians, and I looked forward to getting into touch with them and interesting them in the work in South Africa. Gokhale frequently went to this Club to play billiards, and when he knew that I was to stay in Calcutta for some time, he invited me to stay with him. I thankfully accepted the invitation, but did not think it proper to go there by myself. He waited for a day or two and then took me personally. He discovered my reserve and said: 'Gandhi, you have to stay in the country, and this sort of reserve will not do. You must get into touch with as many people as possible. I want you to do Congress work.'

I shall record here an incident in the India Club, before I proceed to talk of my stay with Gokhale.

Lord Curzon held his darbar about this time. Some Rajas and Maharajas who had been invited to the darbar were members of the Club. In the Club I always found them wearing fine Bengali dhotis and shirts and scarves. On the darbar day they put on trousers befitting khansamas* and shining boots. I was pained and inquired of one of them the reason for the change.

'We alone know our unfortunate condition. We alone know the insults we have to put up with, in order that we may possess our wealth and titles,' he replied.

'But what about these khansama turbans and these shining boots?' I asked.

'Do you see any difference between khansamas and us?' he replied, and added, 'they are our khansamas, we are Lord Cruzon's khansamas. If I were to absent myself from the levée, I should have to suffer the consequences. If I were to attend it in my usual dress, it would be an offence. And do you think I am going to get any opportunity there of talking to Lord Curzon? Not a bit of it!'

I was moved to pity for this plain-spoken friend.

This reminds me of another darbar.

At the time when Lord Hardinge laid the foundation-stone of the Hindu University, there was a darbar. There were Rajas and Maharajas of course, but Pandit Malaviyaji specially invited me also to attend it, and I did so.

I was distressed to see the Maharajas bedecked like women — silk pyjamas and silk achkans, pearl necklaces round their necks, bracelets on their wrists, pearl and diamond tassels on their turbans and, besides all this, swords with golden hilts hanging from their waist-bands.

I discovered that these were insignia not of their royalty, but of their slavery. I had thought that they must be wearing these badges of impotence of their own free will, but I was told that it was obligatory for these Rajas to wear all their costly jewels at such functions. I also gathered that some of them had a positive dislike for wearing these jewels,

---

* Waiters

and that they never wore them except on occasions like the darbar.

I do not know how far my information was correct. But whether they wear them on other occasions or not, it is distressing enough to have to attend viceregal darbars in jewels that only some women wear.

How heavy is the toll of sins and wrongs that wealth, power and prestige exact from man!

Chapter 17: A month with Gokhale—I

From the very first day of my stay with him Gokhale made me feel completely at home. He treated me as though I were his younger brother; he acquainted himself with all my requirements and arranged to see that I got all I needed. Fortunately my wants were few, and as I had cultivated the habit of self-help, I needed very little personal attendance. He was deeply impressed with my habit of fending for myself, my personal cleanliness, perseverance and regularity, and would often overwhelm me with praise.

He seemed to keep nothing private from me. He would introduce me to all the important people that called on him. Of these the one who stands foremost in my memory is Dr. (now Sir) P. C. Ray. He lived practically next door and was a very frequent visitor.

This is how he introduced Dr. Ray: 'This is Professor Ray, who, having a monthly salary of Rs. 800, keeps just Rs. 40 for himself and devotes the balance to public purposes. He is not, and does not want to get, married.'

I see little difference between Dr. Ray as he is today and as he used to be then. His dress used to be nearly as simple as it is, with this difference of course, that whereas it is Khadi now, it used to be Indian mill-cloth in those days. I felt I could never hear too much of the talks between Gokhale and Dr. Ray, as they all pertained to public good or were of educative value. At times they were painful too, containing, as they did, strictures on public men. As a result, some of those whom I had regarded as stalwart fighters began to look quite puny.

To see Gokhale at work was as much a joy as an education. He never wasted a minute. His private relations and friendships were all for public good. All his talks had reference only to the good of the country and were absolutely free from any trace of untruth or insincerity. India's poverty and subjection were matters of constant and intense concern to him. Various people sought to interest him in different things. But he gave every one of them the same reply: 'You do the thing yourself. Let me do my own work. What I want is freedom for my country. After that is won, we can think of other things. Today that one thing is enough to engage all my time and energy.'

His reverence for Ranade could be seen every moment. Ranade's authority was final in every matter, and he would cite it at every step. The anniversary of Ranade's death (or birth,

I forget which) occurred during my stay with Gokhale, who observed it regularly. There were with him then, besides myself, his friends Professor Kathavate and a Sub-Judge. He invited us to take part in the celebration, and in his speech he gave us his reminiscences of Ranade. He compared incidentally Ranade, Telang and Mandlik. He eulogized Telang's charming style and Mandlik's greatness as a reformer. Citing an instance of Mandlik's solicitude for his clients, he told us an anecdote as to how once, having missed his usual train, he engaged a special train so as to be able to attend the court in the interest of his client. But Ranade, he said, towered above them all, as a versatile genius. He was not only a great judge, he was an equally great historian, economist and reformer. Although he was a judge, he fearlessly attended the Congress, and everyone had such confidence in his sagacity that they unquestioningly accepted his decisions. Gokhale's joy knew no bounds, as he described these qualities of head and heart which were all combined in his master.

Gokhale used to have a horse-carriage in those days. I did not know the circumstances that had made a horse-carriage a necessity for him, and so I remonstrated with him: 'Can't you make use of the tramcar in going about from place to place? Is it derogatory to a leader's dignity?'

Slightly pained he said, 'So you also have failed to understand me! I do not use my Council allowances for my own personal comforts. I envy your liberty to go about in tramcars, but I am sorry I cannot do likewise. When you are the victim of as wide a publicity as I am, it will be difficult, if not impossible, for you to go about in a tramcar. There is no reason to suppose that everything that the leaders do is with a view to personal comfort. I love your simple habits. I live as simply as I can, but some expense is almost inevitable for a man like myself.'

He thus satisfactorily disposed of one of my complaints, but there was another which he could not dispose of to my satisfaction.

'But you do not even go out for walks,' said I. 'Is it surprising that you should be always ailing? Should public work leave no time for physical exercise?'

'When do you ever find me free to go out for a walk?' he replied.

I had such a great regard for Gokhale that I never strove with him. Though this reply was far from satisfying me, I remained silent. I believed then, and I believe even now, that, no matter what amount of work one has, one should always find some time for exercise, just as one does for one's meals. It is my humble opinion that, far from taking away from one's capacity for work, it adds to it.

Chapter 18: A month with Gokhale—II

Whilst living under Gokhlae's roof I was far from being a stay-at-home.

I had told my Christian friends in South Africa that in India I would meet the Christian Indians and acquaint myself with their condition. I had heard of Babu Kalicharan Banerji and held him in high regard. He took a prominent part in the Congress, and I had none of the misgivings about him that I had about the average Christian Indian, who stood aloof from the Congress and isolated himself from Hindus and Musalmans. I told Gokhale that I was thinking of meeting him. He said: 'What is good of your seeing him? He is a very good man, but I am afraid he will not satisfy you. I know him very well. However, you can certainly meet him if you like?'

I sought an appointment, which he readily gave me. When I went, I found that his wife was on her death-bed. His house was simple. In the Congress I had seen him in a coat and trousers, but I was glad to find him now wearing a Bengal dhoti and shirt. I liked his simple mode of dress, though I myself then wore a Parsi coat and trousers. Without much ado I presented my difficulties to him. He asked: 'Do you believe in the doctrine of original sin?'

'I do,' said I.

'Well then, Hinduism offers no absolution therefrom, Christianity does;' and added: 'The wages of sin is death, and the Bible says that the only way of deliverance is surrender unto Jesus.'

I put forward Bhakti-marga (the path of devotion) of the Bhagavad Gita, but to no avail. I thanked him for his goodness. He failed to satisfy me, but I benefited by the interview.

During these days I walked up and down the streets of Calcutta. I went to most places on foot. I met Justice Mitter and Sir Gurdas Banerji, whose help I wanted in my work in South Africa. And about this time I met Raja Sir Pyarimohan Mukarji.

Kalicharan Banerji had spoken to me about the Kali temple, which I was eager to see, especially as I had read about it in books. So I went there one day. Justice Mitter's house was in the same locality, and I therefore went to the temple on the same day that I visited him. On the way I saw a stream of sheep going to be sacrificed to Kali. Rows of beggars lined the lane leading to the temple. There were religious mendicants too, and even in those days I was sternly opposed to giving alms to sturdy beggars. A crowd of them pursued me. One of such men was found seated on a verandah. He stopped me, and accosted me: 'Whither are you going, my boy?' I replied to him.

He asked my companion and me to sit down, which we did.

I asked him: 'Do you regard this sacrifice as religion?'

'Who would regard killing of animals as religion?'

'Then, why don't you preach against it?'

'That's not my business. Our business is to worship God.'

'But could you not find any other place in which to worship God?'

'All places are equally good for us. The people are like a flock of sheep, following where leaders lead them. It is no business of us sadhus.'

We did not prolong the discussion but passed on to the temple. We were greeted by rivers of blood. I could not bear to stand there. I was exasperated and restless. I have never forgotten that sight.

That very evening I had an invitation to dinner at a party of Bengali friends. There I spoke to a friend about this cruel form of worship. He said: 'The sheep don't feel anything. The noise and the drum-beating there deaden all sensation of pain.'

I could not swallow this. I told him that, if the sheep had speech, they would tell a different tale. I felt that the cruel custom ought to be stopped. I thought of the story of Buddha, but I also saw that the task was beyond my capacity.

I hold today the same opinion as I held then. To my mind the life of a lamb is no less precious than that of a human being. I should be unwilling to take the life of a lamb for the sake of the human body. I hold that, the more helpless a creature, the more entitled it is to protection by man from the cruelty of man. But he who has not qualified himself for such service is unable to afford to it any protection. I must go through more self-purification and sacrifice, before I can hope to save these lambs from this unholy sacrifice. It is my constant prayer that there may be born on earth some great spirit, man or woman, fired with divine pity, who will deliver us from this heinous sin, save the lives of the innocent creatures, and purify the temple. How is it that Bengal with all its knowledge, intelligence, sacrifice, and emotion tolerates this slaughter?

Chapter 19: A month with Gokhale — III

The terrible sacrifice offered to Kali in the name of religion enhanced my desire to know Bengali life. I had read and heard a good deal about the Brahmo Samaj. I knew something about the life of Pratap Chandra Mazumdar. I had attended some of the meetings addressed by him. I secured his life of Keshav Chandra Sen, read it with great interest, and understood the distinction between Sadharan Brahmo Samaj, and Adi Brahmo Samaj. I met Pandit Shivanath Shastri and in company with Professor Kathavate went to see Maharshi Devendranath Tagore; but as no interviews with him were allowed then, we could not see him. We were, however, invited to a celebration of the Brahmo Samaj held at his place, and there we had the privilege of listening to fine Bengali music. Ever since I have been a lover of Bengali music.

Having seen enough of the Brahmo Samaj, it was impossible to be satisfied without seeing Swami Vivekanand. So with great enthusiasm I went to Belur Math, mostly, or maybe all the way, on foot. I loved the sequestered site of the Math. I was disappointed and sorry to be told that the Swami was at his Calcutta house, lying ill, and could not be seen.

I then ascertained the place of residence of Sister Nivedita, and met her in a Chowringhee mansion. I was taken aback by the splendour that surrounded her, and even in our conversation there was not much meeting ground. I spoke to Gokhale about this, and he said he did not wonder that there could be no point of contact between me and a volatile* person like her.

I met her again at Mr. Pestonji Padshah's place. I happened to come in just as she was talking to his old mother, and so I became an interpreter between the two. In spite of my failure to find any agreement with her, I could not but notice and admire her overflowing love for Hinduism. I came to know of her books later.

I used to divide my day between seeing the leading people in Calcutta regarding the work in South Africa, and visiting and studying the religious and public institutions of the city. I once addressed a meeting, presided over by Dr. Mullick, on the work of the Indian Ambulance Corps in the Boer War. My acquaintance with The Englishmanstood me in good stead on this occasion too. Mr. Saunders was ill then, but rendered me as much help as in 1896. Gokhale liked this speech of mine, and he was very glad to hear Dr. Ray praising it.

Thus my stay under the roof of Gokhale made my work in Calcutta very easy, brought me into touch with the foremost Bengali families, and was the beginning of my intimate contact with Bengal.

I must needs skip over many a reminiscence of this memorable month. Let me simply mention my flying visit to Burma, and the foongis† there. I was pained by their lethargy. I saw the golden pagoda. I did not like the innumerable little candles burning in the temple, and the rats running about the sanctum brought to my mind thoughts of Swami Dayanand's experience at Morvi. The freedom and energy of the Burmese women charmed just as the indolence of the men pained me. I also saw, during my brief sojourn, that just as Bombay was not India, Rangoon was not Burma, and that just as we in India have become commission agents of English merchants, even so in Burma have we combined with the English merchants, in making the Burmese people our commission agents.

On my return from Burma I took leave of Gokhale. The separation was a wrench, but my work in Bengal, or rather Calcutta, was finished, and I had no occasion to stay any longer.

Before settling down I had thought of making a tour through India travelling third class, and acquainting myself with the hardships of third class passengers. I spoke to Gokhale about this. To begin with he ridiculed the idea, but when I explained to him what I hoped to see, he cheerfully approved. I planned to go first to Benares to pay my respects to Mrs. Besant, who was then ill.

It was necessary to equip myself anew for the third class tour. Gokhale himself gave me a metal tiffin-box and got it filled with sweet-balls and puris. I purchased a canvas

---

* Regarding the use of the word 'volatile', see note 'In Justice to Her Memory', Young India, 30th June, 1927.

† Monks

bag worth twelve annas and a long coat made of Chhay* wool. The bag was to contain this coat, a dhoti, a towel and a shirt. I had a blanket as well to cover myself with and a water-jug. Thus equipped I set forth on my travels, Gokhale and Dr. Ray came to the station to see me off. I had asked them both not to trouble to come, but they insisted. 'I should not have come if you had gone first class, but now I had to,' said Gokhale.

No one stopped Gokhale from going on to the platform. He was in his silk turban, jacket and dhoti. Dr. Ray was in his Bengali dress. He was stopped by the ticket collector, but on Gokhale telling him that he was his friend, he was admitted. Thus with their good wishes I started on my journey.

Chapter 20: In Benaras

The journey was from Calcutta to Rajkot, and I planned to halt at Benares, Agra, Jaipur and Palanpur en route. I had not the time to see any more places than these. In each city I stayed one day and put up in dharmashalas or with pandas† like the ordinary pilgrims, excepting at Palanpur. So far as I can remember, I did not spend more than Rs. 31 (including the train fare) on this journey.

In travelling third class I mostly preferred the ordinary to the mail trains, as I knew that the latter were more crowded and the fares in them higher.

The third class compartments are practically as dirty, and the closet arrangements as bad, today as they were then, there may be a little improvement now, but the difference between the facilities provided for the first and the third classes is out of all proportion to the difference between the fares for the two classes. Third class passengers are treated like sheep and their comforts are sheeps' comforts. In Europe I travelled third — and only once first, just to see what it was like — but there I noticed no such difference between the first and the third classes. In South Africa third class passengers are mostly negros, yet the third class comforts are better there than here. In parts of South Africa third class compartments are provided with sleeping accommodation, and cushioned seats. The accommodation is also regulated, so as to prevent overcrowding, whereas here I have found the regulation limit usually exceeded.

The indifference of the railway authorities to the comforts of the third class passengers, combined with the dirty and inconsiderate habits of the passengers themselves, makes third class travelling a trial for a passenger of cleanly ways. These unpleasant habits commonly include throwing of rubbish on the floor of the compartment, smoking at all hours and in all places, betel and tobacco chewing, converting of the whole

---

* A place in Porbandar State noted for its coarse woollen fabrics.
† Priests

carriage into a spittoon, shouting and yelling, and using foul language, regardless of the convenience or comfort of fellow passengers. I have noticed little difference between my experience of the third class travelling in 1902 and that of my unbroken third class tours from 1915 to 1919.

I can think of only one remedy for this awful state of things — that educated men should make a point of travelling third class and reforming the habits of the people, as also of never letting the railway authorities rest in peace, sending in complaints wherever necessary, never resorting to bribes or any unlawful means for obtaining their own comforts, and never putting up with infringements of rules on the part of anyone concerned. This, I am sure, would bring about considerable improvement.

My serious illness in 1918-19 has unfortunately compelled me practically to give up third class travelling, and it has been a matter of constant pain and shame to me, especially because the disability came at a time when the agitation for the removal of the hardships of third class passengers was making fair headway. The hardships of poor railway and steamship passengers, accentuated by their bad habits, the undue facilities allowed by Government to foreign trade, and such other things, make an important group of subjects, worthy to be taken up by one or two enterprising workers who could devote their full time to it.

But I shall leave the third class passengers at that, and come to my experience in Benares. I arrived there in the morning. I had decided to put up with a panda. Numerous Brahmans surrounded me, as soon as I got out of the train, and I selected one who struck me to be comparatively cleaner and better than the rest. It proved to be a good choice. There was a cow in the courtyard of his house and an upper storey where I was given a lodging. I did not want to have any food without ablution in the Ganges in the proper orthodox manner. The panda made preparations for it. I had told him beforehand that on no account could I give him more than a rupee and four annas as dakshina*, and that he should therefore keep this in mind while making the preparations.

The panda readily assented. 'Be the pilgrim rich or poor,' said he, 'the service is the same in every case. But the amount of dakshina we receive depends upon the will and the ability of the pilgrim.' I did not find that the panda at all abridged the usual formalities in my case. The puja† was over at twelve o'clock, and I went to the Kashi Vishvanath temple for darshan. I was deeply pained by what I saw there. When practising as a barrister in Bombay in 1891, I had occasion to attend a lecture on 'Pilgrimage to Kashi' in the Prarthana Samaj hall. I was therefore prepared for some measure of disappointment. But the actual disappointment was greater than I had bargained for.

The approach was through a narrow and slippery lane. Quiet there was none. The swarming flies and the noise made by the shopkeepers and pilgrims were perfectly insufferable.

---

* Gift
† Worship

Where one expected an atmosphere of meditation and communion it was conspicuous by its absence. One had to seek that atmosphere in oneself. I did observe devout sisters, who were absorbed in meditation, entirely unconscious of the environment. But for this the authorities of the temple could scarcely claim any credit. The authorities should be responsible for creating and maintaining about the temple a pure, sweet and serene atmosphere, physical as well as moral. Instead of this I found a bazar where cunning shopkeepers were selling sweets and toys of the latest fashion.

When I reached the temple, I was greeted at the entrance by a stinking mass of rotten flowers. The floor was paved with fine marble, which was however broken by some devotee innocent of aesthetic taste, who had set it with rupees serving as an excellent receptacle for dirt.

I went near the Jnana-vapi (Well of knowledge). I searched here for God but failed to find Him. I was not therefore in a particularly good mood. The surroundings of the Jnana-vapi too I found to be dirty. I had no mind to give any dakshina. So I offered a pie. The panda in charge got angry and threw away the pie. He swore at me and said, 'This insult will take you straight to hell.'

This did not perturb me. 'Maharaj,' said I, 'whatever fate has in store for me, it does not behove one of your class to indulge in such language. You may take this pie if you like, or you will lose that too.'

'Go away,' he replied, 'I don't care for your pie.' And then followed a further volley of abuse.

I took up the pie and went my way, flattering myself that the Brahman had lost a pie and I had saved one. But the Maharaj was hardly the man to let the pie go. He called me back and said, 'All right, leave the pie here, I would rather not be as you are. If I refuse your pie, it will be bad for you.'

I silently gave him the pie and, with a sigh, went away.

Since then I have twice been to Kashi Vishvanath, but that has been after I had already been afflicted with the title of Mahatma and experiences such as I have detailed above had become impossible. People eager to have my darshan would not permit me to have a darshan of the temple. The woes of Mahatmas are known to Mahatmas alone. Otherwise the dirt and the noise were the same as before.

If anyone doubts the infinite mercy of God, let him have a look at these sacred places. How much hypocrisy and irreligion does the Prince of Yogis suffer to be perpetrated in His holy name? He proclaimed long ago: 'Whatever a man sows, that shall he reap.' The law of Karma is inexorable and impossible of evasion. There is thus hardly any need for God to interfere. He laid down the Law and, as it were, retired.

After this visit to the temple, I waited upon Mrs. Besant. I knew that she had just recovered from an illness. I sent in my name. She came at once. As I wished only to pay my respects to her, I said, 'I am aware that you are in delicate health. I only wanted to pay my respects. I am thankful that you have been good enough to receive me in spite of your indifferent health. I will not detain you any longer.'

So saying, I took leave of her.

Chapter 21 : Settled in Bombay ?

Gokhale was very anxious that I should settle down in Bombay, practise at the bar and help him in public work. Public work in those days meant Congress work, and the chief work of the institution which he had assisted to found was carrying on the Congress administration.

I liked Gokhale's advice, but I was not overconfident of success as a barrister. The unpleasant memories of past failure were yet with me, and I still hated as poison the use of flattery for getting briefs.

I therefore decided to start work first at Rajkot. Kevalram Mavji Dave, my old well-wisher, who had induced me to go to England, was there, and he started me straight-away with three briefs. Two of them were appeals before the Judicial Assistant to the Political Agent in Kathiawad and one was an original case in Jamnagar. This last was rather important. On my saying that I could not trust myself to do it justice, Kevalram Dave exclaimed: 'Winning or losing is no concern of yours. You will simply try your best, and I am of course there to assist you.'

The counsel on the other side was the late Sjt. Samarth. I was fairly well prepared. Not that I knew much of Indian law, but Kevalram Dave had instructed me very thoroughly. I had heard friends say, before I went out to South Africa, that Sir Pherozeshah Mehta had the law of evidence at his finger-tips and that was the secret of his success. I had borne this in mind, and during the voyage had carefully studied the Indian Evidence Act with commentaries thereon. There was of course also the advantage of my legal experience in South Africa.

I won the case and gained some confidence. I had no fear about the appeals, which were successful. All this inspired a hope in me that after all I might not fail even in Bombay.

But before I set forth the circumstances in which I decided to go to Bombay, I shall narrate my experience of the inconsiderateness and ignorance of English officials. The Judicial Assistant's court was peripatetic. He was constantly touring, and vakils and their clients had to follow him wherever he moved his camp. The vakils would charge more whenever they had to go out of headquarters, and so the clients had naturally to incur double the expenses.

The inconvenience was no concern of the judge.

The appeal of which I am talking was to be heard at Veraval where plague was raging. I have a recollection that there were as many as fifty cases daily in the place with a population of 5,500. It was practically deserted, and I put up in a deserted dharmashala at some distance from the town. But where were the clients to stay? If they were poor, they had simply to trust themselves to God's mercy.

A friend who also had cases before the court had wired that I should put in an application for the camp to be moved to some other station because of the plague at Veraval. On my submitting the application, the sahib asked me. 'Are you afraid?'

I answered: 'It is not a question of my being afraid. I think I can shift for myself, but what about the clients?'

'The plague has come to stay in India,' replied the sahib. 'Why fear it? The climate of Veraval is lovely. (The sahib lived far away from the town in a palatial tent pitched on the seashore.) Surely people must learn to live thus in the open.'

It was no use arguing against this philosophy. The sahib told his shirastedar:

'Make a note of what Mr. Gandhi says, and let me know if it is very inconvenient for the vakils or the clients.'

The sahib of course had honestly done what he thought was the right thing. But how could the man have an idea of the hardships of poor India? How was he to understand the needs, habits, idiosyncrasies and customs of the people? How was one, accustomed to measure things in gold sovereigns, all at once to make calculations in tiny bits of copper? As the elephant is powerless to think in the terms of the ant, in spite of the best intentions in the world, even so is the Englishman powerless to think in the terms of, or legislate for, the Indian.

But to resume the thread of story. In spite of my successes, I had been thinking of staying on in Rajkot for some time longer, when one day Kevalram Dave came to me and said: 'Gandhi, we will not suffer you to vegetate here. You must settle in Bombay.'

'But who will find work for me there?' I asked. 'Will you find the expenses?'

'Yes, yes, I will,' said he. 'We shall bring you down here sometimes as a big barrister from Bombay, and drafting work we shall send you there. It lies with us vakils to make or mar a barrister. You have proved your worth in Jamnagar and Veraval, and I have therefore not the least anxiety about you. You are destined to do public work, and we will not allow you to be buried in Kathiawad. So tell me, then, when you will go to Bombay.'

'I am expecting a remittance from Natal. As soon as I get it I will go,' I replied.

The money came in about two weeks, and I went to Bombay. I took chambers in Payne, Gilbert and Sayani's offices, and it looked as though I had settled down.

Chapter 22: Faith on its trial

Though I had hired chambers in the Fort and a house in Girgaum, God would not let me settle down. Scarcely had I moved into my new house when my second son Manilal, who had already been through an acute attack of smallpox some years back, had a severe attack of typhoid, combined with pneumonia and signs of delirium at night.

The doctor was called in. He said medicine would have little effect, but eggs and chicken broth might be given with profit.

Manilal was only ten years old. To consult his wishes was out of the question. Being his guardian I had to decide. The doctor was a very good Parsi. I told him that we were all vegetarians and that I could not possibly give either of the two things to my son. Would he therefore recommend something else?

'Your son's life is in danger,' said the good doctor. 'We could give him milk diluted with water, but that will not give him enough nourishment. As you know, I am called in by many Hindu families, and they do not object to anything I prescribe. I think you will be well advised not to be so hard on your son.'

'What you say is quite right,' said I. 'As a doctor you could not do otherwise. But my responsibility is very great. If the boy had been grown up, I should certainly have tried to ascertain his wishes and respected them. But here I have to think and decide for him. To my mind it is only on such occasions that a man's faith is truly tested. Rightly or wrongly it is part of my religious conviction that man may not eat meat, eggs, and the like. There should be a limit even to the means of keeping ourselves alive. Even for itself we may not so certain things.

Religion, as I understand it, does not permit me to use meat or eggs for me or mine even on occasions like this, and I must therefore take the risk that you say is likely. But I beg of you one thing. As I cannot avail myself of your treatment, I propose to try some hydropathic remedies which I happen to know. But I shall not know how to examine the boy's pulse, chest, lungs, etc. If you will kindly look in from time to time to examine him and keep me informed of his condition, I shall be grateful to you.'

The good doctor appreciated my difficulty and agreed to my request. Though Manilal could not have made his choice, I told him what had passed between the doctor and myself and asked him his opinion.

'Do try your hydropathic treatment,' he said. 'I will not have eggs or chicken broth.'

This made me glad, though I realized that, if I had given him either of these, he would have taken it.

I knew Kuhne's treatment and had tried it too. I knew as well that fasting also could be tried with profit. So I began to give Manilal hip baths according to Kuhne, never keeping him in the tub for more than three minutes, and kept him on orange juice mixed with water for three days.

But the temperature persisted, going up to 104. At night he would be delirious. I began to get anxious. What would people say of me? What would my elder brother think of me? Could we not call in another doctor? Why not have an Ayurvedic physician? What right had the parents to inflict their fads on their children?

I was haunted by thoughts like these. Then a contrary current would start. God would surely be pleased to see that I was giving the same treatment to my son as I would give myself. I had faith in hydropathy, and little faith in allopathy. The doctors could not guarantee recovery. At best they could experiment. The thread of life was in the hands of God. Why not trust it to Him and in His name go on with what I thought was the right treatment?

My mind was torn between these conflicting thoughts. It was night. I was in Manilal's bed lying by his side. I decided to give him a wet sheet pack. I got up, wetted a sheet, wrung the water out of it and wrapped it about Manilal, keeping only his head out, and then covered him with two blankets. To the head I applied a wet towel. The whole body was burning like hot iron, and quite parched. There was absolutely no perspiration.

I was sorely tired. I left Manilal in the charge of his mother, and went out for a walk on Chaupati to refresh myself. It was about ten o'clock. Very few pedestrians were out. Plunged in deep thought, I scarcely looked at them. 'My honour is in Thy keeping, oh Lord, in this hour of trial,' I repeated to myself. Ramanama was on my lips. After a short time I returned, my heart beating within my breast.

No sooner had I entered the room than Manilal said, 'You have returned, Bapu?'

'Yes, darling.'

'Do please pull me out. I am burning.'

'Are you perspiring, my boy?'

'I am simply soaked. Do please take me out.'

I felt his forehead. It was covered with beads of perspiration. The temperature was going down. I thanked God.

'Manilal, your fever is sure to go now. A little more perspiration and then I will take you out.'

'Pray, no. Do deliver me from this furnace. Wrap me some other time if you like.'

I just managed to keep him under the pack for a few minutes more by diverting him. The perspiration streamed down his forehead. I undid the pack and dried his body. Father and son fell asleep in the same bed.

And each slept like a log. Next morning Manilal had much less fever. He went on thus for forty days on diluted milk and fruit juices. I had no fear now. It was an obstinate type of fever, but it had been got under control.

Today Manilal is the healthiest of my boys. Who can say whether his recovery was due to God's grace, or to hydropathy, or to careful dietary and nursing? Let everyone decide according to his own faith. For my part I was sure that God had saved my honour, and that belief remains unaltered to this day.

Chapter 23: To South Africa again

Manilal was restored to health, but I saw that the Girgaum house was not habitable. It was damp and ill-lighted. So in consultation with Shri Revashankar Jagjivan I decided to hire some well-ventilated bungalow in a suburb of Bombay. I wandered about in Bandra and Santa Cruz. The slaughter house in Bandra prevented our choice falling there. Ghatkopar and places near it were too far from the sea. At last we hit upon a fine bungalow in Santa Cruz, which we hired as being the best from the point of view of sanitation.

I took a first class season ticket from Santa Cruz to Churchgate, and remember having frequently felt a certain pride in being the only first class passenger in my compartment. Often I walked to Bandra in order to take the fast train from there direct to Churchgate.

I prospered in my profession better than I had expected. My South African clients often entrusted me with some work, and it was enough to enable me to pay my way.

I had not yet succeeded in securing any work in the High Court, but I attended the 'moot' that used to be held in those days, though I never ventured to take part in it. I recall Jamiatram Nanabhai taking a prominent part. Like other fresh barristers I made a point of attending the hearing of cases in the High Court, more, I am afraid, for enjoying the soporific breeze coming straight from the sea than for adding to my knowledge. I observed that I was not the only one to enjoy this pleasure. It seemed to be the fashion and therefore nothing to be ashamed of.

However I began to make use of the High Court library and make fresh acquaintances and felt that before long I should secure work in the High Court.

Thus whilst on the one hand I began to feel somewhat at ease about my profession, on the other hand Gokhale, whose eyes were always on me, had been busy making his own plans on my behalf. He peeped in at my chambers twice or thrice every week, often in company with friends whom he wanted me to know, and he kept me acquainted with his mode of work.

But it may be said that God has never allowed any of my own plans to stand.

He has disposed them in His own way.

Just when I seemed to be settling down as I had intended, I received an unexpected cable from South Africa: 'Chamberlain expected here. Please return immediately.' I remembered my promise and cabled to say that I should be ready to start the moment they put me in funds. They promptly responded, I gave up the chambers and started for South Africa.

I had an idea that the work there would keep me engaged for at least a year, so I kept the bungalow and left my wife and children there.

I believed then that enterprising youths who could not find an opening in the country should emigrate to other lands. I therefore took with me four or five such youths, one of whom was Maganlal Gandhi.

The Gandhis were and are a big family. I wanted to find out all those who wished to leave the trodden path and venture abroad. My father used to accommodate a number of them in some state service. I wanted them to be free from this spell. I neither could nor would secure other service for them; I wanted them to be self-reliant.

But as my ideals advanced, I tried to persuade these youths also to conform their ideals to mine, and I had the greatest success in guiding Maganlal Gandhi.

But about this later.

The separation from wife and children, the breaking up of a settled establishment, and the going from the certain to the uncertain — all this was for a moment painful, but I had inured myself to an uncertain life. I think it is wrong to expect certainties in this world, where all else but God that is Truth is an uncertainty. All that appears and happens about and around us is uncertain, transient. But there is a Supreme Being hidden therein as a Certainty, and one would be blessed if one could catch a glimpse of that Certainty and hitch one's wagon to it. The quest for that Truth is the summum bonum of life.

I reached Durban not a day too soon. There was work waiting for me. The date for the deputation to wait on Mr. Chamberlain had been fixed. I had to draft the memorial to be submitted to him and accompany the deputation.

PART IV

Chapter 1 : 'Love's labour's lost?'

Mr. Chamberlain had come to get a gift of 35 million pounds from South Africa, and to win the hearts of Englishmen and Boers. So he gave a cold shoulder to the Indian deputation.

'You know,' he said 'that the Imperial Government has little control over self-governing Colonies. Your grievances seem to be genuine. I shall do what I can, but you must try your best to placate the Europeans, if you wish to live in their midst.'

The reply cast a chill over the members of the deputation. I was also disappointed. It was an eye-opener for us all, and I saw that we should start with our work de novo. I explained the situation to my colleagues.

As a matter of fact there was nothing wrong about Mr. Chamberlain's reply. It was well that he did not mince matters. He had brought home to us in a rather gentle way the rule of might being right or the law of the sword.

But sword we had none. We scarcely had the nerve and the muscle even to receive sword-cuts.

Mr. Chamberlain had given only a short time to the sub-continent. If Shrinagar to Cape Comorin is 1,900 miles, Durban to Capetown is not less than 1,100 miles, and Mr. Chamberlain had to cover the long distance at hurricane speed.

From Natal he hastened to the Transvaal. I had to prepare the case for the Indians there as well and submit it to him. But how was I to get to Pretoria? Our people there were not in a position to procure the necessary legal facilities for my getting to them in time. The War had reduced the Transvaal to a howling wilderness. There were neither provisions nor clothing available. Empty or closed shops were there, waiting to be replenished or opened, but that was a matter of time. Even refugees could not be allowed to return until the shops were ready with provisions. Every Transvaaller had therefore to obtain a permit. The European had no difficulty in getting one, but the Indian found it very hard.

During the War many officers and soldiers had come to South Africa from India and Ceylon, and it was considered to be the duty of the British authorities to provide for such of them as decided to settle there. They had in any event to appoint new officers, and these experienced men came in quite handy. The quick ingenuity of some of them created a new department. It showed their resourcefulness. There was a special department for the negroes. Why then should there not be one for the Asiatics? The argument seemed to be quite plausible. When I reached the Transvaal, this new department had already been opened and was gradually spreading its tentacles. The officers who issued permits to the returning refugees might issue them to all, but how could they do so in respect of the Asiatics without the intervention of the new department? And if the permits were to be issued on the recommendation of the new department, some of the responsibility and burden of the permit officers could thus be lessened. This was how they had argued.

The fact, however, was that the new department wanted some apology for work, and the men wanted money. If there had been no work, the department would have been unnecessary and would have been discontinued. So they found this work for themselves.

The Indians had to apply to this department. A reply would be vouchsafed many days after. And as there were large numbers wishing to return to the Transvaal, there grew up an army of intermediaries or touts, who with the officers, looted the poor Indians to the tune of thousands. I was told that no permit could be had without influence, and that in some cases one had to pay up to a hundred pounds in spite of the influence which one might bring to bear. Thus there seemed to me no way open to me. I went to my old friend, the Police Superintendent of Durban, and said to him: 'Please introduce me to the Permit Officer and help me to obtain a permit. You know that I have been a resident of the Transvaal.' He immediately put on his hat, came out and secured me a permit. There was hardly an hour left before my train was to start. I had kept my luggage ready. I thanked Superintendent Alexander and started for Pretoria.

I now had a fair idea of the difficulties ahead. On reaching Pretoria I drafted the memorial. In Durban I do not recollect the Indians having been asked to submit in advance the names of their representatives, but here there was the new department and it asked to do so. The Pretoria Indians had already come to know that the officers wanted to exclude me.

But another chapter is necessary for this painful though amusing incident.

Chapter 2: 'Love's labour's lost?'

Mr. Chamberlain had come to get a gift of 35 million pounds from South Africa, and to win the hearts of Englishmen and Boers. So he gave a cold shoulder to the Indian deputation.

'You know,' he said 'that the Imperial Government has little control over self-governing Colonies. Your grievances seem to be genuine. I shall do what I can, but you must try your best to placate the Europeans, if you wish to live in their midst.'

The reply cast a chill over the members of the deputation. I was also disappointed. It was an eye-opener for us all, and I saw that we should start with our work de novo. I explained the situation to my colleagues.

As a matter of fact there was nothing wrong about Mr. Chamberlain's reply. It was well that he did not mince matters. He had brought home to us in a rather gentle way the rule of might being right or the law of the sword.

But sword we had none. We scarcely had the nerve and the muscle even to receive sword-cuts.

Mr. Chamberlain had given only a short time to the sub-continent. If Shrinagar to

Cape Comorin is 1,900 miles, Durban to Capetown is not less than 1,100 miles, and Mr. Chamberlain had to cover the long distance at hurricane speed.

From Natal he hastened to the Transvaal. I had to prepare the case for the Indians there as well and submit it to him. But how was I to get to Pretoria? Our people there were not in a position to procure the necessary legal facilities for my getting to them in time. The War had reduced the Transvaal to a howling wilderness. There were neither provisions nor clothing available. Empty or closed shops were there, waiting to be replenished or opened, but that was a matter of time. Even refugees could not be allowed to return until the shops were ready with provisions. Every Transvaaller had therefore to obtain a permit. The European had no difficulty in getting one, but the Indian found it very hard.

During the War many officers and soldiers had come to South Africa from India and Ceylon, and it was considered to be the duty of the British authorities to provide for such of them as decided to settle there. They had in any event to appoint new officers, and these experienced men came in quite handy. The quick ingenuity of some of them created a new department. It showed their resourcefulness. There was a special department for the negroes. Why then should there not be one for the Asiatics? The argument seemed to be quite plausible. When I reached the Transvaal, this new department had already been opened and was gradually spreading its tentacles. The officers who issued permits to the returning refugees might issue them to all, but how could they do so in respect of the Asiatics without the intervention of the new department? And if the permits were to be issued on the recommendation of the new department, some of the responsibility and burden of the permit officers could thus be lessened. This was how they had argued. The fact, however, was that the new department wanted some apology for work, and the men wanted money. If there had been no work, the department would have been unnecessary and would have been discontinued. So they found this work for themselves.

The Indians had to apply to this department. A reply would be vouchsafed many days after. And as there were large numbers wishing to return to the Transvaal, there grew up an army of intermediaries or touts, who with the officers, looted the poor Indians to the tune of thousands. I was told that no permit could be had without influence, and that in some cases one had to pay up to a hundred pounds in spite of the influence which one might bring to bear. Thus there seemed to me no way open to me. I went to my old friend, the Police Superintendent of Durban, and said to him: 'Please introduce me to the Permit Officer and help me to obtain a permit. You know that I have been a resident of the Transvaal.' He immediately put on his hat, came out and secured me a permit. There was hardly an hour left before my train was to start. I had kept my luggage ready. I thanked Superintendent Alexander and started for Pretoria.

I now had a fair idea of the difficulties ahead. On reaching Pretoria I drafted the memorial. In Durban I do not recollect the Indians having been asked to submit in advance the names of their representatives, but here there was the new department and it asked to do so. The Pretoria Indians had already come to know that the officers wanted to exclude me. But another chapter is necessary for this painful though amusing incident.

Chapter 3: 'Love's labour's lost?'

Mr. Chamberlain had come to get a gift of 35 million pounds from South Africa, and to win the hearts of Englishmen and Boers. So he gave a cold shoulder to the Indian deputation.

'You know,' he said 'that the Imperial Government has little control over self-governing Colonies. Your grievances seem to be genuine. I shall do what I can, but you must try your best to placate the Europeans, if you wish to live in their midst.'

The reply cast a chill over the members of the deputation. I was also disappointed. It was an eye-opener for us all, and I saw that we should start with our work de novo. I explained the situation to my colleagues.

As a matter of fact there was nothing wrong about Mr. Chamberlain's reply. It was well that he did not mince matters. He had brought home to us in a rather gentle way the rule of might being right or the law of the sword.

But sword we had none. We scarcely had the nerve and the muscle even to receive sword-cuts.

Mr. Chamberlain had given only a short time to the sub-continent. If Shrinagar to Cape Comorin is 1,900 miles, Durban to Capetown is not less than 1,100 miles, and Mr. Chamberlain had to cover the long distance at hurricane speed.

From Natal he hastened to the Transvaal. I had to prepare the case for the Indians there as well and submit it to him. But how was I to get to Pretoria? Our people there were not in a position to procure the necessary legal facilities for my getting to them in time. The War had reduced the Transvaal to a howling wilderness. There were neither provisions nor clothing available. Empty or closed shops were there, waiting to be replenished or opened, but that was a matter of time. Even refugees could not be allowed to return until the shops were ready with provisions. Every Transvaaller had therefore to obtain a permit. The European had no difficulty in getting one, but the Indian found it very hard.

During the War many officers and soldiers had come to South Africa from India and Ceylon, and it was considered to be the duty of the British authorities to provide for such of them as decided to settle there. They had in any event to appoint new officers, and these experienced men came in quite handy. The quick ingenuity of some of them created a new department. It showed their resourcefulness. There was a special department for the negroes. Why then should there not be one for the Asiatics? The argument seemed to be quite plausible. When I reached the Transvaal, this new department had already been opened and was gradually spreading its tentacles. The officers who issued permits to the returning refugees might issue them to all, but how could they do so in respect of the Asiatics without the intervention of the new department? And if the permits were to be issued on the recommendation of the new department, some of the responsibility and burden of the permit officers could thus be lessened. This was how they had argued. The fact, however, was that the new department wanted some apology for work, and the men wanted money. If there had been no work, the department would have been unnecessary and would have been discontinued. So they found this work for themselves.

The Indians had to apply to this department. A reply would be vouchsafed many days after. And as there were large numbers wishing to return to the Transvaal, there grew up an army of intermediaries or touts, who with the officers, looted the poor Indians to the tune of thousands. I was told that no permit could be had without influence, and that in some cases one had to pay up to a hundred pounds in spite of the influence which one might bring to bear. Thus there seemed to me no way open to me. I went to my old friend, the Police Superintendent of Durban, and said to him: 'Please introduce me to the Permit Officer and help me to obtain a permit. You know that I have been a resident of the Transvaal.' He immediately put on his hat, came out and secured me a permit. There was hardly an hour left before my train was to start. I had kept my luggage ready. I thanked Superintendent Alexander and started for Pretoria.

I now had a fair idea of the difficulties ahead. On reaching Pretoria I drafted the memorial. In Durban I do not recollect the Indians having been asked to submit in advance the names of their representatives, but here there was the new department and it asked to do so. The Pretoria Indians had already come to know that the officers wanted to exclude me.

But another chapter is necessary for this painful though amusing incident.

Discovery Publisher is a multimedia publisher whose mission is to inspire and support personal transformation, spiritual growth and awakening. We strive with every title to preserve the essential wisdom of the author, spiritual teacher, thinker, healer, and visionary artist.